Adaptations for
SAXON MATH™
Intermediate 3

Student Workbook

For Use with *Saxon Math Intermediate 3*

SAXON™
A Harcourt Education Imprint

www.SaxonPublishers.com
800-531-5015

2012 Edition

Printed in the U.S.A.

ISBN 978-1-600-32330-0

15 2266 22

4500844663   ^ B C D E F G

TABLE OF CONTENTS

This workbook is designed to supplement and support the instruction and exercises in *Saxon Math Intermediate 3* and cannot be used independently of the textbook. Included are Lesson and Investigation Worksheets.

Each Lesson Worksheet contains brief instruction on the lesson's topics, workspace for every Practice Set and Written Practice problem, and assistance for many of the solutions. Many worksheets also include teacher notes indicating resources (such as Teaching Guide hints, manipulatives, or masters) that will help students understand the lesson.

Support for individual problems takes many forms, including:

- identifying a starting point

- restating the problem

- crafting partial solutions

- citing a *Student Reference Guide* page

- referring students to a page in the textbook (with the textbook icon, 📖)

- reminding students to include units in the answer (by showing unit prompters in relevant answer boxes)

Investigation Worksheets are much like Lesson Worksheets. They summarize the contents of Investigations, aid in solving problems, and supply teacher-support information.

Assignment	Date	Assignment	Date	Assignment	Date	Assignment	Date
1		26		47		Test 12	
2		TP 26		TP 47		Inv. 7	
3		27		48		71	
4		28		TP 48		72	
TP 4		TP 28		49		73	
5		29		50		74	
6		30		TP 50		75	
7		Test 4		Test 8		Test 13	
8		Inv. 3		Inv. 5		76	
9		31		51		77	
10		32		52		TP 77	
Inv. 1		TP 32		53		78	
11		33		54		79	
12		34		55		80	
13		35		Test 9		Test 14	
14		TP 35		56		Inv. 8	
TP 14		Test 5		57		81	
15		36		58		82	
TP 15		37		59		83	
Test 1		38		60		TP 83	
16		39		Test 10		84	
17		40		Inv. 6		85	
18		TP 40		61		Test 15	
19		Test 6		62		86	
TP 19		Inv. 4		63		TP 86	
20		41		TP 63		87	
Test 2		42		64		88	
Inv. 2		43		65		89	
21		TP 43		Test 11		90	
22		44		66		Test 16	
23		45		67		Inv. 9	
24		Test 7		68		91	
25		46		69		92	
Test 3		TP 46		70		TP 92	

Name_____

Assignment	Date	Assignment	Date	Assignment	Date	Assignment	Date
93		102					
94		103					
95		104					
Test 17		Test 19					
96		105					
97		TP 105					
TP 97		106					
98		107					
99		Test 20					
100		108					
TP 100		109					
Test 18		TP 109					
Inv. 10		110					
101		Test 21					
TP 101		Inv. 11					

Name _____

Teacher Notes:

• Refer students to "Days of the Week" and "Months of the Year" on page 3 and "Time" on page 2 in the *Student Reference Guide*.

• Students need a copy of **Lesson Activity 1** to complete this lesson.

• Months and Years

• Calendar

New Concepts

• **Months and Years**

• A **common year** has 365 days.

• A **leap year** has 366 days. The extra day is added to February.

• This rhyme tells the months that have **30 days.**

Thirty days hath September,
April, June, and November.

• All other months, except February, have **31 days.**

Math Language

Ordinal numbers name a position in a line.

first, second, third, ...

1st, 2nd, 3rd, ...

• Dates are written in different ways:

1. **name** of the month day, year

   July 4, 1776

2. **number** of the month/day/year

   7/4/1776

   July is the seventh (7th) month.

3. **name** of the day of month, year.

   Fourth of July, 1776

© Saxon

- **Calendar**
  - A **calendar** shows one month of numbered days.
  - This calendar has 7 **columns** that go *up and down*.

	JULY 2006					
S	M	T	W	T	F	S
						1
2	3	4	5	6	7	8
9	10	11	12	13	14	15
16	17	18	19	20	21	22
23	24	25	26	27	28	29
30	31					

- Each column is for one day of the week. The first column is for all the Sundays in a month and the last column is for all the Saturdays in a month.

- The calendar has 5 **rows** that go *across*. Each row is for one week of the month.

	JULY 2006					
S	M	T	W	T	F	S
						1
2	3	4	5	6	7	8
9	10	11	12	13	14	15
16	17	18	19	20	21	22
23	24	25	26	27	28	29
30	31					

Activity 📖 page 9

Make a Calendar

Use your textbook to complete this activity.

© Saxon

a. Read out loud this rhyme that tells the months that have 30 days:
"Thirty days hath September, April, June, and November."

Use your calendar to answer **b–f.**

b. On **which day of the week** did this month begin? _____
Find the day numbered 1.

c. **How many days** are in this month? _____ days

d. On which day of the week will this month **end?** _____

e. How many **rows** did you use in your calendar? _____
Rows go across.

f. How many **columns** did you use in your calendar? Why?

_____ columns, one column for each d_____ of the week.

Use the *Student Reference Guide* to answer **g–i.**

g. How many days are in a leap year? _____ days

h. What month is the **tenth month** of the year? O_____

i. How many months have 31 days? _____ months

Use your calendar to answer **j** and **k.**

j. How many days are there from the 16th of the month through the 21st?

_____ days
Count from the 17th to the 21st.

k. What date is **two weeks after** the 3rd? the _____
Go down two rows from the 3rd.

1. How many years old are you?

_____

2. your birthday

Use the name of the month.

_____ _____, _____
        month   day   year

Use the number of the month.

_____ / _____ / _____
month   day   year

Use work area.

3. ninth month

_____

4. Thirty days hath S_____, A_____,

J_____, and N_____.

Use work area.

5. 1 week = _____ days

© Saxon

6. How many days are not in full rows?

Use your calendar.

7. 5th through the 11th?

Do not count the 11th.

8. Circle the 7th person.

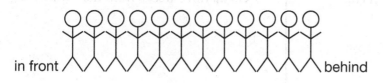

in front ... behind

a. in front

b. behind

Do not count the circled person.

a. _____ b. _____

9. between Michael and Janet

Michael ... Janet

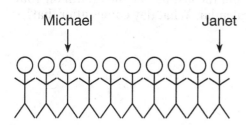

10. first, _____, third,

fourth, _____,

sixth, _____, _____,

ninth, _____

Use work area.

11. one week after the 9th

Use your calendar. Go down one row from the 9th.

12. two weeks after the 11th

Go down two weeks from the 11th.

13. three weeks before the 27th

Go **up** three weeks from the 27th.

14. month with less than 30 days

See the *Student Reference Guide.*

15. day that next month begins

Find the last day of the month on your calendar. What day comes after that?

© Saxon

Name _____

📖 page 13

Teacher Notes:
• Introduce Hint #1 "Finding Patterns in Sequences."
• Refer students to "Hundred-Number Chart" on page 11 in the *Student Reference Guide.*
• Students need their calendar from Lesson 1 to complete this lesson.

• Counting Patterns

New Concept

• A **counting pattern** is a pattern of numbers that follows a rule.

  3, 6, 9, 12, …

  Rule: Count up by 3.

• A counting pattern can also go down.

  10, 8, 6, 4, …

  Rule: Count down by 2.

• To find a rule and continue a pattern:

  1. Use the "Hundred-Number Chart" from the *Student Reference Guide.*

  2. Put your finger or pencil tip on the first number in the pattern.

  3. Count by ones to the second number in the pattern. Now we know the rule.

  4. Count on the Hundred-Number Chart by the rule to find more numbers in the pattern.

Example

Find the next three numbers in this sequence:

7, 14, 21, 28, _____, _____, _____, …

1. Use the Hundred-Number Chart.

2. Put your pencil tip on 7.

3. Count by ones to 14.

   8, 9, 10, 11, 12, 13, 14

We counted **up 7** times to get to 14.

The rule is "Count up by 7."

4. Counting up by 7 from 28 goes to **35,** then to **42,** and then to **49.**

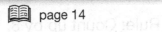 📖 page 14

Skip Counting

Materials needed:

• student calendar from Lesson 1

We can count patterns on a calendar. A counting pattern is also called **skip counting** because we skip over some of the numbers.

1. Skip count by *threes* from 3 to 30.

   Start at 3 on the calendar. Count up by 3 to 30.

   3, 6, _____, 12, _____, _____, 21, _____, _____, 30

2. Skip count by *fours* from 4 to 28.

   Start at 4. Count up by 4 to 28.

   4, _____, 12, _____, _____, _____, 28

3. Skip count by *twos* from 30 **down** to 2.

   Start at 30. Count down by 2 to 2.

   30, 28, _____, _____, _____, 20, _____, _____, _____,

   12, _____, _____, _____, _____, 2

Find the next 3 numbers in each pattern and write the rule.

Use the Hundred-Number Chart from the *Student Reference Guide*.

a. 3, 6, 9, 12, _____, _____, _____, ...

Rule: Count up by _____.

b. 10, 9, 8, 7, _____, _____, _____, ...

Rule: Count d_____ by 1.

c. 80, 70, 60, 50, _____, _____, _____, ...

Rule: Count down by _____.

d. Skip count **by sevens** from 7 to 35.

7, _____, _____, _____, 35

Written Practice 📖 page 15

1. 1 week = 7 days

2 weeks = _____ days

2. last month of the year

See the *Student Reference Guide*.

3. 4 months with **30 days**

A _____, J _____,

S _____, N _____

Use work area.

4. shortest month

_____

5. seventh month

_____

6. fourth day of the week

_____

7. Find the pattern.
Use the Hundred-Number Chart for help.

7, 14, 21, _____, _____, _____, ...

Rule: Count _____ by 7.

Use work area.

8. 5, 10, 15, _____, _____, _____, ...

Rule: Count up by _____.

Use work area.

9. 50, 60, 70, _____, _____, _____, ...

Rule: Count _____ by _____.

Use work area.

10. 4, 8, 12, _____, _____, _____, ...

Rule: Count _____ by _____.

Use work area.

11.

MARCH 2007						
S	M	T	W	T	F	S
				1	2	3
4	5	6	7	8	9	10
11	12	(13)	14	15	16	17
18	19	20	21	22	23	24
25	26	27	28	29	30	31

Use the name of the month.

_____ _____, _____
month   day   year

Use the number of the month.

_____ / _____ / _____
month   day   year

Use work area.

12. What **day** of the week was the 1st?

13. first Saturday of the month

Use the number of the month.

_____ / _____ / _____
month   day   year

Use work area.

14. first day of April, 2007

Find the last day on the calendar. What day of the week comes after that?

15. a. Put an X on the tenth person.

in front ☺☺☺☺☺☺☺☺☺☺☺☺☺☺☺☺☺☺☺☺☺☺ behind

             ↑   ↑

           John   Beth

in front: _____ people

behind: _____ people

b. between John and Beth

_____ people

Use work area.

Name _____

Teacher Notes:

• Introduce Hint #2 "Reading Clocks."

• Review "Time" on page 2 in the *Student Reference Guide.*

• Use geared mini clocks to enhance this lesson.

• Reading a Clock to the Nearest Five Minutes

New Concept

• An *analog clock* shows time on a circular face.

• The *short hand* tells the **hour.**

   Each number on a clock is one hour.

• The *long hand* tells the **minutes.**

   Each number on the clock is five minutes.

• On the clock below the hour hand points between the 12 and the 1.

   It is after 12 and before 1.

• The minute hand points to the 6.

   Skip count by 5 to find the minutes:

   5, 10, 15, 20, 25, 30

• To write this time in *digital form,* use **"hours:minutes."**

   12:30

• **Noon** is 12:00 in the day (lunch time).

• **Midnight** is 12:00 at night.

Math Language

The abbreviation **a.m.** means the 12 hours *before* noon (morning).

The abbreviation **p.m.** means the 12 hours *after* noon (afternoon and evening).

© Saxon

 page 19

Setting a Clock

This activity is optional.

Lesson Practice

It is morning. What time is shown by each clock?

Remember to write a.m. or p.m.

hours:minutes

a.

_____:_____

b.

_____:_____

c.

_____:_____

© Saxon

1.

Remember to write a.m. or p.m.
hours:minutes

2. eighth month

3. leap year

4. A, B, C, D, E, F, G, H, I, J, K

_____ and _____

5. Find the pattern. Use the Hundred-Number Chart for help.

7, 14, 21, _____, _____, _____, _____, ...

Rule: Count _____ by 7.

_____ ⌐ ‑ ‑ ‑ ‑ ‑ ‑ ‑ ‑ ¬
                                                   ¦ Use work area. ¦
                                                   ∟ ‑ ‑ ‑ ‑ ‑ ‑ ‑ ‑ ⌐

6. 15, 20, 25, _____, _____, _____, _____, ...

Rule: Count up by _____.

_____ ⌐ ‑ ‑ ‑ ‑ ‑ ‑ ‑ ‑ ¬
                                                   ¦ Use work area. ¦
                                                   ∟ ‑ ‑ ‑ ‑ ‑ ‑ ‑ ‑ ⌐

7. 3, 6, 9, _____, _____, _____, _____, ...

Rule: Count _____ by _____.

_____ ⌐ ‑ ‑ ‑ ‑ ‑ ‑ ‑ ‑ ¬
                                                   ¦ Use work area. ¦
                                                   ∟ ‑ ‑ ‑ ‑ ‑ ‑ ‑ ‑ ⌐

8.

The minute hand is the long hand.

© Saxon

9. month **before** the tenth month

_____

10. 1 week = 7 days

3 weeks = _____ days

11.

Remember to write a.m. or p.m.
hours:minutes

_____

12. Add one to the hours.

© Saxon

13. Add one more to the hours.

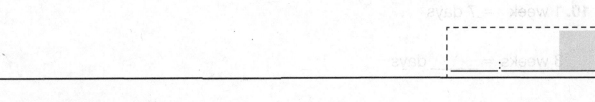

14. four days after Saturday

Use a calendar.

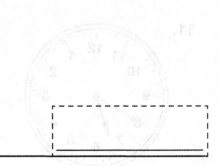

15. 7/15/99

What month?

Which month is the **seventh** month?

Name _____

Teacher Notes:

• Refer students to "Temperature" on page 2 in the *Student Reference Guide*.

• For additional practice, students may complete Targeted Practice 4.

• Number Line
• Thermometer

New Concepts

• **Number Line**

• A **number line** shows numbers on a line in order. **Tick marks** represent numbers. Some of the tick marks are labeled.

Number Line

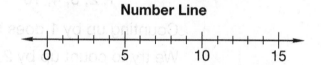

• Each tick mark on this number line counts up by 1.

1, 2, 3, 4, 5

• A dot, or **point,** can tell where a number is on a number line.

Example

What numbers do the points labeled a, b, and c show?

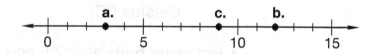

Each tick mark counts up by 1.
a. Count up from 0 by 1 to **a.**

1, 2, **3**

b. Count up from 10 by 1 to **b.**

10, 11, **12**

c. Count *down* from 10 by 1 to **c.**

10, **9**

© Saxon

• On some number lines, each tick mark counts up by 2, 5, or 10.

Example

What number does point *A* show?

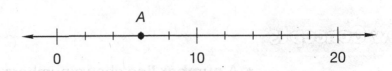

We try to count up by 1 on the tick marks from 0 to 10:

1, 2, 3, 4, 10

Counting up by 1 does not work.

We try to count up by 2 on the tick marks:

2, 4, 6, 8, 10

Each tick mark counts up by 2. Point *A* shows the number **6.**

• **Thermometer**

• We use a **thermometer** to measure temperature in **degrees.**

Some thermometers show temperature in degrees **Fahrenheit** (°F).

Others show temperature in degrees **Celsius** (°C).

• Hot water **boils** at 212°F and 100°C.

• Cold water **freezes** at 32°F and 0°C.

Math Language

A **scale** is a type of number line used for measuring.

• To read a thermometer:

1. Find if the scale on the thermometer counts up by 1 or counts up by 2.

2. Look at where the temperature mark ends on the thermometer.

3. Count up to the mark. Write that number and °F or °C.

© Saxon

Example

What is the temperature on the thermometer?

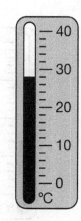

1. Counting up by 1 on the tick marks does not work. Counting up by 2 does work: 2, 4, 6, 8, 10.

2. The temperature mark ends almost at the 30.

3. We count up to the mark by 2: 20, 22, 24, 26, **28.**
   The thermometer shows °C, so the temperature is **28°C.**

Activity 📖 page 25

Reading and Recording Temperature
This activity is optional.

Lesson Practice

Write the number shown by each point **a–c.**

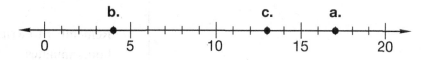

a. _____   b. _____   c. _____

© Saxon

What temperature is shown on each thermometer?

d. _____    e. _____   f. _____

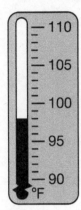   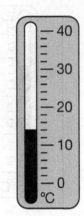   

g. The temperature is 35°F. Is it a hot or a cold day? _____

Water freezes at 32°F.

Written Practice   📖 page 26

1. middle two months

See the *Student Reference Guide.*

2. It is morning.

Remember to write a.m. or p.m.

hours:minutes

_____ and _____

_____ : _____

© Saxon

3. Remember that p.m. is after noon.

_____

4. Find the pattern. Use the Hundred-Number Chart for help.

14, 21, 28, _____, _____, _____, _____, ...

Rule: Count up by _____.

Use work area.

5. 4, 8, 12, _____, _____, _____, _____, ...

Rule: Count up by _____.

Use work area.

6. six days **after** Friday

_____

7.

The minute hand is the long hand.

_____

8. July 5, 2001

Use a number for the month.

_____ / _____ / _____

9. temperature water freezes in °F

_____

10.

Count up by 1.
Remember to write °F or °C.

_____

11. Give the month and day.

Use your calendar.

M_____

12. between Dan and Jan

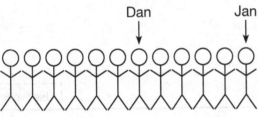

_____

13.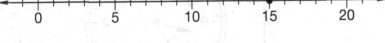

Count up by 1.

_____

14. last three months

_____,

_____,

_____

Use work area.

15. temperature on a **cool** day

A 60°F   **B** 90°F

C 100°F   **D** 80°F

_____

Name _____

Teacher Notes:

• Introduce Hint #3 "Abbreviations and Symbols."

• Review "Time" on page 2 in the *Student Reference Guide*.

• Students need a copy of **Lesson Activity 4** to complete this lesson.

• Use geared mini clocks to enhance this lesson.

• Fractions of an Hour

New Concept

Math Language

A **fraction** is a number that names part of a whole.

• One hour is 60 minutes.

• One **half hour** is 30 minutes.

6:30
"Half past 6"

• One **quarter hour** is 15 minutes.

6:15
"A quarter after 6"

5:45
"A quarter to 6"

© Saxon

Activity page 30

Fractions of an Hour

Materials needed:
- **Lesson Activity 4**

Follow the instructions to draw hands on the clock faces for these times.

1. A quarter to three

"Quarter to" means **15 minutes before.**

- Draw the long hand to 9.
- Draw the short hand in between 2 and 3.

    The time is _____:45.

2. Half past four

"Half past" means **30 minutes after.**

- Draw the long hand to 6.
- Draw the short hand in between 4 and 5.

    The time is _____:30.

3. A quarter after ten

"Quarter after" means **15 minutes after.**

- Draw the long hand to 3.
- Draw the short hand in between 10 and 11.

    The time is _____:15.

4. A quarter of eight

"Quarter of" means **15 minutes before.**

- Draw the long hand to 9.
- Draw the short hand in between 7 and 8.

    The time is 7:_____.

a. The clock says 1:15. Write the time in words using a fraction of an hour.

q_____ after one

Remember to write a.m. or p.m.

b. Write a **quarter to eight** in the **evening** in digital form.

_____:45_____

c. Cory gets up at **half past six** in the **morning**. Write that time in digital form.

6:_____

Written Practice 📖 page 31

1. One half hour = _____ minutes

See page 2 in the *Student Reference Guide*.

2. What is the **sixth month?**

3. How many days after Wednesday?

See page 3 in the *Student Reference Guide*.

© Saxon

4. Find the pattern. Use the
Hundred-Number Chart for help.

18, 24, 30, _____, _____, _____, _____, ...

Rule: Count _____ by 6.

┌─────────────────┐
│ Use work area. │
└─────────────────┘

5. 7, 14, 21, _____, _____, _____, _____, ...

Rule: Count up by _____.

┌─────────────────┐
│ Use work area. │
└─────────────────┘

6. 50, 45, 40, _____, _____, _____, _____, ...

Rule: Count _____ by 5.

┌─────────────────┐
│ Use work area. │
└─────────────────┘

7. morning

hours:minutes

Remember to write a.m. or p.m.

┌─────────────────┐
│ _____ : _____   │
└─────────────────┘

© Saxon

8.

Count up by 1.

_____

9. Count up by 5.

5, _____, _____, _____, _____

Use work area.

10. quarter past 4 in the **afternoon**

Remember to write a.m. or p.m.

_____ : _____

11.

Count up by 1.
Remember to write °F or °C.

_____

12. See page 2 in the *Student Reference Guide*.

water freezes: _____ °F

water boils: _____ °F

Use work area.

13. Count up by 7.

   A 8, 6, 4, 2

   B 5, 7, 9, 11

   C 21, 28, 35, 42

   D 25, 20, 15, 10

14.

Remember to write a.m. or p.m.

hours:minutes

15.

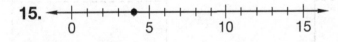

Count up by 1.

© Saxon

Name _____

📖 page 33

• Addition

Teacher Notes:

• Refer students to "Arithmetic with Two Numbers" on page 6 in the *Student Reference Guide*.

• Review "Hundred-Number Chart" on page 11 in the *Student Reference Guide*.

• Students need color tiles to complete this lesson.

New Concept

Math Language

A **number sentence** is a sentence that uses numbers and symbols but not words.

$$4 + 3 = 7$$

• The numbers that are added are called **addends.**

• The answer to an addition problem is called the **sum.**

• Here are two ways to add 4 and 3.

$$\begin{array}{r} 4 \\ + 3 \\ \hline 7 \end{array}\ \begin{array}{l} \text{addend} \\ \text{addend} \\ \text{sum} \end{array}\qquad \begin{array}{r} 3 \\ + 4 \\ \hline 7 \end{array}$$

• + is a plus sign.

• = is an equal sign.

• One way to add is to **count up by 1** on the Hundred-Number Chart.

$$4 + 3 = 7$$

Start at 4 and count up 3 more numbers:

$$4 \;\rightarrow\; 5 \;\rightarrow\; 6 \;\rightarrow\; 7$$

• We can show addition by counting groups of squares.

Example

Use words and numbers to show this addition.

$$\square\square + \square\square\square\square = \begin{array}{ccc}\square&\square&\square\\\square&\square&\square\end{array}$$

Count the squares in the first group: **2** squares.

Count the squares in the second group: **4** squares.

Count all the squares: **6** squares.

Two **plus** four **equals** six.

$$2 + 4 = 6$$

- **Adding 0 to a number does not change the number.**

$$6 + 0 = 6$$

Lesson Practice

a. Use words and numbers to show this addition.

$$\square\square\square + \square\square\square\square\square = \begin{array}{c}\square\square\square\\\square\square\square\square\end{array}$$

words: _____ plus _____ equals eight.

numbers: _____ + _____ = 8

b. Follow the instructions to show this addition.

$$6 + 4 = 10$$

1. Put 6 color tiles on your desk.

2. Put 4 more color tiles on your desk.

3. Count all the tiles on your desk.

How many are there? _____

c. What is the name for **numbers that are added?**

a_____

d. What is the name for the **total** when we add?

s_____

Add. Count up by 1 or use color tiles.

e. 4 + 0 = _____

f. 2 + 8 = _____

g. 9
     + 6

h. 7
      + 5

Written Practice page 36

1. Count up by 2.
Remember to write °F or °C.

temperature = _____

Is that temperature cool or hot? _____

Use work area.

2. half past seven in the **morning**

Remember to write a.m. or p.m.

3. Find the pattern. Use the Hundred-Number Chart for help.

7, 14, 21, 28, _____, _____, _____, _____, ...

¡ Use work area. ¡

4. 3, 6, 9, 12, _____, _____, _____, _____, ...

¡ Use work area. ¡

5.

Remember to write a.m. or p.m.

hours:minutes

6.

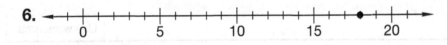

Count up by 1.

7. five days **after** Thursday

Use a calendar.

8. five months **after** July

See page 3 in the *Student Reference Guide*.

© Saxon

9. quarter to three in the **afternoon**

Remember to write a.m. or p.m.

_____ : _____

10. water **freezes** in °**F**

A 0°F

B 32°F

C 212°F

D 100°F

11. Use a mini clock.

a. Point the short hand between 2 and 3. Is the hour 2 or 3? _____

b. Point the long hand at 5. Count up by 5 to find the minutes. _____

c. It is night time. Write the time in digital form.

Remember to write a.m. or p.m.

hours:minutes

_____ : _____

Use work area.

© Saxon

12. Count each group of squares.

_____ + _____ = _____

13. Draw circles to show the **total**.

○○○ ○○○
○○○ + ○○○ =

Use work area.

14. half past six in the **morning**

Remember to write a.m. or p.m.

15. 5 + 4 = 9

　a. addends

　b. sum

a. _____ and _____

b. _____

© Saxon

• Subtraction

Teacher Notes:

• Introduce Hint #4 "Word Problem Cues, Part 1."

• Refer students to "Word Problem Keywords" on page 6 in the *Student Reference Guide*.

• Review "Arithmetic with Two Numbers" on page 6 and "Hundred-Number Chart" on page 11 in the *Student Reference Guide*.

New Concept

• The answer to a subtraction problem is called the **difference.**

• – is a minus sign.

$$\begin{array}{r} 6 \\ -2 \\ \hline 4 \end{array} \text{ difference}$$

• One way to subtract is to **count** *down* **by 1** on the Hundred-Number Chart.

$6 - 2 = 4$

Start at 6 and count down 2 numbers:

$6 \longrightarrow 5 \longrightarrow 4$

• We can show subtraction by crossing out circles.

Example

Show the subtraction.

10 – 3 = 7

1. Draw 10 circles.

2. Mark out 3 circles.

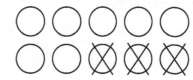

© Saxon

> **3.** Count the circles that are left: **7** circles.
>
> Ten **minus** three **equals** seven.

Lesson Practice

a. There are **7** days in a week. **Five** days have passed. How many days of the week are **left?**

_____ days

Start at 7. Count back 5.

b. There are 12 months in a year. How many months are left in a year after February? Write a subtraction sentence that shows the answer.

February is the **second** month.

$12 - 2 =$ _____

c. Use words and numbers to write the subtraction shown.

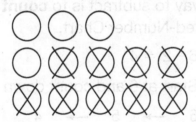

There are 13 circles in all.

Count the crossed out circles: _____ circles

Count the circles that are not crossed out: _____ circles

Thirteen minus n_____ equals f_____.

$13 -$ _____ $=$ _____

d. Follow the instructions to show this subtraction.

$11 - 5 = 6$

1. Start with 11 circles:

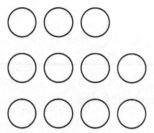

2. Cross out five circles.

3. How many circles are left? _____

Subtract. Count **down** by 1 or draw circles.

e. $5 - 1 =$ _____   **f.** $10 - 2 =$ _____

g.   4   **h.**   6
      -3 -4
      ____   ____

Written Practice   page 42

1. Explain how to count down on the number line to find $8 - 2$.

Start at 8 and count   d_____   to get _____.

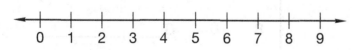

Use work area.

2. Draw circles to show the **sum.**

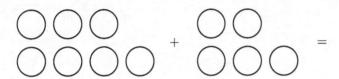

| Use work area. |

3. Find the pattern. Use the Hundred-Number Chart for help.

18, 24, 30, _____, _____, _____, _____, ...

| Use work area. |

4. 18, 27, 36, _____, _____, _____, _____, ...

| Use work area. |

5. Which month has an extra day in a leap year?

See page 3 in the *Student Reference Guide.*

6. morning

Remember to write a.m. or p.m.

hours:minutes

7.   7   addend
   + 3   addend

       sum

8.   8   a _____

    + 5   a _____

       s _____

| Use work area. | | Use work area. |

© Saxon

9. Count up to 5 and write 5 below the mark.

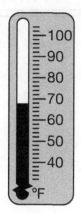

Draw a dot at 8.

Use work area.

10. Count up by 2.

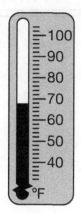

Remember to write °F or °C.

11. **quarter to noon**	12. **half past four** in the **afternoon**

Remember to write a.m. or p.m.	

© Saxon

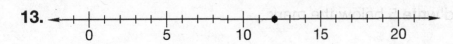
13.

Count up by 1.

14. morning

Remember to write a.m. or p.m.

15. 6:15 p.m.

q _____ past

s _____

Name _____

Teacher Note:
• Introduce Hint #5 "Addition/
  Subtraction Fact Families."

• Addition and Subtraction Fact Families

New Concept

• A **fact family** is a group of 3 numbers that make 2 addition facts and 2 subtraction facts.

$$\begin{array}{cccc}
3 & 4 & 7 & 7 \\
+\,4 & +\,3 & -\,4 & -\,3 \\
\hline
7 & 7 & 3 & 4
\end{array}$$

• When you learn **one** fact family, you know **four** facts.

Lesson Practice

a. Write two addition facts and two subtraction facts using the numbers 2, 5, and 7.

$$\begin{array}{cccc}
2 & 5 & 7 & 7 \\
+\,5 & +\,2 & -\,2 & -\,5 \\
\end{array}$$

b. Write two addition facts and two subtraction facts using the numbers 4, 6, and 10.

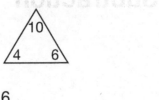

```
        6                        10
   4                  10
 + 6        +        - 6        -
```

c. Three months plus 9 months total 12 months. Write two addition facts and two subtraction facts using 3, 9, and 12.

```
   3          9          12          12

 +          +          -           -
```

d. Which of these sets of numbers **can** be used to make an addition and subtraction fact family? Circle your answer.

Which two numbers add up to the third?

A 3, 4, 5   **B** 3, 6, 9   **C** 6, 8, 10

© Saxon

1. There are 12 months.
September is the **ninth** month.

12 − 9 = _____

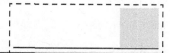

2.

Count up by 1.

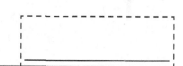

3. quarter to seven in the **morning**

Remember to write a.m. or p.m.

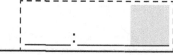

4. Find the pattern. Use the Hundred-Number Chart for help.

60, 55, 50, _____, _____, _____, _____, ...

Use work area.

© Saxon

5. 4, 8, 12, _____, _____, _____, _____, ...

> Use work area.

6. Add.

   $7 + 8 =$

7. $9 + 9 =$

8. Subtract.

   $10 - 1 =$

9. $8 - 7 =$

_____

10. Who came home earlier?

Bob

quarter after four

Sister

half past four

_____

11. fact family

1	4	5	5
+_____	+_____	−_____	−_____

_____

Use work area.

12. Which is **not** a fact family?

Which two numbers do not add up to the third?

A 2, 7, 9

B 3, 5, 8

C 2, 4, 7

D 2, 9, 11

13. Remember to write a.m. or p.m.
hours:minutes

14. What is the **seventh** month?

15. Is 32°F hot or cold? Why?

Use the *Student Reference Guide.*

_____, because water f_____ at 32°F.

Use work area.

© Saxon

📖 page 48

Name _____

Teacher Notes:

• Introduce Hint #6 "Finding Missing Numbers."

• Refer students to "Missing Numbers" on page 7 in the *Student Reference Guide*.

• Review "Word Problem Keywords" on page 6 in the *Student Reference Guide*.

• Unknown Addends

New Concept

Math Language

An **addend** is one of the numbers that is added in an addition problem.

• Some addition problems have a missing **addend.**

• The missing number is shown with a letter or a box.

$$\begin{array}{r} 3 \\ + m \\ \hline 8 \end{array} \quad \begin{array}{r} 3 \\ + \square \\ \hline 8 \end{array}$$

• To find a missing addend, **subtract.**

$$\begin{array}{r} 4 \\ + m \\ \hline 7 \end{array} \rightarrow \begin{array}{r} \\ - 4 \\ \hline m = 3 \end{array} \qquad \begin{array}{r} \square \\ + 4 \\ \hline 9 \end{array} \rightarrow \begin{array}{r} 9 \\ - 4 \\ \hline \square = 5 \end{array}$$

• Watch for these addition cue words:

  some more
  total
  in all

Lesson Practice

Find the missing addend:

Subtract.

a. $\square$ = _____

$$\begin{array}{r} 3 \\ + \square \\ \hline 7 \end{array} \rightarrow \begin{array}{r} 7 \\ - 3 \\ \hline \end{array}$$

© Saxon

b. $a =$ _____

$$\begin{array}{r} 5 \\ + \ a \\ \hline 7 \end{array} \rightarrow \begin{array}{r} 7 \\ - \ 5 \\ \hline \end{array}$$

c. ▢ = _____

$$\begin{array}{r} 16 \\ 9 \\ + \ ▢ \\ \hline 16 \end{array} \rightarrow \begin{array}{r} \\ - \\ \hline \end{array}$$

d. $n =$ _____

$$\begin{array}{r} 2 \\ + \ n \\ \hline 7 \end{array} \rightarrow \begin{array}{r} \\ - \ 2 \\ \hline \end{array}$$

e. Maria had 5 pencils. Her friend gave her **some more.** Then she had

9 pencils. How many pencils did Maria's friend give her? _____ pencils

$$\begin{array}{r} 5 \\ + \ m \\ \hline 9 \end{array} \rightarrow \begin{array}{r} 9 \\ - \ 5 \\ \hline \end{array}$$

 Written Practice 📖 page 50

1. fact family

$$\begin{array}{r} 3 \\ + \\ \hline \end{array} \qquad \begin{array}{r} 6 \\ - \\ \hline \end{array}$$

Use work area.

© Saxon

2. 30 minutes is what fraction of an hour?

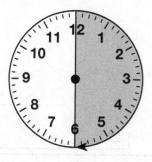

3. Add.

6 + 3 =

4. 2 + 5 =

5. _____; Amy used four numbers. A fact family has only

_____ numbers.

Use work area.

6. Subtract.

$$\begin{array}{r} 6 \\ + \square \\ \hline 10 \end{array} \quad \longrightarrow \quad \begin{array}{r} 10 \\ - 6 \\ \hline \end{array}$$

$\square =$ _____

7.

$$\begin{array}{r} 3 \\ + m \\ \hline 12 \end{array} \quad \longrightarrow \quad \begin{array}{r} 12 \\ - \\ \hline \end{array}$$

$m =$ _____

8.

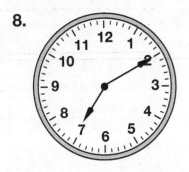

The minute hand is the long hand.

_____

9. Subtract.

$9 - 3 =$

_____

10. $4 - 4 =$

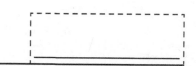

11.

$$\xleftarrow{\hspace{0.3cm}} \overset{\displaystyle\downarrow}{\underset{20}{|}} + + \underset{30}{|} + + + \underset{40}{|} + + + \xrightarrow{\hspace{0.3cm}}$$

Count up by 2.

12. 1 hour = _____ minutes

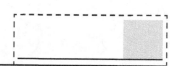

13. February 24, 1992

Use a number for the month.

_____ / _____ / _____

© Saxon

14. Write noon in digital form.

_____:_____ p.m.

15. 9, _____, _____, ⊖

Count up by 9.

© Saxon

Name _____

📖 page 52

Teacher Notes:

• Introduce Hint #7 "Column Addition (Sets of Ten)."

• Refer students to "Sets of Ten" on page 13 in the *Student Reference Guide*.

• Adding Three Numbers

New Concept

• To add three numbers:

1. Add two of the numbers.

2. Add the third number to the sum of the first two.

Example

Add 4 + 3 + 5.

1. Add 4 and 3:

$$4 + 3 = 7$$

2. Add 5 to the sum of the first two numbers:

$$7 + 5 = 12$$

• We can add 4, 3, and 5 in any order. The sum is always 12.

$$4 + 3 + 5 = 12$$
$$3 + 4 + 5 = 12$$
$$5 + 4 + 3 = 12$$

• Add **sets of 10** first.

Example

Add 8 + 3 + 2.

1. 8 and 2 make 10, so we add them first.

$$8 + 2 = 10$$

2. Add 3 and 10:

$$3 + 10 = 13$$

• This chart shows the numbers that add to 10:

Sets of 10

9 + 1 = 10
8 + 2 = 10
7 + 3 = 10
6 + 4 = 10
5 + 5 = 10

Lesson Practice

Add.

a. $1 + 3 + 2 =$

First, $1 + 3 =$ _____

Then, $2 +$ _____ $=$ _____

b. $4 + 4 + 4 =$ _____

c. Find sets of ten.

$\overset{\bullet}{6} + 5 + \overset{\bullet}{4} =$ _____

d. $5 + 4 + 1 =$ _____

e. Carol has 8 sheets of orange paper, 5 sheets of black paper, and 2 sheets of blue paper on her desk. How many sheets of paper does she have in total? _____

Find sets of ten.

```
    8 • orange
    5   black
 +  2 • blue
 _____
    total
```

© Saxon

1. last three months of the year

_____, _____, _____

Which has 30 days? _____

Use work area.

2. Use a student clock.

• Point the hour hand between 1 and 2.

• Point the minute hand at 8.

• It is dark outside.

Remember to write a.m. or p.m.

3. Find the pattern. Use the Hundred-Number Chart for help.

7, 14, 21, 28, _____, _____, _____, _____, ...

Use work area.

4. 3, 6, 9, 12, _____, _____, _____, _____, ...

Use work area.

5. 6, 12, 18, _____, 30, _____, 42, _____, ...

| Use work area. |

6. Subtract.

$$\begin{array}{r} 8 \\ + n \\ \hline 14 \end{array} \longrightarrow \begin{array}{r} 14 \\ - \\ \hline \end{array}$$

| $n =$ _____ |

7.

$$\begin{array}{r} 1 \\ + \square \\ \hline 9 \end{array} \longrightarrow \begin{array}{r} \\ - 1 \\ \hline \end{array}$$

| $\square =$ _____ |

8. 1 week = 7 days

5 weeks = _____ days

© Saxon

9. Add.

$$9 + 2 + 7 =$$

First, $9 + 2 =$ _____.

Then, $7 +$ _____ $=$ _____.

10. $6 + 3 + 5 =$

11. Subtract.

$$8 - 3 =$$

12. $7 - 1 =$

© Saxon

13. fact family

         1   4   5   5

    + __   + __   − __   − __

> Use work area.

14. ◯◯ + ◯◯ = ◯◯◯◯
◯◯ ◯◯◯ ◯◯◯◯◯

Words: four plus f_____ = n_____

numbers: 4 + _____ = _____

> Use work area.

15. $5 + 4 + 3 = 12$

   a. addends: _____, _____, and _____

   b. sum: _____

> Use work area.

Teacher Note:
- Students will need a copy of **Lesson Activity 5** to complete this Investigation.

 page 56

Focus on
• Pictographs and Bar Graphs

- Jan counted the number of sunny days in three months: January, February, and March.

- For every sunny day, Jan made a tally mark in a chart.

Sunny Days

Month	Tally
January	卌 卌 ‖
February	卌 ‖‖
March	卌 卌 ‖‖‖

Math Language
A **graph is a** diagram that shows data in an organized way.

- Each mark is a piece of **data.**

- A **pictograph** uses pictures to show data. The pictograph below shows the data for sunny days.

Sunny Days	
January	☼ ☼ ☼ ☼ ☼ ☼
February	☼ ☼ ☼ ☼
March	☼ ☼ ☼ ☼ ☼ ☼ ☼

Key
☼ = 2 days

- At the bottom of the pictograph is a **key.** The key shows that **1 sun stands for 2 sunny days.**

- To count the number of sunny days, *count up by 2.*

© Saxon

1. The row for **March** shows how many **sun pictures?** _____

2. How many **sunny days** did Jan count in **March?**

_____ days

Count up by 2 on the sun pictures.

3. If Jan counts 10 sunny days in April, how many suns will

she draw? _____ suns

One sun is 2 sunny days.

How many suns is 10 sunny days?

- The chart below shows the high temperature in degrees Celsius for the first five days of March.

High Temperatures in March

Date	1st	2nd	3rd	4th	5th
°C	8	10	14	12	10

- A **bar graph** shows data with bars of different heights. The bar graph below shows the temperature data.

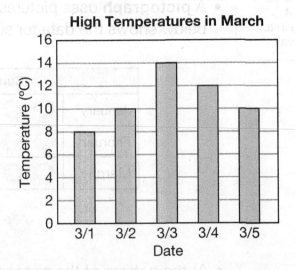

- The left side of the bar graph has a scale that shows temperature.

4. What is the **title** of the graph?

H_____ Temperatures in

M_____

5. What does the label on the **bottom** of the bar graph say?

D_____

What does the label on the **left side** of the graph say?

T_____ (°C)

6. What was the high temperature on **March 4?**

_____

Find the bar labeled 3/4.
Remember to write °C or °F.

How do you know?

The top of the bar is at _____ on the

t_____ scale.

7. How can you tell which day had the **highest temperature?**

The tallest bar shows the h_____
temperature.

Activity 📖 page 57

Pictograph and Bar Graph

Materials needed:

- **Lesson Activity 5**

Pictograph: Follow the instructions to create a pictograph titled *Rainy Days* from the chart below.

Rainy Days

Month	Number of Days
January	9
February	12
March	6

- The pictograph will be the top graph on **Lesson Activity 5.**

- Write *Rainy Days* on the **title** line.

- In the left column, write the three months from the chart.

- Find the **key.**

  Draw a cloud in the empty box.

- **One cloud equals 3 rainy days.**

  Write *3 rainy days* on the line next to the box.

- January had 9 rainy days.

  One cloud equals 3 rainy days, so 3 clouds equal 9 rainy days.

- Draw **3 clouds** in the box next to **January.**

- February had 12 rainy days. How many clouds will equal 12 rainy days?

  _____ clouds

- Draw the clouds in the box next to February.

- March had how many rainy days?

  _____ rainy days

- How many clouds does March need?

  _____ clouds

- Draw the clouds in the box next to March. Your pictograph is done!

Bar Graph: Write *Sunny Days in Spring* for the title of your bar graph on **Lesson Activity 5.**

8. Write *Months* at the bottom label of the graph.

9. Write *April, May,* and *June* in order above the months label.

10. Turn your paper and write *Number of Days* on the label along the left.

11. Turn your paper back. Find the scale on the left of the graph where 0 and 30 are written. The scale counts up by 5. Write the numbers *5, 10, 15, 20,* and *25* going up the scale.

12. The chart below shows the data for the bar graph.

Sunny Days in Spring

Month	Number of Days
April	10
May	15
June	25

- April had 10 sunny days.

- Find "April" on your graph.
  Find "10" on the scale.

- Draw a rectangle above "April" that goes up to 10.
  Color in your rectangle.

- Look at the chart above. How many sunny days did **May** have?

  _____ sunny days

- Find "May" on your graph.
  Find "15" on the scale.

- Draw a rectangle above "May" that goes up to 15.
  Color in your rectangle.

- How many sunny days did **June** have?

  _____ sunny days

- Draw a rectangle for "June" on your graph.
  Color in your rectangle.

- Your bar graph is done!

Name _____

📖 page 59

Teacher Notes:

• Introduce Hint #8 "Place Value (Digit Lines)."

• Refer students to "Expanded Notation" on page 9 and "Place Value Through Thousands" on page 13 in the *Student Reference Guide*.

• Students need a copy of **Lesson Activity 6** to complete this lesson. Money manipulatives can be found in the manipulative kit or on **Lesson Activities 7–9**.

• Place Value

New Concept

• A **digit** is any single number:

0, 1, 2, 3, 4, 5, 6, 7, 8, 9

• Larger numbers use more than one digit.

537 has **three** digits: 5, 3, and 7.

• Where a digit is in a number tells the **place value** of the digit.

Example

537

5 means 5 *hundreds* (500).

3 means 3 *tens* (30).

7 means 7 *ones* (7).

Hundreds	Tens	Ones
5	3	7

© Saxon

- **Expanded form** shows the value of each digit in a number.

Example

$$537 = 500 + 30 + 7$$

5 $100 bills, **3** $10 bills, and **7** $1 bills makes **$537**.

**Activity**   📖 page 61

Place Value

Materials needed:

- **Lesson Activity 6**
- money manipulatives

Cindy's friend counted her money at the end of a game.
*She had **eight** $1 bills, **four** $100 bills, and **nine** $10 bills.*

- How many $100 bills did Cindy have? _____ $100 bills

  Put $100 bills onto the place value chart.

- How many $10 bills did Cindy have? _____ $10 bills

  Put $10 bills onto the place value chart.

- How many $1 bills did Cindy have? _____ $1 bills

  Put $1 bills onto the place value chart.

- How much money is that in all? $_____ _____ _____

a. Nate had seven $10 bills, three $100 bills, and two $1 bills.

How much money is that? _____ _____ _____

Be careful! The digits are not in order.

b. Add: $200 + $5 + $70 = _____ _____ _____

How many hundreds? tens? ones?

Use bills to show each number on **Lesson Activity 6.** Then write each number in **expanded form.**

How many hundreds? tens? ones?

c. 54 = ___50___ + _____

d. 230 = _____ + _____

There are no ones.

e. 403 = _____ + _____

There are no tens.

f. 324 = _____ + _____ + _____

Written Practice   📖 page 63

1. expanded form
520

How many hundreds?
tens? ones?

_____ + _____

2.   5   4

_____ _____

3.   3   5   6

How much money? _____ _____ _____

hundreds place: _____

Use work area.

---

4. quarter of an hour

A 15 minutes

B 30 minutes

C 45 minutes

D 60 minutes

---

5. expanded form
365

How many hundreds? tens? ones?

_____ + _____ + _____

6. Find the pattern. Use the Hundred-Number Chart for help.

7, 14, 21, 28, _____, _____, _____, _____, ...

Rule: Count up by _____.

Use work area.

---

7. 30, 27, 24, _____, _____, _____, _____, ...

Rule: Count _____ by _____.

Use work area.

© Saxon

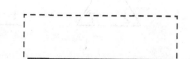

8. Find sets of ten.

$$
\begin{array}{r}
5 \; \bullet \\
9 \\
+ \; 5 \; \bullet \\
\hline
\end{array}
$$

9.

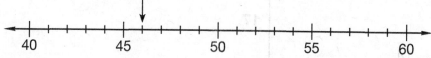

Count up by 1.

10.

The minute hand is the long hand.

11. $200 + $30 + $5 =

How many hundreds? tens? ones?

12. Add.

Find sets of ten.

$8 + 2 + 3 =$

13. $6 + 4 + 2 =$

14. Subtract.

$10 - 6 =$

15. fact family

2   7

+___   +___   −___   −___

Use work area.

---

16. Subtract.

14

6
+ m   →   −___
14

m = ___

17.

7
+ m   →   −___
10

m = ___

---

18. Count up by 2.

Remember to write °F or °C.

___

---

19. quarter after six in the **morning**

hours:minutes
Remember to
write a.m. or p.m.

___ : ___

20.

3 a ___

+ 7 a ___

10 s ___

Use work area.

© Saxon

📖 page 65

Name _____

Teacher Notes:
- Introduce Hint #9 "Writing Numbers."
- Refer students to "Spelling Numbers" on page 12 in the *Student Reference Guide.*

• Reading and Writing Numbers Through 999

New Concept

- We use these number words to write all the numbers from 0 to 999.

0	zero	10	ten	20	twenty
1	one	11	eleven	30	thirty
2	two	12	twelve	40	forty
3	three	13	thirteen	50	fifty
4	four	14	fourteen	60	sixty
5	five	15	fifteen	70	seventy
6	six	16	sixteen	80	eighty
7	seven	17	seventeen	90	ninety
8	eight	18	eighteen	100	one hundred
9	nine	19	nineteen		

- Use a hyphen (-) to write the numbers from 21 to 99.

  24   twenty-four

  37   thirty-seven

  568   five hundred sixty-eight

- Do not write "and" unless you mean dollars and cents.

  $4.52   four dollars **and** fifty-two cents

Lesson Practice

Use numbers and a dollar sign to write the following.

How many hundreds? tens? ones?

a. six hundred twenty-five dollars

_____ _____ _____

b. two hundred eight dollars

_____ 0 ____

Use words to write each amount.

If you need help, use the number word list.

c. $648

_____ hundred _____-_____ dollars

d. 706

_____ hundred _____

e. Write the amount of money shown.

How many hundreds? tens? ones?

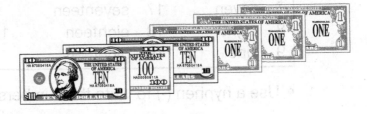

numbers: _____

words: _____ hundred _____-_____ dollars

© Saxon

1.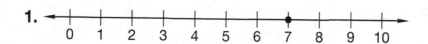

2. expanded form

640 = _____ + _____

How many hundreds? tens? ones?

ones place: _____

There are no ones. What digit means none?

⌐ ‎ ⌐
Use work area.
⌐ ‎ ⌐

3. five $10 bills and nine $1 bills

words: _____ dollars

numbers: _____ _____

Remember to write the dollar sign.

© Saxon

⌐ ‎ ⌐
Use work area.
⌐ ‎ ⌐

4. _____ months in a year

— ___5___ months gone

_____ months left

_____ − 5 = _____

Use work area.

5. 6, 12, 18, 24, _____, _____, _____, _____, …

Rule: Count _____ by _____.

Use work area.

6. 44, 40, 36, _____, _____, _____, _____, …

Rule: Count _____ by _____.

Use work area.

7. $683

_____ hundred _____ -

_____ dollars

Use work area.

8. nine hundred ninety-nine

How many hundreds? tens? ones?

9. $600 + $7 + $50 =

Remember to write the dollar sign.

10. Add.

    $6 + 8 =$

11. $4 + 2 + 7 =$

12. $9 + 7 =$

13. Subtract.

    $9 - 5 =$

14. $8 - 5 =$

15. Number the tick marks. Then draw a dot at 2.

$$\begin{array}{ccccccc} & & & & & & \\ \hline 0 & & & & 5 & & \end{array}$$

Use work area.

16. Subtract.

$$\begin{array}{r} 9 \\ 5 \\ + x \\ \hline 9 \end{array} \rightarrow \begin{array}{r} \\ - \\ \hline \end{array}$$

$x =$

© Saxon

17.

hours:minutes

Remember to write a.m. or p.m.

_____ : _____

18. fact family

3   5

+ _____   + _____   − _____   − _____

Use work area.

19. between Ben and Brenda

Find Ben and Brenda. Circle them.

20. 1 week = 7 days

2 weeks = _____ days

Add 2 days to that.

A 14 days

B 15 days

C 16 days

© Saxon

• Adding Two-Digit Numbers

New Concept

- To add two-digit numbers:

    1. Add the ones.
    2. Add the tens.
    3. With money, write the dollar sign.

Example

Add: 31 + 40

Line up the numbers to add.

3

1

+

4

7   1

Add the ones: $1 + 0 = 1$. Write "1" below the ones.

Add the tens: $3 + 4 = 7$. Write "7" below the tens.

The sum is **71**.

- **Regroup** if there are more than 10 ones.

- Regrouping means *trading 10 ones for 1 ten.*

 **Activity** 📖 page 71

Regrouping

This activity is optional.

Example

Add: 36 + 27

Line up the numbers.

Add the ones: 6 + 7 = 13. We must **regroup.**

Write "3" below the ones and write "1" above the tens.

Now add the tens: 1 + 3 + 2 = 6. Write "6" below the tens.

Add ones. ⎤
Add tens. ⎦

$$\begin{array}{r} \overset{1}{} \\ 3\,6 \\ +\,2\,7 \\ \hline 6\,3 \end{array}$$

The sum is **63.**

Lesson Practice

Add.

Remember to write the dollar sign in money problems.

a.
$$\begin{array}{r} \$60 \\ +\ \$22 \\ \hline \end{array}$$

b.
$$\begin{array}{r} 1\,0 \\ 4\,9 \\ +\,3\,0 \\ \hline \end{array}$$

© Saxon

c.
```
    3|0
    2|0
  + ||5
  ——
```

d.
```
    $20
  + $20
  ——
```

e. How much money is **four** $10 bills and **eleven** $1 bills? _____ _____

Regroup. 11 is 1 ten and 1 one.

Add.

f. Regroup.
```
    1
   $39
  + $23
  ——
```

g.
```
   26
  + 52
  ——
```

h. Regroup.
```
    1
   35
  + 16
  ——
```

Written Practice 📖 page 73

1. $526

_____ hundred _____-_____ dollars

tens place: _____

⌐ ‾ ‾ ‾ ‾ ‾ ‾ ‾ ⌐
¦ Use work area. ¦
└ _ _ _ _ _ _ _ ┘

2. $30
```
  + $30
  ——
```

Remember to write the dollar sign.

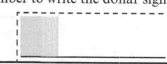

© Saxon

3. expanded form
256

How many hundreds? tens? ones?

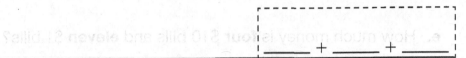

_____ + _____ + _____

4. Count the months after September.

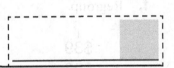

5. 55, 50, 45, 40, _____, _____, _____, _____, ...

Rule: Count _____ by _____.

Use work area.

6. 14, 21, 28, 35, _____, _____, _____, _____, ...

Rule: Count _____ by _____.

Use work area.

7. $53
    + $10

Remember to write the dollar sign.

8. five hundred twenty-four dollars

How many hundreds? tens? ones?
Remember to write the dollar sign.

9. half an hour

10. Add.

$60
+ $20

Remember to write the dollar sign.

11. Regroup.

15
+ 19

12.
$ 80
+ $5 0 0

13.
$. 5
$3 0 0
+ $ 4 0

14. Subtract.

$12 - 2 =$

15. $9 - 2 =$

16. fact family

3   7

+____   +____   -____   -____

Use work area.

17. quarter to eight in the **morning**

____ : ____

18. Add $6 + 7$. Then subtract the sum.

```
  6        14
  g
+ 7   →   -____
____
 14
```

$g =$ ____

19.
```
  45
+ m    →    - 45
____        ____
  55
```

$m =$ ____

20. November 10, 1998

____ / ____ / ____
month   day   year

How many months **before** November? _____ months

See page 3 in the *Student Reference Guide.*

Use work area.

Name _____

Teacher Notes:
- Introduce Hint #10 "Borrowing."
- For additional practice, students may complete Targeted Practice 14.

• Subtracting Two-Digit Numbers

New Concept

- To subtract two-digit numbers:

    1. Subtract the ones.
    2. Subtract the tens.
    3. With money, write the dollar sign.

Example

Subtract: 35 – 12

Line up the numbers to subtract.

First subtract ones. ⎯⎯⎯⎯⎐
Then subtract tens. ⎯⎯⎯⎯⎐

$$\begin{array}{r} 3\,5 \\ -\,1\,2 \\ \hline 2\,3 \end{array}$$

1. Subtract the ones: $5 - 2 = 3$. Write "3" below the ones.
2. Subtract the tens: $3 - 1 = 2$. Write "2" below the tens.
The difference is **23**.

- Sometimes there are not enough ones in the top number to subtract.

- **Borrow** one ten from the tens.

    1. Borrow one ten from the neighbor.
    Write a small "1" next to the ones digit.

    2. Leave a note.
    Cross out the tens digit and write the number that is one less.

    3. Subtract the ones and the tens.

 **page 76**

Regrouping For Subtraction

This activity is optional.

Example

Subtract: 61 – 15

Line up the numbers.

Subtract the ones: 1 – 5. We cannot subtract 5 from 1. **Borrow** from the neighbor.

1. Borrow one ten from the neighbor. Write "1" next to the ones digit.

2. Leave a note. Cross out the "6" and write "5."

$$\begin{array}{r} \overset{5}{\cancel{6}}{}^{1}1 \\ -15 \\ \hline 46 \end{array}$$

3. Subtract the ones: 11 – 5 = 6. We write "6" below the ones.

   Subtract the tens: 5 – 1 = 4. We write "4" below the tens.

   The difference is **46**.

Lesson Practice

Subtract.

Remember to write the dollar sign in money problems.

a.	b.	c.
81 − 30	$97 − $55	14 − 10

© Saxon

d. Borrow.

$$\begin{array}{r} 4 \\ \$\,\cancel{5}^{1}6 \\ -\;\$\,2\,7 \\ \hline \end{array}$$

e. Borrow.

$$\begin{array}{r} 2 \\ \cancel{3}^{1}5 \\ -\;\;1\,9 \\ \hline \end{array}$$

f. Borrow.

$$\begin{array}{r} \$\,4\,3 \\ -\;\$\,3\,5 \\ \hline \end{array}$$

Written Practice page 78

1. $247

_____ hundred _____-_____ dollars

!-------------------!
! Use work area. !
!-------------------!

2. expanded form
247

How many hundreds? tens? ones?

_____ + _____ + _____

3. months with 30 days

See page 3 in the *Student Reference Guide.*

_____, _____,

_____, _____

!-------------------!
! Use work area. !
!-------------------!

4. _____, _____, _____, _____, 90, 100, 110, 120, ...

Start at the end and count down.

!-------------------!
! Use work area. !
!-------------------!

5. _____, _____, _____, _____, 54, 63, 72, 81, ...

!-------------------!
! Use work area. !
!-------------------!

6. $50
   − $40

Remember to write the dollar sign.

7. $50
  + $20

8. $46
  − $32

9. $37
  + $20

10. eight hundred nineteen dollars

How many hundreds? tens? ones?

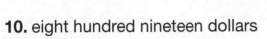

Remember to write the dollar sign.

© Saxon

11. fact family

15   15

+ ___   + ___   − ___   − ___

¡ Use work area. ¡

12. Regroup.

$27
+ $28
___

Remember to write the dollar sign.

13. 7 + 5 + 2 =

14. Subtract.

Borrow.

$55
− $27
___

Remember to write the dollar sign.

15. Find sets of ten.

5 + 5 + 5 =

16. quarter after four in the **morning**

_____:_____

---

17. Which has a **sum** of 10?

A 5 + 10 = 15   **B** 10 = 6 + 4

C 10 + 3 = 13   **D** 10 + 10 = 20

---

18. Add 90 + 10. Then subtract the sum.

```
   90              110
    m
 +  10     →     − _____
  110
```

_m =_ _____

19.
```
     5
     m
 +  10     →     − _____
    25
```

_m =_ _____

---

20. 11 − 4 =

© Saxon

📖 page 79

Name _____

Teacher Notes:

• Introduce Hint #11 "Estimating or Rounding."

• Refer students to "Estimate" on page 8 in the *Student Reference Guide.*

• For additional practice, students may complete Targeted Practice 15.

• Rounding to the Nearest Ten and Hundred

New Concept

Math Language

The numbers 0, 1, 2, 3, 4, 5, 6, 7, 8, and 9 are **digits**.

Larger numbers use more than one **digit**.

• To **round** a number:

1. <u>Underline</u> the place value which you are rounding to.

2. (Circle) the digit to its right.

3. Ask: Is the circled digit 5 or more? (5, 6, 7, 8, 9)

   Yes → **Add 1** to the underlined digit.
   No → The underlined digit **stays the same.**

4. Replace the circled digit and all digits to the right with **zero.**

Example

Round 63 to the *nearest ten*.

This number line shows that 63 is between 60 and 70. Is 63 closer to 60 or 70?

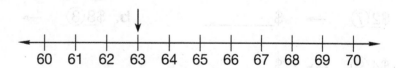

1. Underline the *tens digit,* 6.
2. Circle the digit to the right, 3.

$$6③$$

3. Ask, "Is 3 more or less than 5?"

   Three is **less than** 5, so the 6 stays the same.

4. The 3 becomes zero.

$$6③ → 60$$

63 rounds to **60.**

Example

Round 367 to the *nearest hundred*.

This number line shows that 367 is between 300 and 400.
Is 367 closer to 300 or 400?

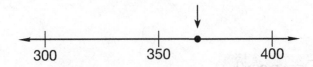

300   350   400

1. Underline the *hundreds digit*, 3.
2. Circle the digit to the right, 6.

3⑥7

3. Ask, "Is 6 more or less than 5?"

   Six is **more than** 5, so we add 1 to 3 and write 4.

4. The 6 and the 7 become zeros.

3⑥7 ⟶ 400

367 rounds to **400.**

• **About** and **estimate** are cue words for rounding.

Lesson Practice

Round each price to the **nearest ten.**

a. $2⑦ ⟶ $_____   **b.** $8③ ⟶ $_____

c. $4⑨ ⟶ $_____

Round each price to the **nearest hundred.**

d. $3①7 ⟶ $_____   **e.** $1⑥8 ⟶ $_____

f. $7②9 ⟶ $_____

© Saxon

g. Round each of the numbers in the story below.

Last weekend Frank made muffins to sell at the carnival. He made **38 muffins** *on Saturday and* **23 muffins** *on Sunday.* **About** *how many muffins did Frank make on Saturday and Sunday?*

3⃞8 ⟶ _____   2⃞3 ⟶ _____

Use your rounded numbers to write a number sentence.

_____ + _____ = _____

Complete this sentence that solves the problem.

On Saturday and Sunday, Frank made about _____ muffins.

Written Practice
📖 page 82

1. $894

_____ hundred _____ -

_____ dollars

¡ Use work area. ¡

---

2. expanded form
894

How many hundreds? tens? ones?

_____ + _____ + _____

---

3. $2⃞8 ⟶

$3⃞3 ⟶ + __

A $50

B $60

C $70

D $80

_____

4. nearest ten

Remember to write the dollar sign.

a. $2④ →

b. $3⑥ →

a. _____

b. _____

5. nearest hundred

a. $6②1 →

b. $8⑦6 →

a. _____

b. _____

6. $75
    − $50

7. $5:0:0
     + $: :5:0

8. Borrow.

    $31
    − $15

9. Regroup.

    $35
    + $16

10. fact family

___ + ___   ___ + ___   ___ − ___   ___ − ___

Use work area.

© Saxon

11. Label 55 on the number line. Then draw dots at 52, 54, and 57.

Use work area.

12. Is $768 closer to $700 or $800?

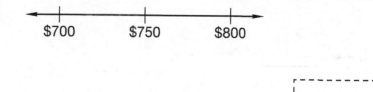

13. seven hundred eighty-six dollars

How many hundreds? tens? ones?

Remember to write the dollar sign.

14.
```
  $30
  $30
+ $30
```

15.
```
  $42
- $12
```

16. 8, 16, 24, 32, _____, _____, _____, _____, ...

Rule: Count _____ by _____.

Use work area.

© Saxon

17. Subtract.

$$\begin{array}{r} 60 \\ + \; m \\ \hline 100 \end{array} \quad \rightarrow \quad \underline{-}$$

$$m = \underline{}$$

18.

$$\begin{array}{r} 4 \\ + \; q \\ \hline 11 \end{array} \quad \rightarrow \quad \underline{-}$$

$$q = \underline{}$$

19. 27 is closer to _____ than to _____ .

....

!Use work area.!

20. morning

digits: _____ : _____

words: q _____ after e _____

!Use work area.!

Name _____

• Adding Three-Digit Numbers

New Concept

• To add three-digit numbers:

  1. Add the ones.
  2. Add the tens.
  3. Add the hundreds.

• **Regroup** when a sum is more than 10.

Example

Add: $154 + $382

Line up the numbers to add.

1. Add the ones: 4 + 2 = 6. Write "6" below the ones.

2. Add the tens: 5 + 8 = 13.

13 is more than 10, so **regroup.**

Write "3" below the tens and write "1" above the hundreds.

Add ones ⎯⎯⎯⎯⎯⎯⎯⎯⎯⎯⎯⎯⎯⎯⎯⎯┐
  Add tens ⎯⎯⎯⎯⎯⎯⎯⎯⎯⎯⎯⎯┐ │
    Add hundreds ⎯⎯⎯⎯⎯┐ │ │
                      ↓ ↓ ↓

$$\begin{array}{r} 1 \\ \$154 \\ +\$382 \\ \hline \$536 \end{array}$$

3. Add the hundreds: 1 + 1 + 3 = 5. Write "5" below the hundreds.

The sum is **$536.**

© Saxon

Add.

Remember to write the dollar sign in money problems.

a. $430
    + $120

b.   123
    + 245

c. Regroup the ones.

    249
   + 325

d. Regroup the tens.

    $571
   + $364

e. How much money is **five** $100 bills, **three** $10 bills, and **thirteen** $1 bills?

_____ _____ _____

Regroup. 13 is 1 ten and 3 ones.

Add.

f.   431
    + 263

g. Regroup.

    $648
   + $237

h. Regroup.

    362
   + 194

Written Practice   📖 page 90

1. Add.

Regroup.

    $162
   + $253

Remember to write the dollar sign.

© Saxon

2. $444

_____ hundred _____-_____ dollars

Use work area.

3.

4. expanded form
560
How many hundreds? tens? ones?

_____ + _____

5. 3, 6, 9, 12, _____, _____, _____, _____, ...

Use work area.

6. 6, 12, 18, 24, _____, _____, _____, _____, …

Use work area.

7.

Jess

  1   3   9

Jess has $ _____.

Gayle

  4   2   3

Gayle has $ _____.

Now add.

Regroup.

$$+ \underline{}$$

© Saxon

8. nearest hundred

Remember to write the dollar sign.

a. $8⑦2 →

b. $4⑥3 →

9. nearest ten

a. 8① →

b. 1⑥ →

a. _____

b. _____

a. _____

b. _____

10. The **minute hand** points to what number?

_____

11. quarter of an hour plus half an hour

A 4 + 30

B 25 + 30

C 15 + 30

D 25 + 50

_____

12. Remember to write the dollar sign.

$16
− $ 5

13. 58
+ 10

14. 8
8
+ 8

© Saxon

15. Borrow.
Remember to write the dollar sign.

$$\begin{array}{r} \$25 \\ -\ \$17 \\ \hline \end{array}$$

16.
$$\begin{array}{r} 1\,2\,7 \\ +\ 6\,3\,1 \\ \hline \end{array}$$

17.
$$\begin{array}{r} \$58 \\ -\ \$30 \\ \hline \end{array}$$

18. Subtract.

$$\begin{array}{r} 35 \\ +\ m \\ \hline 55 \end{array} \longrightarrow \begin{array}{r} - \\ \hline \end{array}$$

$m =$

19.

$$\begin{array}{r} 30 \\ +\ \square \\ \hline 100 \end{array} \longrightarrow \begin{array}{r} - \\ \hline \end{array}$$

$\square =$

20. fact family

_____ + _____   _____ + _____   _____ − _____   _____ − _____

Use work area.

© Saxon

Name _____

Teacher Notes:
- Introduce Hint #12 "Comparing Numbers."
- Refer students to "Comparison Symbols" on page 12 in the *Student Reference Guide*.

• Comparing and Ordering, Part 1

New Concept

- **Comparing** numbers is telling which number is greater (bigger) or lesser (smaller).

- A **comparison symbol (>)** shows which number is greater.

- The **big end** of the comparison symbol points to the **bigger number.**

$$6 > 3 \qquad\qquad 4 < 8$$
Six is greater than 3.   Four is less than 8.

- To compare three-digit numbers:

   1. Compare the **hundreds.**
      The number with more hundreds is the greater number.

   2. If the hundreds are the same, compare the **tens.**
      The number with more tens is the greater number.

   3. If the tens are the same, compare the **ones.**
      The number with more ones is the greater number.

Example

Write < or > in the circle to compare the numbers.

475 ◯ 425

1. Compare the hundreds.

   Both numbers have 4 hundreds, so go to the next digit.

© Saxon

2. Compare the tens.

7 is more than 2.

So 475 is greater than 425.

Write the symbol so the big end points to the bigger number.

475 (>) 425

Example

Write these numbers in order from least to greatest:

424, 428, 324

Compare three numbers in the same way.

1. Compare the hundreds.

Two of the numbers have 4 hundreds.

The other has 3 hundreds.

324 is the least number.

2. Compare the tens.

Both numbers left have 2 tens.

3. Compare the ones.

8 is more than 4.

428 is the greatest number.

Write the numbers from *least to greatest.*

324, 424, 428

Lesson Practice

a. Write < or > in the circle to compare:

Compare tens.

$29 ( ) $57

b. Which costs less, a basketball for **$15** or a baseball bat for **$30?**

_____

Compare tens.

c. Write < or > in the circle to compare:

Compare hundreds.
Compare tens.

$193 ◯ $163

d. Put these numbers in order from **least to greatest:**

273, 615, 480

Compare hundreds.

_____, _____, _____
    least   greatest

Written Practice page 95

1. Add.

$$\$\,5\,2\,4$$
$$+\ \$\,1\,1\,2$$

2. Which is greater, $432 or $423?

Compare hundreds.
Compare tens.

3. $405

_____ hundred _____ dollars

Use work area.

4. nearest hundred

three hundred forty-seven

How many hundreds? tens? ones?

$\$\_\_\_\_$ ⊖ $\_\_\_\_$ →

Remember to write the dollar sign.

5. Regroup.

$$\begin{array}{r} \$1\,1\,9 \\ + \ \$1\,1\,9 \\ \hline \end{array}$$

Remember to write the dollar sign.

6. 6, 12, 18, 24, _____, _____, _____, _____, ···

Find the pattern. Use the Hundred-Number Chart for help.

Use work area.

7. 60, 70, 80, 90, _____, _____, _____, _____, ···

Use work area.

8. nearest ten

a. 9② →

b. 6⑧ →

a. _____

b. _____

9. nearest hundred

Remember to write the dollar sign.

a. \$4③8 →

b. \$3⑨8 →

a. _____

b. _____

© Saxon

10.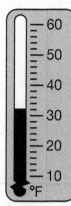

Gia should wear a _____ because

the temperature is _____.

Use work area.

11. Add.

$$
\begin{array}{r}
\$2\,4\,8 \\
+\ \$3\,0\,0 \\
\hline
\end{array}
$$

12. Subtract.

$$
\begin{array}{r}
\$36 \\
-\ \$12 \\
\hline
\end{array}
$$

13.
$$
\begin{array}{r}
7 \\
7 \\
+\ 7 \\
\hline
\end{array}
$$

14.
$$
\begin{array}{r}
36 \\
-\ 34 \\
\hline
\end{array}
$$

15. Regroup.

$$
\begin{array}{r}
52 \\
+\ 28 \\
\hline
\end{array}
$$

16. Remember to write the dollar sign.

$$
\begin{array}{r}
\$26 \\
-\ \$23 \\
\hline
\end{array}
$$

© Saxon

17. Subtract.

$$
\begin{array}{r}
25 \\
+\ m \\
\hline
100
\end{array}
\quad \rightarrow \quad
\begin{array}{r}
- \\
\hline
\end{array}
$$

$m = $

18.

$$
\begin{array}{r}
\square \\
+\ 36 \\
\hline
66
\end{array}
\quad \rightarrow \quad
\begin{array}{r}
- \\
\hline
\end{array}
$$

$\square = $

19.

digits: _____ : _____

words: q _____ to S _____

Use work area.

20.

$$
\begin{array}{r}
\quad\quad \text{December} \\
+\ \underline{\quad\quad}\quad \text{January} \\
\hline
\quad\quad \text{days}
\end{array}
$$

A 60 days

B 61 days

C 62 days

© Saxon

Name _____

Teacher Notes:
- Review Hint #4 "Word Problem Cues, Part 1."
- Review "Word Problem Keywords" on page 6 in the *Student Reference Guide*.

• Some and Some More Stories, Part 1

New Concept

- **Some and some more** stories have an addition formula.

  John had $5. Then he earned $7. Now John has $12.

Some	$\longrightarrow$	$ 5
+ Some more	$\longrightarrow$	+$ 7
Total	$\longrightarrow$	$12

- A **number sentence** for the story is:

  $5 + $7 = $12

- In some stories, the total is missing. **Add** to find the total.

Example

Write a number sentence for the story. Then answer the question.

> Mickey saw 15 rabbits. Then he saw 7 more rabbits. How many rabbits did he see in all?

This is an addition story. The total number of rabbits is missing.

15 rabbits + 7 rabbits = t rabbits

Add to find the total: $15 + 7 = 22$. **Mickey saw 22 rabbits in all.**

- Look for these addition cue words:

total	altogether
in all	both

© Saxon

a. Write a number sentence for the following story.

> Gus had **seven dollars**. He received **five dollars** more in a birthday card. Then Gus had **twelve dollars.**

$_____ + $_____ = $_____

b. The following story has a missing number. Write a number sentence for this story.

> Diane ran **5 laps** in the morning. She ran **8 laps** in the afternoon. How many laps did she run **in all?**

_____ laps + _____ laps = ☐ laps

Add and complete the sentence to answer the question.

Diane ran _____ laps in a_____.

c. Write a number sentence for this story.

> Dan had some play money in his pockets. He had $50 in his left pocket and $25 in his right pocket. How much play money did Dan have in both pockets?

$_____ + $_____ = ☐

Add and complete the sentence to answer the question.

Dan had $_____ in _____ pockets.

d. Complete the some and some more story for this number sentence.

> 7 birds + 8 birds = ? birds

Jen saw _____ birds. Then she saw _____ more birds.

How many birds did Jen see in _____?

© Saxon

1. $\$\_\_\_\_ + \$\_\_\_\_ = \square$

S_____ had _____ dollars.

Use work area.

2. nearest hundred
seven hundred sixty-seven
How many hundreds? tens? ones?

 →

_____

3. $\$\_\_\_\_ + \$\_\_\_\_ = \square$

Nate had _____.

Use work area.

4. $919

_____ hundred _____ dollars

Use work area.

5. expanded form
919

How many hundreds? tens? ones?

____ + ____ + ____

6. Regroup.

$$\begin{array}{r} \$167 \\ + \$528 \\ \hline \end{array}$$

Remember to write the dollar sign.

---

7. 4, 8, 12, _____, _____, _____, _____, 32, ...

Use work area.

---

8. 9, 18, _____, _____, _____, _____, 63, 72, ...

Use work area.

---

9. Is $248 closer to $200 or $300?

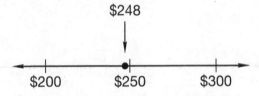

$248

$200 $250 $300

© Saxon

10.

The minute hand is the long hand.

---

11. $65
     − $24

12.   56
        − 54

---

13.   38
        − 15

14.   6
        6
      + 6

---

15. $56
     − $32

16. $100
        $ 60
      + $ 4

---

17. Subtract.

$$
\begin{array}{r}
m \\
+\ 32 \\
\hline
52
\end{array}
\qquad \longrightarrow \qquad
\begin{array}{r}
- \\
\hline
\end{array}
$$

m = _____

18.

$$
\begin{array}{r}
\square \\
+\ 10 \\
\hline
100
\end{array}
\qquad \longrightarrow \qquad
\begin{array}{r}
- \\
\hline
\end{array}
$$

□ = _____

19. quarter to nine o'clock in the **morning**

hours:minutes

Remember to write a.m. or p.m.

_____:_____

20. quarter of an hour plus half an hour

A 15 minutes

B 30 minutes

C 45 minutes

D 60 minutes

© Saxon

Name _____

Teacher Notes:

• Review Hint #10 "Borrowing."

• For additional practice, students may complete Targeted Practice 19.

• Subtracting Three-Digit Numbers, Part 1

New Concept

• To subtract three-digit numbers:

    1. Subtract the ones.

    2. Subtract the tens.

    3. Subtract the hundreds.

• If there are not enough ones or tens in the top number, **borrow.**

Example

Subtract: $430 − $70

Line up the numbers.

    1. Subtract the ones: $0 − 0 = 0$. Write "0" below the ones.

    2. Subtract the tens: $3 − 7$. You cannot subtract 7 from 3. **Borrow.**

    Borrow "1" from the next number and write that "1" next to the tens digit.

    Leave a note. Cross out the "4" and write "3."

$$
\begin{array}{ccc}
\text{Start} & & \\
\downarrow & {\scriptstyle 3} & {\scriptstyle 3} \\
\$4\,3\,0 & \$\cancel{4}{}^{1}3\,0 & \$\cancel{4}{}^{1}3\,0 \\
-\$\ \ 7\,0 & -\$\ \ 7\,0 & -\$\ \ 7\,0 \\
\hline
0 & 0 & \mathbf{\$3\ 6\,0}
\end{array}
$$

$13 − 7 = 6$. We write "6" below the tens.

© Saxon

3. Subtract the hundreds: 3 − 0 = 3. Write "3" below
the hundreds.

The difference is **$360.**

Lesson Practice

Subtract to solve the story problems. Remember to write the dollar sign.

a. Cindy had $843. She landed on a property that had a house. She had to
pay Matt $125. How much money did she have left?

Borrow.

$$
\begin{array}{r}
{\scriptstyle 3} \\
\$ 8\ 4\ 3 \\
-\ \$ 1\ 2\ 5 \\
\hline
\end{array}
$$

b. Matt had $720. He had to pay Cindy $250. How much money did he have left?

Borrow.

$$
\begin{array}{r}
{\scriptstyle 6} \\
\$ 7\ 2\ 0 \\
-\ \$ 2\ 5\ 0 \\
\hline
\end{array}
$$

Subtract.
Borrow.

c.

$$
\begin{array}{r}
{\scriptstyle 5} \\
\$ 6\ 3 \\
-\ \$ 4\ 7 \\
\hline
\end{array}
$$

d.

$$
\begin{array}{r}
\$ 3\ 5\ 4 \\
-\ \$ 1\ 8\ 2 \\
\hline
\end{array}
$$

© Saxon

1. $321
   + $123

Remember to write the dollar sign.

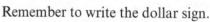

---

2. $_____ + $_____ = ?

   N_____ and Julie had _____ together.

Use work area.

---

3. $_____ + $_____ = ?

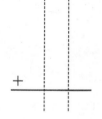

Yolanda had _____.

Use work area.

---

4. $6⟨7⟩ → _____

   $6⟨7⟩0 → _____

Use work area.

---

5. expanded form
   330

   How many hundreds? tens? ones?

   _____ + _____

© Saxon

6. Subtract.

$$
\begin{array}{r}
\$5\,6\,7 \\
-\ \$2\,3\,2 \\
\hline
\end{array}
$$

Remember to write the dollar sign.

7. 14, 21, 28, 35, _____, _____, _____, _____, ...

Use work area.

8. 25, 50, 75, 100, _____, _____, _____, _____, ...

Use work area.

9. nearest ten

$\$9\,①\ \rightarrow$ _____

nearest hundred

$\$9\,①0\ \rightarrow$ _____

Use work area.

© Saxon

10. quarter past nine in the **morning**

Was Terrance on time?

_____ because quarter past

nine in the morning is

_____:_____ and Terrance arrived at 9:30 a.m.

> Use work area.

11. $56
     + $43

Remember to write the dollar sign.

12. $59
     − $35

13.   6
           8
        + 10

14. $14
     − $ 4

Remember to write the dollar sign.

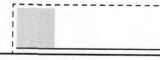

© Saxon

15. Find sets of ten.

$$
\begin{array}{r}
5 \\
7 \; \bullet \\
+ \; 3 \; \bullet \\
\hline
\end{array}
$$

16. Remember to write the dollar sign.

$$
\begin{array}{r}
\$35 \\
- \; \$20 \\
\hline
\end{array}
$$

17. Add 6 and 4. Then subtract the sum.

$$
\begin{array}{r}
m \\
6 \\
+ \; 4 \\
\hline
10
\end{array}
\qquad
\begin{array}{r}
10 \\
- \\
\hline
\end{array}
$$

m = _____

18. Subtract.

$$
\begin{array}{r}
\square \\
+ \; 36 \\
\hline
40
\end{array}
\rightarrow
\begin{array}{r}
- \\
\hline
\end{array}
$$

□ = _____

19. Show how to write five minutes after six o'clock in the morning in digital form.

_____ : _____

20. Which does **not** say 9:45 a.m.?

A a quarter after nine in the morning

B nine forty-five in the morning

C a quarter of ten a.m.

D a quarter to ten in the morning

© Saxon

Name _____

Teacher Notes:

• Review Hint #4 "Word Problem Cues, Part 1."

• Review "Word Problem Keywords" on page 6 in the *Student Reference Guide*.

• Some Went Away Stories, Part 1

New Concept

• **Some went away** stories have a subtraction formula.

John had $12. He spent $5 for a book. Then he had $7.

Some	$12
− Some went away	− $ 5
What is left	$ 7

Math Language

The answer in a subtraction problem is called the **difference**.

• A number sentence for the story is:

$$\$12 - \$5 = \$7$$

• In some stories, the answer is missing.

Subtract to find what is left.

Example

Write a number sentence for the story. Then answer the question.

Rebecca had $65. Then she spent $13. How much money did Rebecca have left?

This is a subtraction story. The money left is missing.

$$\$65 - \$13 = \square$$

Subtract to find what is left:

$$\begin{array}{r} \$65 \\ - \$13 \\ \hline \$52 \end{array}$$

Rebecca had $52 left.

- Look for these subtraction story cue words:

    left

    change

Lesson Practice

Write a number sentence for each story. Subtract to find each answer. Complete the sentence to answer the question. Remember to write the dollar sign.

a. Donald had **$26.** He **spent $12** on a new game. How much money did he have **left?**

$_____ – $_____ =

$26
– $12

Donald had _____ left.

b. Sarah had **$43.** Then she bought a new coat for **$36.** How much money did Sarah have after she bought the coat?

$_____ – $_____ =

Borrow.

$43
– $36

Sarah had _____ after she bought the   C_____.

c. Jim had **$40.** He bought a shirt that cost $25. How much **change** did he get?

$_____ – $_____ =

Borrow.

$40
– $25

J_____ got _____ in change.

Written Practice 📖 page 110

1. first three months

See page 3 in the *Student Reference Guide*.

Month	Days
_____	_____
_____	_____
_____	_____

‹ Use work area. ›

2. $_____ + $_____ = ☐

\+

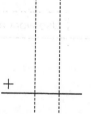M_____ had  _____.

‹ Use work area. ›

© Saxon

3. $\$$_____ – $\$$_____ = ☐

–_____   Jenny had   ▢_____ .

Use work area.

4. $\$647$

_____ hundred _____-_____ dollars

Use work area.

5. expanded form
647
How many hundreds? tens? ones?

_____ + _____ + _____

6. How many hundreds? tens? ones?
Remember to write the dollar sign.

_____ _____ _____

7. 18, 27, 36, 45, _____, _____, _____, _____, …

Use work area.

8. 18, 24, 30, 36, _____, _____, _____, _____, …

Use work area.

© Saxon

9. Subtract.

Borrow.

Remember to write the dollar sign.

$$\begin{array}{r} \$3\,4\,0 \\ -\ \$1\,2\,6 \\ \hline \end{array}$$

10.

```
  15
 7   8
```

___ + ___ + ___ - ___ - ___

Use work area.

11. Remember to write the dollar sign.

$$\begin{array}{r} \$57 \\ -\ \$52 \\ \hline \end{array}$$

12.
$$\begin{array}{r} 25 \\ +\ 73 \\ \hline \end{array}$$

13.
$$\begin{array}{r} 3\,4\,0 \\ -\ 1\,4\,0 \\ \hline \end{array}$$

14. Regroup.

Remember to write the dollar sign.

$$\begin{array}{r} \$2\,7\,9 \\ +\ \$1\,1\,9 \\ \hline \end{array}$$

15. Regroup.

$$\begin{array}{r} 5 \\ 7 \\ 4 \\ +\ 1\,0 \\ \hline \end{array}$$

16. Remember to write the dollar sign.

$$\begin{array}{r} \$34 \\ +\ \$51 \\ \hline \end{array}$$

© Saxon

17. in all

Alan

Kalia

+___ Alita

fish in all

18.

$$
\begin{array}{r} 8 \\ + m \\ \hline 15 \end{array} \rightarrow \; \underline{}
$$

m = _____

19.

$$
\begin{array}{r} 56 \\ + \square \\ \hline 86 \end{array} \rightarrow \; \underline{}
$$

□ = _____

20.   shoes

+_____ socks

3   3

total

Is this the right amount of money?

_____ because the total was $ _____ and the money

shown is $ _____.

Use work area.

© Saxon

page 112

Focus on
• Working with Money

Teacher Note:

• This Investigation has been adapted for individual work without money manipulatives. If students wish to use money manipulatives for the work, they can follow the activity on pages 112–113.

• In this Investigation, Anne and Bob take turns **exchanging** money.

• When Anne gives Bob money, subtract from Anne's total and add to Bob's total.

• When Bob gives Anne money, subtract from Bob's total and add to Anne's total.

• **Show all your work on this paper. Remember to write the dollar sign.**

 page 112

Money Exchanges

Materials needed:

• none

• Anne and Bob both start with **three** $100 bills, **four** $10 bills, and **five** $1 bills.

3   4   5

• How much money is that? _____ _____ _____

How many hundreds? tens? ones?

© Saxon

- After each exchange see if your answers match the starting amount for the next exchange.

First Exchange

- Anne gives Bob $32.

- Subtract $32 from Anne. Add $32 to Bob.

Anne	Bob
$3|4|5	$3|4|5
− $ |3|2	+ $ |3|2

- Anne now has $_____. Bob now has $_____.

Second Exchange

- Bob gives Anne $43.

- Add $43 to Anne. Subtract $43 from Bob.

Anne	Bob
$3|1|3	$3|7|7
+ $ |4|3	− $ |4|3

- Anne now has $_____. Bob now has $_____.

© Saxon

Third Exchange

- Anne gives Bob $128.

- Subtract $128 from Anne. Add $128 to Bob.

Anne	**Bob**
Borrow.	Regroup.
$3⋮5⋮6	$3⋮3⋮4
− $1⋮2⋮8	+ $1⋮2⋮8

- Anne now has $_____. Bob now has $_____.

Fourth Exchange

- Bob gives Anne $114.

- Add $114 to Anne. Subtract $114 from Bob.

Anne	**Bob**
Regroup.	Borrow.
$2⋮2⋮8	$4⋮6⋮2
+ $1⋮1⋮4	− $1⋮1⋮4

- Anne now has $_____. Bob now has $_____.

© Saxon

Fifth Exchange

- Anne gives Bob $161.

- Subtract $161 from Anne. Add $161 to Bob.

Anne	Bob
Borrow.	Regroup.
$3 4 2	$3 4 8
− $1 6 1	+ $1 6 1

- Anne now has $_____. Bob now has $_____.

Sixth Exchange

- Bob gives Anne $164.

- Add $164 to Anne. Subtract $164 from Bob.

Anne	Bob
Regroup.	Borrow.
$1 8 1	$5 0 9
+ $1 6 4	− $1 6 4

- Anne now has $_____. Bob now has $_____.

- How much money did Anne and Bob have at the

  beginning? _____

- Anne and Bob have as much money as they started with!

Teacher Note:
• Refer students to "Money" on page 4 in the *Student Reference Guide*.

• Naming Dollars and Cents
• Exchanging Dollars, Dimes, and Pennies

New Concepts

• **Naming Dollars and Cents**

• To show cents (pennies), we can write money with a **cent sign (¢).**

    324¢   20¢   4¢

• Cents can also be shown using a dollar sign and a **decimal point.**

• The **two digits after the decimal point** show cents.

    $3.24   3 dollars **and** 24 cents

    $0.20   20 cents

    $0.04   4 cents

• **Do not use a dollar sign and a cent sign together.**

• **Exchanging Dollars, Dimes, and Pennies**

• A **penny** is 1 cent.   1¢ $0.01

• A **dime** is 10 cents.   10¢ $0.10

• 10 pennies = 1 dime

• 10 dimes = 1 dollar

© Saxon

Activity 📖 page 115

Exchanging Pennies for Dimes

Materials needed:

- **Lesson Activity 11,** money manipulatives

  1. Count the number of pennies in this picture. Write the number of pennies in the chart below.

Dimes	Pennies
0	

How many cents is that? _____¢

  2. Trade ten pennies for 1 dime. On the drawing above, cross out 10 pennies. Write the number of pennies that are left in the chart below.

Dimes	Pennies
1	

  3. How many cents is 1 dime and 2 pennies? _____¢

  4. What do the digits "1" and "2" mean in 12¢?

     _____ dime and _____ pennies

© Saxon

Exchanging Dimes for Dollars

5. The chart below shows 0 dollars, 14 dimes, and 5 pennies. Take those coins from your money kit.

How much money is that? _____¢

Count up by 10 for the dimes. Then count up by 1 for the pennies.

Dollars	Dimes	Pennies
0	14	5

6. Trade ten dimes for 1 dollar. In the chart below, write the number of dimes that are left.

Dollars	Dimes	Pennies
1		5

7. How much money is that? $_____ . _____ _____

8. What do the digits "1," "4," and "5" mean in $1.45?

_____ dollar, _____ dimes, and _____ pennies

Lesson Practice

a. Describe three ways to make 21¢ using dimes and pennies.

_____ dimes and 1 penny

1 dime and _____ pennies

_____ pennies

b. Describe how to make $3.45 using $1 bills, dimes, and pennies.

_____ $1 bills, _____ dimes, and _____ pennies

c. How much money is three $1 bills, 11 dimes, and 12 pennies?

$_____ . _____ _____

Written Practice

📖 page 117

1. See page 3 in the *Student Reference Guide*.

Month	Days
_____	_____
_____	_____
_____	_____

Use work area.

2. $_____ – $_____ = /

M_____ had 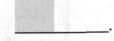 _____ .

Use work area.

3.

_____
+ _____
_____

Jenny had _____ .

Use work area.

4. Subtract.
Borrow.

$62
– $28

© Saxon

5. $873

_____

_____ dollars

Use work area.

---

6. Subtract.

Borrow.

$80
− $54

---

7. 8, 16, 24, _____, _____,

_____, _____, ...

Use work area.

8. 4, 8, 12, _____, _____,

_____, _____, ...

Use work area.

---

9. ten minutes before midnight

10.

    8
    9
+ 10

---

11. $54
      − $12

12. Regroup.

    $36
+ $47

© Saxon

13. $56
      − $21

14. Regroup.

$4 9 5
+ $ 1 0

15. Borrow.

   34
 − 25

16. 99 cents

$0.____

____¢

Use work area.

17.   9
          4
       + m   →   − ____
         15

m = ____

18.   75
        + □   →   − ____
         100

□ = ____

19. Minute hand points to what?

20. Thirty days hath September,

_____, _____,

and _____.

Use work area.

© Saxon

• Adding Dollars and Cents

New Concept

Math Language

A **decimal point** is a symbol that separates dollars from cents.

decimal point

↓

$ 9 . 5 3

dollars ↑ ↑ ↑ pennies
dimes

• To add dollars and cents:

1. Write the numbers with the decimal points lined up.

2. Add the pennies.

3. Add the dimes.

4. Add the dollars.

• **Regroup** when a sum is more than 10.

• The decimal point goes straight down.

Example

Add: $4.85 + $3.72

1. Line up the numbers to add. The decimal points go in a line.

2. Add the pennies.

5 + 2 = 7. Write "7" below the pennies.

3. Add the dimes.

8 + 7 = 15. 15 is more than 10. **Regroup.**

Write "5" below the dimes and write "1" above the dollars.

$$
\begin{array}{r}
1 \\
\$4.85 \\
+ \ \$3.72 \\
\hline
\$8.57
\end{array}
$$

4. Add the dollars.

$1 + 4 + 3 = 8$. Write "8" below the dollars.

The decimal point in the answer is straight down from the decimal points in the problem.

The sum is **$8.57** (8 dollars and 57 cents).

Lesson Practice

Add.

Remember to write the dollar sign and decimal point in money problems.

a. Regroup.

$$\begin{array}{r} \$6.44 \\ + \ \$3.38 \\ \hline \end{array}$$

b. Regroup.

$$\begin{array}{r} \$2.72 \\ + \ \$5.18 \\ \hline \end{array}$$

c. Nathan bought a game for $6.29 plus $0.44 tax. What was the total price?

$$\begin{array}{r} \$6.29 \\ + \ \$0.44 \\ \hline \end{array}$$

Written Practice

 page 122

1. five $1 bills, **twelve** dimes, **fifteen** pennies

10 pennies = 1 dime

10 dimes = 1 dollar

© Saxon

2. ┆┆┆ first turn

  + ┆┆┆ second turn

3. three $100 bills and **four** $10 bills

  − $ ┆3┆0

4. Subtract.

Borrow.

$81
− $27

5. one hundred five dollars

6. See page 3 in the *Student Reference Guide.*

7. 18, 24, 30, _____, _____, _____, _____, …

┆ Use work area. ┆

8. Which **rounds** to $80?

____ ◯ → $80

A $73

B $93

C $82

D $89

Use work area.

9. $79
  − $55

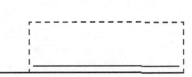

10. Regroup.

  25
+ 25

11. $46
  − $35

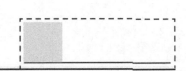

12. Regroup.

  48
+ 63

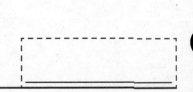

13. $52
        − $32

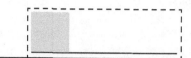

14. Regroup.

```
   4
   7
+ 10
```

15. Borrow.

$60
− $24

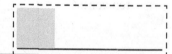

16.

```
  350
+   m  →  − ____
  450
```

$m =$

17.

```
   □
  10
+ 15  →  − ____
  30
```

$□ =$

© Saxon

18. after dinner

19. 2¢ = \$_____ . _____ _____

two cents

\$0.10 = _____¢

ten cents

Use work area.

20. Label the mark at 20. Draw a dot at 25.

Use work area.

© Saxon

Name _____

Teacher Note:
• Review Hint #10 "Borrowing."

• Subtracting Three-Digit Numbers, Part 2

New Concept

- To subtract three-digit numbers:

  1. Subtract the ones.

  2. Subtract the tens.

  3. Subtract the hundreds.

- If there are not enough ones or tens in the top number, **borrow.**

Example

Subtract: $465 − $247

Line up the numbers.

1. Subtract the ones: 5 − 7. There are not enough ones. **Borrow.**

Borrow one ten from the neighbor.

Write that "1" next to the ones digit.

Leave a note. Cross out the "6" and write "5."

$$\begin{array}{r} \overset{5}{\$4\,\cancel{6}^{1}5} \\ -\ \$2\,4\,7 \\ \hline \$2\,1\,8 \end{array}$$

15 − 7 = 8. Write "8" below the ones.

2. Subtract the tens: 5 − 4 = 1. Write "1" below the tens.

3. Subtract the hundreds: 4 − 2 = 2. Write "2" below the hundreds.

The difference is **$218.**

Lesson Practice

Subtract.

a. Borrow.

$$
\begin{array}{r}
\$4\,2\,6 \\
-\ \$1\,7\,6 \\
\hline
\end{array}
$$

b. Borrow.

$$
\begin{array}{r}
\$5\,8\,4 \\
-\ \$1\,2\,6 \\
\hline
\end{array}
$$

c. Borrow.

$$
\begin{array}{r}
\$7\,1\,4 \\
-\ \$3\,4\,2 \\
\hline
\end{array}
$$

d. The groceries cost $70. The customer has $130. How much money will the customer have **left?**

Borrow.

$$
\begin{array}{r}
\$1\,3\,0 \\
-\ \$\ \,7\,0 \\
\hline
\end{array}
$$

e. Margie went to the mall with $242. She spent $28. Then how much money did Margie have?

Borrow.

$$
\begin{array}{r}
\$2\,4\,2 \\
-\ \$\ \,2\,8 \\
\hline
\end{array}
$$

Written Practice

 page 127

1. $_____ + $_____ = t

$$
\begin{array}{r}
\quad\quad \text{Saturday} \\
+\ \quad\quad \text{Sunday} \\
\hline
\end{array}
$$

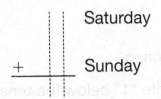

_____ spent $_____ in all.

Use work area.

© Saxon

2. $_____ – $_____ = /

        –_____   The clerk gave _____ $____.

3. $_____ – $_____ = /
Borrow.

_____ raisins are |_____.

4. Add.

    $6.45
  + $5.35

Remember to write the decimal point.

5. expanded form

    375

_____ + _____ + _____

6. fact family

+ _____   + _____   − _____   − _____

!¡ Use work area. ¡!

7. 9, 12, 15, _____, _____, _____, _____, …

!¡ Use work area. ¡!

8. 21, 28, 35, _____, _____, _____, _____, …

!¡ Use work area. ¡!

9. six $1 bills, **eleven** dimes, **sixteen** pennies

10 pennies = 1 dime
10 dimes = 1 dollar

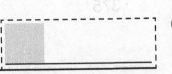

10. $24
      + $50

11. Borrow.

$$\begin{array}{r} \$3\,|3\,|0 \\ -\ \$2\,|5\,|0 \\ \hline \end{array}$$

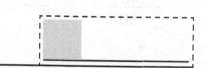

12.
$$\begin{array}{r} 5 \\ 8 \\ +\ 6 \\ \hline \end{array}$$

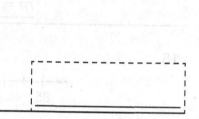

13. Borrow.

$$\begin{array}{r} \$5\,|1\,|6 \\ -\ \$\ \ |7\,|0 \\ \hline \end{array}$$

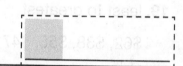

14.
$$\begin{array}{r} 4\,|6\,|3 \\ +\ 2\,|5\,|0 \\ \hline \end{array}$$

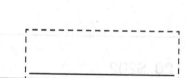

15.
$$\begin{array}{r} \$6\,|8\,|7 \\ -\ \$5\,|0\,|0 \\ \hline \end{array}$$

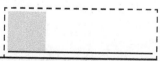

© Saxon

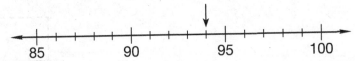

16.

$$\begin{array}{r} m \\ +\ 45 \\ \hline 50 \end{array} \rightarrow \ -\ \underline{\qquad}$$

m = \underline{\qquad}

17.

$$\begin{array}{r} \square \\ +\ 40 \\ \hline 100 \end{array} \rightarrow \ -\ \underline{\qquad}$$

$\square$ = \underline{\qquad}

18.

```
  ←——+——+——+——+——+——+——↓+——+——+——+——+——→
     85        90        95        100
```

\underline{\qquad}

19. least to greatest

$62, $38, $58, $47

Compare tens.

__$38__ , _____ , _____ , _____

Use work area.

20. $202

\underline{\qquad} dollars

Use work area.

© Saxon

Teacher Notes:

• Review Hint #7 "Column Addition (Sets of Ten)."

• Review "Sets of 10" on page 13 in the *Student Reference Guide*.

• Column Addition

New Concept

• To add several numbers:

1. Line up the numbers. Put all the ones digits in a column.

2. Add the ones.

3. Add the tens.

4. Add the hundreds.

• **Regroup** when a sum is more than 10.

Example

Math Language

A **column** is a vertical (up and down) arrangement of numbers.

ones column

```
    6 : 0
      : 9
 +  1 : 4
```

tens column

Add: $345 + $76 + 120

1. Line up the numbers. Put the ones digits in a column.

2. Add the ones: $5 + 6 + 0 = 11$. **Regroup.**

   Write "1" below the ones and "1" above the tens.

$$
\begin{array}{r}
1\,1 \\
\$345 \\
\$\ 76 \\
+\ \ \$120 \\
\hline
\mathbf{\$541}
\end{array}
$$

3. Add the tens: $1 + 4 + 7 + 2 = 14$. **Regroup.**

   Write "4" below the tens and "1" above the hundreds.

4. Add the hundreds: $1 + 3 + 1 = 5$.

   Write "5" below the hundreds.

The total is **$541**.

Add. Regroup when needed.

a. $4 2
      $5 6
  + $2 5

b. $2 4
      $3 5
  + $6 0

c. $2 5
      $2 5
  + $2 5

d. $1 2 5
     $ 5 0
  + $ 2 5

Written Practice   page 132

1.

      had

  − _____ gave

2. $2.65 sandwich
  + $0.21 tax

Remember to write the decimal point.

3. least to greatest

58, 52, 63

Compare tens.

Compare ones.

_____, _____, _____

least   greatest

Use work area.

4. Add.

$3.54
+ $8.65

Remember to write the decimal point.

5. $2<u>1</u>① →

$8<u>3</u>③ →

$1<u>6</u>⑥ → + _____

$_____ + $_____ + $_____ = t

6. closer to 80°F or 90°F?

Count up by 2.

Remember to write °F or °C.

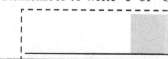

7. $450

_____

_____ dollars

Use work area.

8.

+ _____   + _____   − _____   − _____

Use work area.

9. half past _noon_

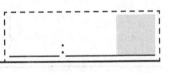

10. 14, 21, 28, 35, _____, _____, _____, _____, …

Use work area.

11. 8, 12, 16, 20, _____, _____, _____, _____, …

Use work area.

© Saxon

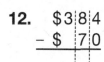

12. $3|8|4
       − $ |7|0

13. |8
          |7
          |5
       + 1|0

14.   450
        − 400

15. $5|8|7
       − $1|0|0

16. $8|7|5
       − $2|5|0

17.
```
  $1:5
  $2:5
+ $2:5
```

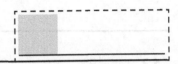

18. Subtract.

```
   37
 + m    →    −
  137
```

$m =$

19.

```
   □
 + 25    →    +
  75
```

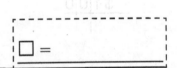

$□ =$

20. Count up by 2.

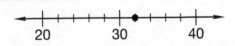

📖 page 134

Name _____

Teacher Note:
• Review "Money" on page 4 in the *Student Reference Guide*.

• Counting Dollars and Cents

New Concept

• A **penny** = 1¢   *Count up by 1.*

• A **nickel** = 5¢   *Count up by 5.*

• A **dime** = 10¢   *Count up by 10.*

• A **quarter** = 25¢   *Count up by 25.*

• To count bills and coins:

   1. Count the number of each kind of coin or bill.

   2. Start with the money that has the *greatest value* (bills, quarters, dimes, nickels, pennies).

   3. Count up by the value of the other money.

Example

Find the total value of these bills and coins.

Count **each kind** of money.

The $1 bills have the greatest value, so start counting with them.

Count up the *$1 bills.* $1.00, $2.00
Count up the *quarters by 25.* $2.25, $2.50
Count up the *dime by 10.* $2.60
Count up the *nickel by 5.* $2.65
Count up the *pennies by 1.* $2.66, $2.67
The total is **$2.67.**

 page 137

Counting Money
Materials needed:
- **Lesson Activity 12**
Use your textbook to complete this activity.

Lesson Practice

a. What is the total value of these coins?
Count each kind of coin.

_____ quarters   _____ dimes

_____ nickels   _____ pennies

Now count up the value of the coins, starting with the quarters. _____¢

© Saxon

b. What is the total value of these bills and coins?

Count each kind of bill or coin.

_____ $5 bill   _____ $1 bill

_____ quarters   _____ dimes

_____ nickels   _____ pennies

Now count up the value of the bills and coins, starting with the $5 bill.

$_____

Write number sentences and find the total value of the following:

c. a **quarter** plus a **dime** plus a **nickel**

_____¢ + _____¢ + _____¢ = _____¢

d. **two quarters** plus **three dimes**

Count up quarters by 25.
Count up dimes by 10.

_____¢ + _____¢ = _____¢

e. This table shows the values of certain numbers of **nickels.**
Complete the table through six nickels.

Number of nickels	1	2	3	4	5	6
Value in cents	5	10	15			

© Saxon

1. $\$\underline{\hspace{1cm}} + \$\underline{\hspace{1cm}} = t$

   Bus

$+ \underline{\hspace{1cm}}$ Taxi

Remember to write the decimal point.

The cost of both rides was

$\$\underline{\hspace{2cm}}$.

Use work area.

2. $\$\underline{\hspace{1cm}} - \$\underline{\hspace{1cm}} = l$

$-\underline{\hspace{1cm}}$

$\underline{\hspace{3cm}}$ had

$\$\underline{\hspace{2cm}}$.

Use work area.

3. 2 quarters, 1 dime, and 3 pennies

Count up quarters by 25.
Count up dimes by 10.
Count up pennies by 1.

$\underline{\hspace{1cm}}¢ + \underline{\hspace{1cm}}¢ + \underline{\hspace{1cm}}¢ = \underline{\hspace{1cm}}¢$

Use work area.

4. Add.

$$\begin{array}{r} \$7.27 \\ + \ \$1.45 \\ \hline \end{array}$$

Remember to write the decimal point.

5. nearest **ten**

   a. $28 \rightarrow$

   b. $11 \rightarrow$

Use work area.

6. nearest **hundred**

   a. $185 \rightarrow$

   b. $299 \rightarrow$

Use work area.

© Saxon

7. two hundred three dollars

8. After May 10, how many days are left in May?

See page 3 in the *Student Reference Guide*.

9.

___ + ___ + ___ − ___ − ___

10. 18, 27, 36, _____, _____, _____, _____, ...

Use work area.

Use work area.

11. 18, 24, 30, 36, _____, _____, _____, _____, ...

12. $89
      − $11

Use work area.

13. $4.25
      + $3.50

Remember to write the decimal point.

14. $3 8 7
      − $ 5 5

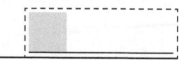

© Saxon

15.
```
  5 7 0
+   2 5
```

16.
```
  $8 6 5
- $3 3 0
```

17. Find sets of ten.
```
  8 •
1 0
+ 2 •
```

18.
```
  6 5
+ m
───
  7 5
```

$m =$ _____

19.
```
    5
    8
+   □
───
   15
```

$□ =$ _____

20. Is it closer to 11:15 p.m. or 11:20 p.m.?

It is closer to _____ p.m. because the time is

_____ minutes after 11:15 p.m. and _____ minutes

before 11:20 p.m.

Use work area.

Name _____

Teacher Notes:
- Review Hint #10 "Borrowing."
- For additional practice, students may complete Targeted Practice 26.

• Subtracting Dollars and Cents

New Concept

Math Language

A **decimal point** is a symbol that separates dollars from cents.

decimal point

↓

$ 9 . 5 3

dollars ⤴ ↑ ⤴ pennies
dimes

• To subtract dollars and cents:

1. Write the numbers with the decimal points lined up.

2. Subtract the pennies.

3. Subtract the dimes.

4. Subtract the dollars.

• If there are not enough ones or tens in the top number, **borrow.**

• The decimal point goes straight down.

Example

Subtract: $4.32 − $2.48

Line up the numbers. The decimal points go in a line.

1. Subtract the pennies: 2 − 8. **Borrow.**

Borrow "1" from the neighbor. Write that "1" next to the pennies. Cross out the "3" and write "2."

Subtract the pennies: 12 − 8 = 4.

2. Subtract the dimes: 2 − 4. **Borrow** again.

Borrow "1" from the neighbor. Write that "1" next to the dimes. Cross out the "4" and write "3."

$$
\begin{array}{r}
\overset{3}{}\overset{12}{} \\
\$4.\,\cancel{3}^1 2 \\
-\ \$2.\,4\,8 \\
\hline
\$1.\,8\,4
\end{array}
$$

Now subtract the dimes: 12 − 4 = 8.

3. Subtract the dollars: 3 − 2 = 1.

The decimal point in the answer is straight down from the decimal points in the problem.

The difference is **$1.84.**

Lesson Practice

Subtract.

Borrow.

a. $4.30
− $1.17

b. $6.28
− $3.56

c. $5.25
− $3.78

d. Karen had $6.25. She paid the taxi driver $4.50. Then how much money did Karen have?

$6.25
− $4.50

Written Practice

 page 144

1. $0.64 had

−   spent

_____

Remember to write the dollar sign and decimal point.

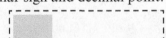

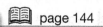

2. $0.39

$+$ _____

____ . ____

---

3. Subtract.

$5.75
$- $4.56

.

---

4. Add.

$6.89
$+ $4.56

.

---

5. nearest **ten**

$12 $\longrightarrow$

---

6. nearest **hundred**

$322 $\longrightarrow$

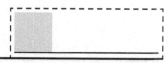

© Saxon

7. $24

_____ dollars

‎ Use work area.

8. 1 quarter, 2 dimes, 1 nickel, and 4 pennies

Count up quarters by 25.
Count up dimes by 10.
Count up nickels by 5.
Count up pennies by 1.

total = ____¢

Is that $1.00 or more? _____

Use work area.

9. quarter to nine in the **morning**

____ : ____

10. 48, 44, 40, 36, ____, ____, ____, ____, ...

Use work area.

11. 70, 63, 56, ____, ____, ____, ____, ...

Use work area.

12. $3.48
+ $2.60

Remember to write the dollar sign and decimal point.

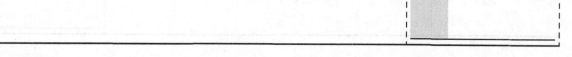

13. $385
− $250

14. 3|8
4|7
+ 1|0

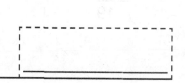

15. $3|4|6
+ $ |3|4

Remember to write the dollar sign.

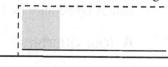

16. 8
7
5
+ 9

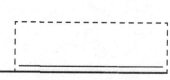

© Saxon

17. $1.77
    − $1.25

Remember to write the dollar sign and decimal point.

18.   *m*
        + 5
        ──
        25

m =

19.   6
            □
          + 3
          ──
           19

□ =

20. Which does **not** equal one dollar?

Count up quarters by 25.
Count up dimes by 10.
Count up nickels by 5.
Count up pennies by 1.

A four quarters

B ten dimes

C fifteen nickels

D one hundred pennies

© Saxon

📖 page 146

Name _____

Teacher Note:
• Review "Comparison Symbols" on page 12 in the *Student Reference Guide*.

• Comparing and Ordering Numbers, Part 2

New Concept

Math Language

0, 1, 2, 3, 4, 5, 6, 7, 8, and 9 are **digits**.

Larger numbers use more than one **digit**.

• **Least to greatest** means *smallest to biggest*.

• **Greatest to least** means *biggest to smallest*.

• To compare three-digit numbers:

　1. Compare the hundreds.

　2. Compare the tens.

　3. Compare the ones.

Example

Four students kept track of how many minutes they read at home in a week. Write the numbers in order from *least to greatest*.

Minutes Read in One Week

Student	Minutes
Cindy	327
Juan	432
Mikel	321
Marissa	486

1. Compare the hundreds.

　　　　　　　　327

　　　　　　　　432

　　　　　　　　321

　　　　　　　　486

Four hundreds is more than 3 hundreds.

432 and 486 are greater than 327 and 321.

2. Compare the tens in 432 and 486.

$$4\underline{3}2$$

$$4\underline{8}6$$

Eight tens is more than 3 tens, so 486 is greater than 432.

$$486 > 432$$

_____, _____, 432, 486

    least   greatest

Compare the tens in 327 and 321.

$$3\underline{2}7$$

$$3\underline{2}1$$

Both numbers have 2 tens.

3. Compare the ones in 327 and 321.

$$32\underline{7}$$

$$32\underline{1}$$

Seven ones is more than 1 one, so 327 is greater than 321.

$$327 > 321$$

The **least** (smallest) number is **321.**

From least to greatest, the numbers are:

321,   327,   432,   486

 least   greatest

Write the numbers in order from _greatest to least._

Greatest to least is least to greatest backwards.

486,   432,   327,   321

 greatest   least

Use the table to answer problems **a–d.**

Minutes Read in One Week

Student	Minutes
Alana	470
Diego	473
Kita	312
Loc	486

a. Which student read the **greatest** number of minutes?

Compare hundreds.
Compare tens.

_____

b. Which student read the **least** number of minutes? _____

c. Write the numbers in order from **least to greatest.**

_____, _____, _____, _____
  least   greatest

d. Write the **names** of the students in order from **greatest to least** number of minutes read.

Greatest to least is least to greatest backwards.

Loc, _____, _____, _____
greatest   least

Written Practice   📖 page 150

1. $3.56   lunch

   − _____ dinner

Remember
to write the
decimal point.

2. 9 dimes and 3 pennies

Count up dimes by 10.
Count up pennies by 1.

   − $0.43

© Saxon

3. Subtract.

$1.52
$$- \$1.48$$

4. Add.

$3.58
$$+ \$2.94$$

5. nearest **ten**

$39 →

6. nearest **ten**

$69 →

7. least to greatest

74°F, 66°F, 68°F, 86°F

_____, _____, _____, _____
least   greatest

Use work area.

8. 1 week = 7 days

5 weeks = _____ days

9. The number line below goes from 10 to 15. Label 10 and 15. Draw a dot at 11.

Use work area.

10. 16, 20, 24, 28, _____, _____, _____, _____, …

Use work area.

11. 16, 24, 32, 40, _____, _____, _____, _____ ...

_____  Use work area.

12. $52
  − $48

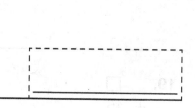

13.   8
     5
   + 10

14. $7⋮9⋮6
    − $7⋮9⋮0

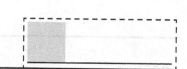

15. $4.25
   + $2.50

Remember to write the decimal point.

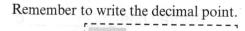

16. $7⋮8⋮6
    − $ ⋮7⋮6

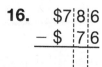

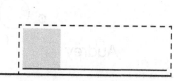

17.   5⎸8
          7⎸6
       + 3⎸0

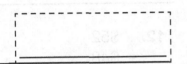

18.   *m*
          8
        + 7
         20

$m =$

19.   ☐
       + 45
          60

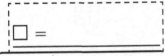

☐ =

20. Count up quarters by 25.
Count up dimes by 10.
Count up nickels by 5.
Count up pennies by 1.

Audrey: 1 quarter, 6 dimes, 2 pennies

Audrey has _____¢.

Kai: 2 quarters, 2 nickels, 3 pennies

Kai has _____¢.

_____¢ ◯ _____¢

Audrey   Kai

Use work area.

Name _____

Teacher Notes:
- Introduce Hint #13 "Borrowing Across Zeros."
- For additional practice, students may complete Targeted Practice 28.

• Subtracting Across Zeros

New Concept

- Sometimes we need to borrow, but the next number is a zero.

- Borrow across **all zeros** in one step.

Example

Subtract: $200 − $127

Line up the numbers.

Subtract the ones: 0 − 7. **Borrow.**

You cannot take away 1 from 0.

You **can** take 1 from 20:

20 − 1 = 19. Cross out the "20" and write "19" above it.

Write the borrowed "1" next to the ones.

$$
\begin{array}{r}
\overset{1\ 9}{\$2\cancel{0}{}^{1}0} \\
-\ \$1\,2\,7 \\
\hline
\$\ \ \ 7\,3
\end{array}
$$

Now subtract the ones: 10 − 7 = 3.

Subtract the tens: 9 − 2 = 7.

Subtract the hundreds: 1 − 1 = 0.

The difference is **$73.**

 📖 page 153

Subtracting Across Zeros

This activity is optional.

© Saxon

Subtract. Borrow across all zeros.

a.
$$\begin{array}{r} \$5\,0\,0 \\ -\ \$3\,7\,1 \\ \hline \end{array}$$

b.
$$\begin{array}{r} \$2\,0\,0 \\ -\ \$1\,4\,4 \\ \hline \end{array}$$

c.
$$\begin{array}{r} \$2\,0\,0 \\ -\ \$\ \,5\,6 \\ \hline \end{array}$$

d.
$$\begin{array}{r} \$1\,0\,0 \\ -\ \$\ \,3\,8 \\ \hline \end{array}$$

Written Practice

 page 154

1. Borrow across all zeros.

$$\begin{array}{rl} \$100 & \text{took} \\ -\ \$\ \,89 & \text{spent} \\ \hline \end{array}$$

2. _____ dollars

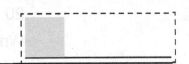

Use work area.

3. Regroup.

$$\begin{array}{rl} \$8.95 & \text{umbrella} \\ +\ \underline{} & \text{tax} \\ \hline \end{array}$$

Remember to write the decimal point.

© Saxon

4. 2 quarters, 1 dime, 1 nickel, 3 pennies

Count up quarters by 25.
Count up dimes by 10.
Count up nickels by 5.
Count up pennies by 1.

¢

5. Add.

Regroup.

$$\begin{array}{r} \$5.48 \\ + \ \$3.64 \\ \hline \end{array}$$

Remember to write the decimal point.

6. nearest **ten**

$18 →

7. nearest **hundred**

$781 →

8. 1 nickel = 5¢

How many nickels equal 100¢?

Count up by 5 to 100. Use the Hundred-Number Chart for help.

```
_____ nickels
```

9. 66¢

2 quarters, _____ dime, _____ nickel, _____ penny

Use work area.

10. Find the pattern. Use the Hundred-Number Chart for help.

12, 18, 24, _____, _____, _____, _____, …

Use work area.

11. 99, 90, 81, _____, _____, _____, _____, …

Use work area.

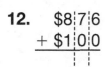

12. $8 7 6
     + $1 0 0

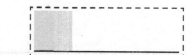

13. $4 8 9
     − $ 5 0

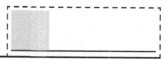

14. Regroup.

     2 5
     3 5
   + 4 5

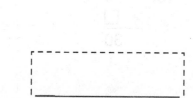

15. $279
     − $119

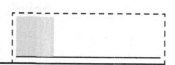

16.   6
       5
       4
    + 10

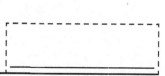

17. $\begin{array}{r} \$2\,8\,0 \\ -\ \$1\,8\,0 \\ \hline \end{array}$

18. $\begin{array}{r} 25¢ \\ +\ m \\ \hline 75¢ \end{array}$

$m = \underline{\hspace{3cm}} ¢$

19. $\begin{array}{r} 24 \\ +\ \square \\ \hline 30 \end{array}$

$\square =$ \underline{\hspace{2cm}}

20. Regroup.

$4.75 adult ticket

$+$ \underline{\hspace{2cm}} child's ticket

A $7.00   **B** $7.75

C $8.00   **D** $8.25

© Saxon

Teacher Notes:
- Introduce Hint #14 "Naming Fractions/Identifying Fractional Parts."
- Review "Spelling Numbers" on page 12 in the *Student Reference Guide.*

• Fractions of a Dollar

New Concept

- A **fraction** tells part of a whole.

- A fraction has two numbers.

  The **bottom** number is the number of *total parts*.

  The **top** number is the number of *shaded parts*.

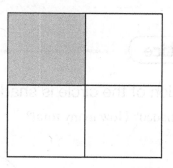

1 out of 4 ⟶ $\frac{1}{4}$ Parts shaded / Total parts

Example

What fraction of this circle is shaded?

The circle is divided into **3** total parts.

There are **2** shaded parts.

Two out of three parts are shaded: $\frac{2}{3}$ of the circle is shaded.

© Saxon

- A coin is a part of a dollar. You can use fractions to name coins.

  A quarter is $\frac{1}{4}$ of a dollar.   *4 quarters make a dollar.*

  A dime is $\frac{1}{10}$ of a dollar.   *10 dimes make a dollar.*

  A nickel is $\frac{1}{20}$ of a dollar.   *20 nickels make a dollar.*

  A penny is $\frac{1}{100}$ of a dollar.   *100 pennies make a dollar.*

Example

Mia has 7 dimes. What fraction of a dollar is 7 dimes?

One dime is $\frac{1}{10}$ of a dollar.

Seven dimes is $\frac{7}{10}$ of a dollar.

Lesson Practice

a. What fraction of the circle is shaded? _____

How many shaded? How many total?

b. What fraction of the rectangle is shaded? _____

How many shaded? How many total?

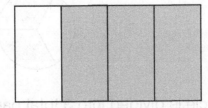

c. Which coin is $\frac{1}{4}$ of a dollar? _____

d. Three dimes is what fraction of a dollar? _____

1 dime is $\frac{1}{10}$ of a dollar.

1. $4.29   sandwich

+ _____   tax

.

Remember to write the decimal point.

---

2. 1 $5 bill, 1 quarter = $_____

− $4.19

.

Remember to write the decimal point.

---

3. nine hundred thirty dollars

How many hundreds? tens? ones?

---

4. 3 quarters, 2 dimes, 1 penny

Count up quarters by 25.
Count up dimes by 10.
Count up pennies by 1.

¢

---

5. nearest **hundred**

$389   ⟶

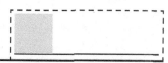

© Saxon

6. nearest **ten**

$28 →

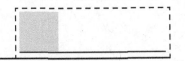

7. $75 ◯ $82

Use work area.

8. least to greatest
$287, $293, $279

———, ———, ———

least   greatest

Use work area.

9. 8, 16, 24, ———, ———, ———, ———, ———, …

Use work area.

10. 4, 8, 12, ———, ———, ———, ———, ———, …

Use work area.

© Saxon

11.   3|1
         2|6
      + 1|5

12.   6
         6
         6
      + 6

13. $3|7|5
      + $3|7|5

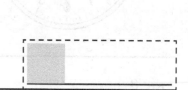

14. $6|2|5
      − $1|2|5

15. Borrow.

      $3.45
    − $1.50

Remember to write the decimal point.

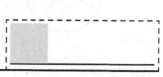

16. $2|5|0
      − $ |1|0

17. 30
     + *m*
  ———
      90

m =

18. 37
     + □
  ———
     100

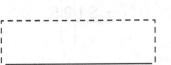

□ =

19. 15 minutes + 15 minutes = 30 minutes
    What fraction of the clock face is shaded?

20. $\frac{3}{4}$

How many shaded? How many total?

A   B

C   D

© Saxon

Name _____

Teacher Notes:
- Review Hint #11 "Estimating or Rounding."
- Review "Estimate" on page 8 in the *Student Reference Guide*.

• Estimating Sums and Differences

New Concept

- In some problems, **estimate** to find an answer that is close to the exact answer.

- Look for the cue word *about* to tell you to estimate.

- To estimate:

  1. *Round* each number.

  2. Add or subtract as the problem tells you to.

Example

Cass had 92 balloons. She used 39 balloons to decorate for a friend's party. About how many balloons does Cass have left?

The problem asks "*about* how many balloons does Cass have left".

This is a "some went away story," so subtract. But first round each number to the nearest ten.

$$9\underline{2} \quad \rightarrow \quad 90$$
$$3\underline{9} \quad \rightarrow \quad \underline{-\ 40}$$
$$\phantom{3\underline{9} \quad \rightarrow \quad -\ } 50$$

Cass has **about 50 balloons** left.

Estimate answers for **a–c**.

a. Rodney's worksheet has 96 subtraction facts. After one minute he has worked 57 facts. **About** how many facts does he have **left** to work?

_____

9(6) →

5(7) → – _____

b. Mr. Neustadt drove 278 miles on Monday and 429 miles on Tuesday.

About how many miles did he travel **in all?** _____ miles

2(7)8 →

4(2)9 → + _____

c. Joni wants a pair of cleats that cost $53 and a pair of kneepads that cost $18. **About** how much money does Joni need to pay for her items?

$5(3) →

$1(8) → + _____

d. What is the best estimate of the **difference** of 687 and 312? (Circle your answer.)

6(8)7 →

3(1)2 → – _____

A 900   **B** 300

C 1000   **D** 400

© Saxon

1. 3 quarters, 2 dimes

Count up quarters by 25.

Count up dimes by 1.

Does Silvia have enough money?

_____ because 3 quarters and 2 dimes is _____ ¢ and

the bagel costs _____ ¢.

Use work area.

2. least to greatest

85¢, 65¢, 45¢

_____ , _____ , _____

least   greatest

Use work area.

3. $0.85

      $0.65

 + $0.45

Remember to write the decimal point.

4. nearest **ten**

$1⑥ →

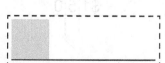

5. nearest **ten**

$6 ①   →

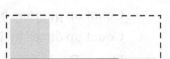

---

6. $849

_____ dollars

Use work area.

---

7. 1 dime = $\frac{1}{10}$ of a dollar

9 dimes =

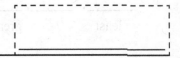

---

8. 99, 90, 81, _____, _____, _____, _____, ...

Use work area.

---

9. 20, 24, 28, _____, _____, _____, _____, ...

Use work area.

---

10. $2 5 0
    − $1 5 0

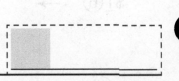

11.
```
   31
   28
 + 31
```

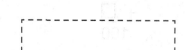

12.
```
  $4|6|5
 -$4|2|0
```

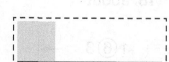

13.
```
   6
   4
   8
 + 2
```

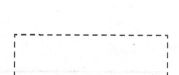

14.
```
  $8|7|5
 -$5|0|0
```

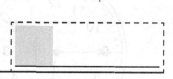

15.
```
   $4.35
 + $2.65
```

Remember to write the decimal point.

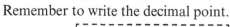

16.
```
   55
 + m
 ───
   66
```

$m =$

© Saxon

17. 20
 30
+ ☐
───
100

☐ =

18. about

1 ⑥ 3 →

1 ① 7 → + ____

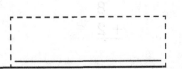

19. sunset

hours:minutes

Remember to write a.m. or p.m.

20. expanded form
 875

© Saxon

Name _____

📖 page 166

Teacher Note:
• Students need a copy of **Lesson Activity 14** to complete this Investigation.

Focus on
• More About Pictographs

• A **pictograph** uses pictures to show data. The pictograph below shows the data for fish in a class aquarium.

Fish in the Class Aquarium	
Angelfish	🐟🐟🐟🐟
Guppies	🐟🐟🐟🐟🐟🐟
Goldfish	🐟🐟🐟

Key
🐟 = 2 fish

• At the bottom of the pictograph is a **key**. The key shows that **1 picture of a fish stands for 2 fish in the aquarium.**

Look at the pictograph above to answer problems **1–6.**

1. What is the **title** of the pictograph?

_____

_____

2. How many **guppies** are in the class aquarium?

_____ guppies

Count up the pictures by 2.

3. Read the key. How many fish does each picture represent?

_____ fish

4. Look at the last picture in the "goldfish" row. It is only half a picture. How many fish do you think that shows?

_____ fish

How many **goldfish** are in the class aquarium?

_____ goldfish

5. Are there more goldfish or more angelfish in the aquarium?

_____

6. If the teacher took away 2 angelfish from the class aquarium, how many angelfish would be left?

_____ angelfish

Activity 📖 page 167

Class Pictograph

Materials needed:

• **Lesson Activity 14**

We will make a pictograph of how many students in a class were born in each season.

There are four seasons in a year: fall, winter, spring, and summer.

© Saxon

The tallies below show how many students were born in each season:

Fall: ⵏ⵰ ||

Winter: ||||

Spring: ⵏ⵰ |

Summer: ⵏ⵰

Copy the data onto the tally chart at the top of **Lesson Activity 14.** Work through problems **7–13** to create your pictograph.

7. What should be the title of your pictograph?

_____

_____

Write the title above the pictograph.

8. Choose a picture to use in your pictograph. The picture can be anything you want. Draw the picture in the **key** on the pictograph.

9. Every picture will represent 1 student. Write "1 student" next to the equal sign in the **key.**

10. Seven students have fall birthdays. Because each picture shows 1 student, you will need 7 pictures. Draw 7 pictures in the row for fall.

11. Four students have winter birthdays.
How many pictures will show four students?

_____ pictures

Draw the pictures in the row for winter.

12. How many students have spring birthdays?

_____ students

How many pictures do you need?

_____ pictures

Draw the pictures in the row for spring.

13. How many students have summer birthdays?

_____ students

How many pictures do you need for summer?

_____ pictures.

Draw the pictures in the row for summer.

Great! Your pictograph is done!

📖 page 169

Teacher Note:
• Refer students to "Directions" on page 3 in the *Student Reference Guide*.

• Writing Directions

New Concept

• Use the direction and the distance to tell how to get from one place to another.

• A **compass** on a map shows the four directions: **north, east, south,** and **west.**

north

N

west **W** ──┼── **E** east

S

south

• To describe a turn, we can use **right** and **left.**

←   →

left side   right side

Activity   📖 page 171

Giving Directions

Materials needed:
• none

The map on the next page shows five locations labeled A–E. Use the map and compass to answer each question.

Example

Start at A. Travel east one block. Turn right and travel south two blocks. Where are you?

Find A on the map. Put your finger on A. Trace along the path as you go.

Travel **east** one block. Look at the compass. Go east (right) from A to the next corner.

Turn **right** and travel **south** two blocks. Look at the compass. Go south (down) two corners. You are at **location C.**

1. Start at B. Travel **west** one block. Turn **left** and travel **south** one block. Where are you?

   location _____

2. Start at C. Travel **west** one block. Turn **right** and travel **north** two blocks. Where are you?

   location _____

3. Start at D. Travel **west** two blocks. Where are you?

   location _____

4. Write directions for traveling from location E to location D.

Start at E. Travel _____ two blocks.

5. Write directions for traveling from location B to location A.

Start at _____. Travel west

_____ blocks. Turn right and travel

_____ one block.

Lesson Practice

Use the map in this lesson. Write directions for traveling from:

a. Location B to location E.

Start at B. Travel _____ one block.

Turn _____ and travel south three blocks.

Turn right and travel _____ one block.

b. Location D to location B.

Start at _____. Travel west _____ block.

Turn right and travel _____ three blocks.

Turn _____ and travel east one block.

c. Location C to location B.

Start at _____. Travel _____ one block.

Turn right and travel _____ one block.

1. $0.75   video game
   $0.85   snack

Remember to write the decimal point.

2. Borrow across all zeros.

$100
− $ 45

3. about

$92 →

$76 → − _____

4. nearest **ten**

$16 →

5. $169

_____ dollars

Use work area.

6. 100 pennies make a dollar, so 1 penny is _____ of a dollar.

10 pennies make a dime, so 1 penny is _____ of a dime.

Use work area.

© Saxon

7. Estimate the **sum.**

231 ⟶

529 ⟶ _____

Use work area.

8. tenth number

36, 33, 30, 27, 24, 21, 18, _____, _____, _____

9. tenth number

Use the 12s column in the Multiplication Table for help.

12, 24, 36, 48, 60, 72, 84, _____, _____, _____

10. $3.49
+ $2.83

Remember to write the decimal point.

11. 2 0 0
– 1 5 0

12. 8
9
+ 4

13. $4.65
– $3.75

Remember to write the decimal point.

© Saxon

14. $0.36
      $0.45
  + $0.60

15. $4|5|0
    − $ |3|0

16.   25
      50
  + _m_
    100

_m_ = _____

17. expanded form
860

_____

18. 2 dimes = _____ ¢

Count up dimes by 10.

− 18¢

_____

19. Name the temperature in °F and °C.

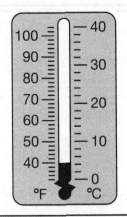

_____ °F

_____ °C

20. quarter to four o'clock in the **afternoon**

_____ : _____

© Saxon

Name _____

• Reading and Writing Numbers Through 999,999

New Concept

• In big numbers with 4, 5, or 6 digits, a **comma** (,) separates the *thousands* places from the *ones* places.

Place Value

Thousands			,	Ones		
Hundred Thousands	Ten Thousands	Thousands	,	Hundreds	Tens	Ones
___	___	___	,	___	___	___

• To write a comma in a big number:

1. Count from the **right**.

2. Write a comma between the third and fourth digit.

Example

Write each of these numbers with a comma.

a. 1760   b. 25071   c. 125000

1. Start on the **right** and count over three digits.

2. Then write a comma.

a. 1,760   b. 25,071   c. 125,000

- To write a big number with words:

  1. Write the part of the number in front of the comma.
  2. Write "thousand," at the comma.
  3. Write the part of the number behind the comma.

Example

Write each of these numbers with words.

a. (1),(760)   b. (25),(071)   c. (125),(000)

It can help to circle the parts of the number that are in front of the comma and behind the comma.

1. Write the part of the number in front of the comma.

2. Write "thousand," at the comma.

3. Write the part of the number behind the comma.

In **c,** you do not have to write a comma after thousand because there are no more numbers to write.

a. **one *thousand,* seven hundred sixty**

b. **twenty-five *thousand,* seventy-one**

c. **one hundred twenty-five *thousand***

- To write a big number with digits:

  1. Find "thousand," in the number.
  2. Write the part of the number in front of "thousand,".
  3. Write a comma for "thousand,".
  4. Write the part of the number behind "thousand,".

Example

A mile is five thousand, two hundred eighty feet.
Write that number with digits.

1. Find "thousand," in the number.

2. The word in front of "thousand," is five.

5

3. Now write a comma for "thousand,".

5,

4. The words behind "thousand," are two hundred eighty. Write that part of the number to finish.

5,280

 page 177

Reading and Writing Big Numbers
• This activity is optional.

Lesson Practice

Write each number with a comma. Then name the numbers.

a. 24800   _____ _____ , _____ _____ _____

_____ thousand, eight hundred

b. 186000   _____ _____ _____ , _____ _____ _____

_____ thousand

Use digits to write these numbers.

c. six **thousand,** four hundred

_____ , _____ _____ _____

d. sixty-four **thousand**

_____ _____ , _____ _____ _____

© Saxon

Write each odometer (mileage counter in a car) display with digits and words.

e.

_____ thousand, _____

f.

_____ thousand, _____

g. Compare: 68,329 $\bigcirc$ 69,235

Compare ten thousands.

Compare thousands.

Written Practice

 page 178

1.

Ann

 $\underline{}$ Tina

\$_____ $\bigcirc$ \$_____

Ann   Tina

Compare hundreds.

Use work area.

2. Borrow across all zeros.

$$\begin{array}{r} \$\cancel{1}0\cancel{0} \\ -\ \$\ 65 \\ \hline \end{array}$$

Use work area.

---

3. nearest **ten**

\$39 $\rightarrow$ _____

Use work area.

4. \$9.12

 ____ dollars and ____ cents

Use work area.

© Saxon

5. location A to location B

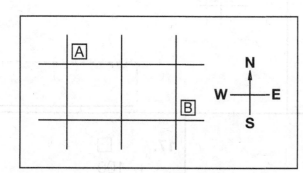

Start at A. Travel east _____

blocks. Turn right and travel

_____ one block.

6. $\frac{2}{4}$ of a dollar

1 quarter = $\frac{1}{4}$ of a dollar

_____ ¢

7. 35694

_____ , _____ _____ _____

_____ thousand,

_____

8. 7, 14, 21, _____ , _____ ,

_____ , _____ , ...

9. 354,382 ◯ 352,847

Compare hundred thousands.

Compare ten thousands.

Compare thousands.

10. $3:0:0
      $-$ $1:5:0

11. $6.47
      $+$ $0.98
   .

12. $7.25
      $-$ $5.35
   .

13.
```
   8
   8
   8
+  8
```

14.
```
  3 7 5
- 2 5 0
```

15.
```
   $0.38
   $0.53
+  $0.72
```

16.
```
   12
   12
+   m
   36
```
m =

17.
```
     □
+  100
   900
```
□ =

18. lunchtime

:

19. 1 quarter, 1 dime, 1 nickel, 3 pennies

Count up quarters by 25.

Count up dimes by 10.   53¢

Count up nickels by 5.

Count up pennies by 1.   _____

¢

20. *Pedro walked one block* **north.**
Then one block **east.**
Then one block **south.**

Draw Pedro's path on the map.

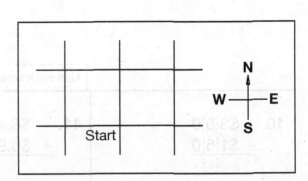

Tell how Pedro can get back to Start.

Walk _____ block _____.

Use work area.

Name _____

• More About Number Lines

New Concept

- A **number line** shows numbers on a line using **tick marks.**

- Some of the tick marks will be numbered and some will not be numbered.

Example

Which point on this number line stands for 126?

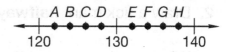

Try counting up by 1 on the marks from 120 to 130:

120, 121, 122, 123, 124, 130

Counting up by 1 does not fit the number line. Try counting up by 2 from 120 to 130:

120, 122, 124, 126, 128, 130

Counting up by 2 fits the number line.

Now count up by 2 from 120 to 126:

120, 122, 124, 126

Point C stands for 126.

Activity    📖 page 181

Making a Timeline

Materials needed:
- none

© Saxon

A **timeline** is a kind of number line. The numbers given on the number line show **years.** Follow the instructions to create a timeline for the following inventions:

A 1876: Telephone   **B** 1975: Personal Computer

C 1927: Television   **D** 1844: Telegraph

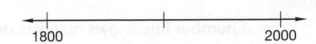

1800   2000

1. The timeline above shows the years 1800 and 2000 and one mark with no year. What number goes at that mark?

_____

   Count up by 100.
   Write 1900 below the unlabeled mark.

2. Draw a tick mark **halfway** between 1800 and 1900.

   What number goes at this mark? _____
   Count up by 50.
   Write 1850 below the mark.

3. Draw a tick mark **halfway** between 1900 and 2000.

   What number goes at this mark? _____
   Count up by 50.
   Write 1950 below the mark.

4. The telephone was invented in **1876.** 1876 is between

   which two marks? 1850 and _____
   Make a dot labeled **A** between those marks.

5. The personal computer was invented in **1975.** 1975

   is between which two marks? _____ and 2000
   Make a dot labeled **B** between those marks.

© Saxon

6. The television was invented in **1927.** 1927 is between

   which two marks? _____ and _____
   Make a dot labeled **C** between those marks.

7. The telegraph was invented in **1844.** 1844 is between

   which two marks? 1800 and _____.

   1844 is very close to which mark? _____
   Make a dot labeled **D** a little to the left of that mark.

Lesson Practice

Use this number line for **a–d.**

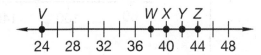

a. What number does *X* stand for? _____

b. Which point stands for 24? point _____

c. What number does *W* stand for? _____

d. Which point stands for 44? point _____

e. Some highways are marked with mileage markers to show the number of miles from the state line. The number line below shows a 10-mile stretch of highway from mile 130 to mile 140. **Draw 9 equally-spaced marks** on the number line. Then label each mark from 130 to 140.

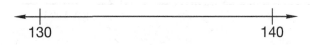

© Saxon

1. 3 quarters = _____ ¢ – 65¢

Count up quarters by 25.

What **coin** is that difference?

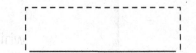

---

2.   184
      52
      _____

3. nearest **hundred**

$685 →

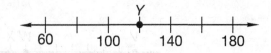

---

4. Estimate the **difference.**

923 →

688 → _____

5.

$Y =$

---

6. least to greatest value

dime, penny, quarter, nickel

_____, _____, _____, _____
least   greatest

Use work area.

© Saxon

7. 1 dime = $\frac{1}{10}$ of a dollar

8 dimes =

8. 18, 24, 30, 36, _____, _____,

_____, _____, ...

Use work area.

9. 375, 400, 425, _____, _____, _____, _____, ...

Use work area.

10. $0.35
$0.48
+ $0.65

11. Borrow across all zeros.

$1̶0̶0
– $ 77

12. $ 4.58
+ $ 4.49

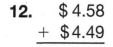

13. 885
– 850

14. 12
12
+ 12

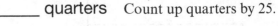

15. $746
      + $ 74

16.   6
          m
        + 8
        ────
         15

m = _____

17. expanded form

605

_____

18.
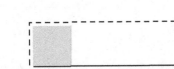

_____ quarters   Count up quarters by 25.

_____ nickels   Count up nickels by 5.

_____ penny   Count up pennies by 1.

19. digits: _____ _____ , _____ _____ _____

words: _____

Use work area.

20. Glenda walked five steps **south.** Then eight steps **west.** Then five steps **north.**

Draw Glenda's path on the grid below. Each line is one step.

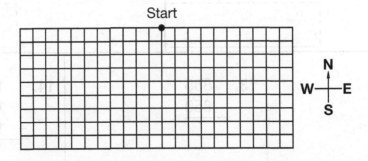

How can Glenda get back to Start?   Walk _____ steps _____.

Use work area.

📖 page 185

Name _____

Teacher Notes:

• Introduce Hint #16 "Measuring" and Hint #17 "Reading Inch Rulers."

• Refer students to "Equivalence Table for Units" on page 1 and "Length" on page 2 in the *Student Reference Guide*.

• Students need an inch ruler to complete this lesson.

• Length: Inches, Feet, and Yards

New Concept

• Length can be measured in **inches, feet,** and **yards.**

Length

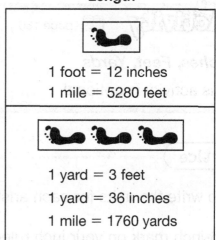

1 foot = 12 inches
1 mile = 5280 feet

1 yard = 3 feet
1 yard = 36 inches
1 mile = 1760 yards

• An inch ruler is **12 inches long** (1 foot).

Every number on the ruler is 1 inch.

• A yardstick is **3 feet long** (1 yard).

3 rulers are as long as 1 yardstick (3 feet = 1 yard).

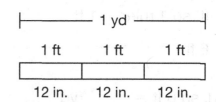

├────── 1 yd ──────┤

1 ft   1 ft   1 ft

12 in. 12 in. 12 in.

© Saxon

- To measure with a ruler, put the **"0" mark** (0 inches) even with the left side of the object.

  - Often **abbreviations** are used to quickly write the units inches, feet, and yards.

Abbreviations	
inch	in.
foot	ft
yard	yd

- **Use these abbreviations when writing answers.**

 📖 page 186

Inches, Feet, Yards

This activity is optional.

Lesson Practice

Remember to write the units for each answer.

a. Find the 6-inch mark on your inch ruler. Put that mark on your first finger and try to balance the ruler. How many **inches** are on each side of the 6-inch mark?

_____ in.

b. Six rulers, each 12 inches long, are laid end to end. How many **yards** do they reach?

12 in. = 1 ft, so 1 ruler = 1 ft

6 rulers = 6 ft

3 ft = 1 yd, so 6 ft = _____ yd

© Saxon

c. Use your ruler to find the distance from point *A* to point *B* to the **nearest inch.**

_____ in.

          A   *B*
          •   •

d. Use your ruler to find the distance from point *C* to point *D* to the **nearest inch.**

_____ in.

                C   *D*
                •   •

e. This table shows how many feet equal 1, 2, or 3 yards. Complete the table to find how many feet equal 5 yards.

1 ft = 3 yd

Yards	1	2	3	4	5
Feet	3	6	9		

Written Practice   📖 page 188

1. Do problem **1** on 📖 page 188.

Remember to write the units.

2.   ticket

     + ____ snacks

3. nearest **ten**

$49   →

4. 549

_____

_____

5. from Tracey's house to school

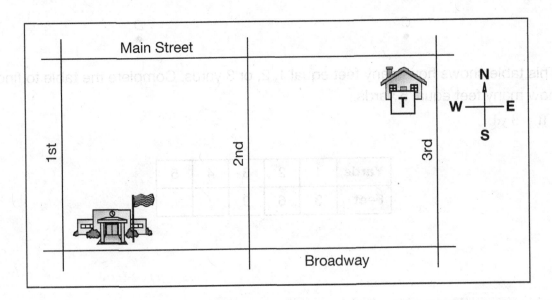

Walk _____ blocks west and 1 block _____.

6. $3.97
         $0.50
         _____

7.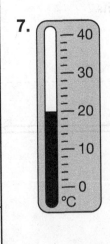

8. 12, 24, 36, _____, _____, _____, _____, …

Use work area.

9. Which is $\frac{3}{100}$ of a dollar?

A 3 quarters
1 quarter = $\frac{1}{4}$ of a dollar

B 3 dimes
1 dime = $\frac{1}{10}$ of a dollar

C 3 nickels
1 nickel = $\frac{1}{20}$ of a dollar

D 3 pennies
1 penny = $\frac{1}{100}$ of a dollar

10. Borrow across all zeros.

$200
− $ 44

11.
    7
    7
    7
  + 7

12.   463
        − 200

13. $567
        + $ 32

14. $2.50
        − $1.49

15. $0.47
          $0.38
        + $1.00

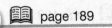

16. Subtract.

$$
\begin{array}{r}
10 \\
m \\
+\ 14 \\
\hline
36
\end{array}
$$

$m = $ _____

17.
$$
\begin{array}{r}
30 \\
+\ \square \\
\hline
100
\end{array}
$$

$\square = $ _____

18. 5,280

words: _____

_____

Use work area.

19. before school

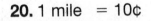

20. 1 mile = 10¢

8 miles = _____ ¢

10¢ + _____ ¢ + _____ ¢ + _____ ¢ + _____ ¢ + _____ ¢ +

_____ ¢ + _____ ¢ = _____ ¢

© Saxon

📖 page 191

• Measuring to the Nearest Quarter Inch

New Concept

• Each inch on a ruler is divided into **half inches** $\left(\frac{1}{2} \text{ inch}\right)$ and **quarter inches** $\left(\frac{1}{4} \text{ inch}\right)$.

• The **long** marks with numbers are inch marks.

• The marks **halfway** between inch marks are $\frac{1}{2}$ inch marks.

• The **short** marks are $\frac{1}{4}$ inch marks.

• Remember: $\frac{2}{4} = \frac{1}{2}$ (Two quarters equal one half.)

• Practice counting up half inches $\left(\frac{1}{2} \text{ inches}\right)$ on the ruler below:

$$\frac{1}{2}, 1, 1\frac{1}{2}, 2, 2\frac{1}{2}, 3, 3\frac{1}{2}, 4$$

• Practice counting up quarter inches $\left(\frac{1}{4} \text{ inches}\right)$ on the ruler:

$$\frac{1}{4}, \frac{1}{2}, \frac{3}{4}, 1, 1\frac{1}{4}, 1\frac{1}{2}, 1\frac{3}{4}, 2, 2\frac{1}{4}, 2\frac{1}{2}, 2\frac{3}{4}, 3, 3\frac{1}{4}, 3\frac{1}{2}, 3\frac{3}{4}, 4$$

• To measure to the nearest quarter inch:

1. Put the "0" mark of the ruler even with the left end of the object.

2. Count up whole inches (the numbers on the ruler).

3. Count up $\frac{1}{4}$ and $\frac{1}{2}$ inches to the right end of the object.

4. If the right end of the object is not on a mark, count to the mark that is closest.

Example

Measure this nail to the nearest quarter inch.

1. Put the "0" mark of the ruler on the left end of the nail.

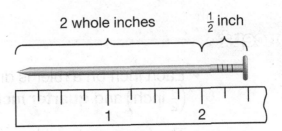

2 whole inches $\frac{1}{2}$ inch

2. Count up 2 whole inches.

3. Then count $\frac{1}{2}$ inch more to the right end of the nail.
The nail is **2$\frac{1}{2}$ inches long.**

**Activity**   📖 page 192

Inch Ruler
This activity is optional.

Lesson Practice

Use a ruler and the map below to find the distance between cities to the **nearest quarter inch.**

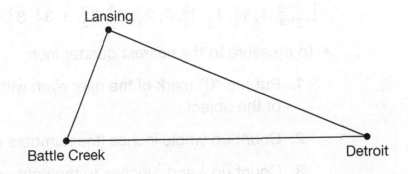

a. From Battle Creek to Detroit _____ in.

© Saxon

b. From Battle Creek to Lansing _____ in.

c. From Lansing to Detroit _____ in.

d. Use a pencil and your ruler to draw a segment that is $1\frac{1}{2}$ inches long.

Written Practice   📖 page 194

1. $9.99   regular price
   $-$ $5.00   off

2. $4.99   stuffed animal
   $+$ $0.35   tax

3. names from **shortest to tallest**

Student	Height
Lindsay	72
Iva	59
Chad	66
Nash	76

_____ , _____ , _____ , _____

shortest   tallest

Use work area.

© Saxon

4. nearest **ten**

$26 →

5. from school to Paula's house

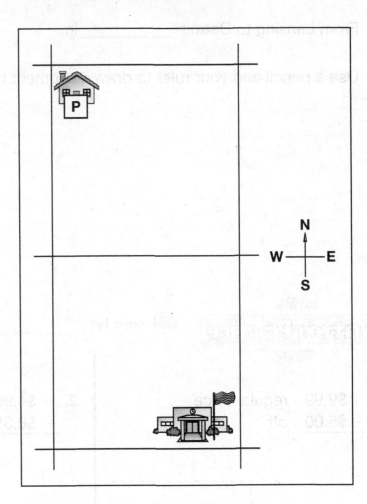

Walk _____ blocks north and

1 block _____.

Use work area.

6. See page 1 in the *Student Reference Guide.*
Remember to write the units.

a. 1 ft = _____ in.

b. 2 ft = _____ in.

a. _____   **b.** _____

7. Draw a segment
$2\frac{1}{4}$ inches long.

Use work area.

© Saxon

8. 9, 18, 27, _____, _____, _____, _____, …

> Use work area.

9. 33, 44, 55, _____, _____, _____, _____, …

> Use work area.

10. Find sets of ten.

$0.64
$0.46
+ $1.00

11.
$4.58
− $2.50

12.
$649
+ $350

13. Borrow across all zeros.

~~100~~
− 33

14.
9
8
+ 7

15.
$625
− $175

16.
10
15
+ ☐
75

☐ =

17. 3 quarters = _____ ¢

− 58¢

What is the **fewest** number of coins to make that difference?

_____ dime, _____ nickel, _____ pennies

> Use work area.

© Saxon

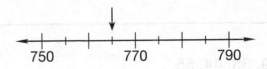

18. 1,760

words: _____

_____

┆ Use work area. ┆

19. Count up by 5.

750   770   790

┆_____┆

---

20. *Simpson walked 3 yards **south**.*
*Then 2 yards **west**.*
*Then 3 yards **south**.*
*Then 4 yards **east**.*
*Then 6 yards **north**.*

Draw Simpson's path on the grid below. Each line is one yard.

Start

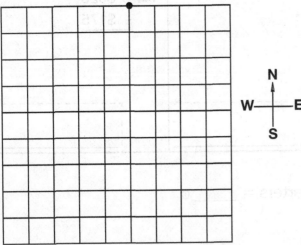

N
W — E
S

How can Simpson get back to Start?

Walk _____ yards _____.

┆ Use work area. ┆

© Saxon

Name _____

Teacher Note:
- Review "Missing Numbers" on page 7 in the *Student Reference Guide.*

• Some and Some More Stories, Part 2

New Concept

- **Some and some more** stories have an addition formula.

$$\begin{array}{r} \text{Some} \\ + \text{ Some more} \\ \hline \text{Total} \end{array}$$

- "Some" and "Some more" are the **addends.** "Total" is the **sum.**

- If the *total* is missing, **add.**

- If one of the *addends* is missing, **subtract.**

Example

John rode his bike nine miles in the morning. He rode his bike some more in the afternoon. In all, John rode his bike fifteen miles. How many miles did he ride in the afternoon?

The total is 15 miles. John rode 9 miles in the morning. You do not know how many miles John rode in the afternoon.

$$\begin{array}{r} 9 \quad \text{morning} \\ + \ m \quad \text{afternoon} \\ \hline 15 \quad \text{total} \end{array} \longrightarrow \begin{array}{r} 15 \\ - \ 9 \\ \hline m \end{array}$$

Subtract to find the missing addend: $15 - 9 = 6$.

John rode his bike **6 miles** in the afternoon.

Subtract to find the missing addend in **a** and **b**. Remember to write the units.

a. The map below shows the distances from Troy to Jackson and from Troy to Denton. How far is it from Jackson to Denton?

_____

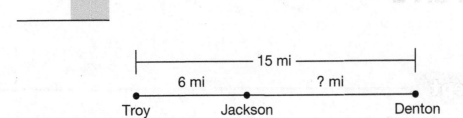

	6	Troy to Jackson
+	m	Jackson to Denton
	15	Troy to Denton

b. A biathlon is a race that includes running and biking. In a biathlon, Jeff ran and biked a **total** of 36 miles. He **biked** 24 miles. How many miles did he run?

_____

        biked

+   _m_ ran

        total

c. Complete the some and some more story with a question for this number sentence.

$$\square \text{ mi} + 6 \text{ mi} = 10 \text{ mi}$$

Lucy walked a total of _____ miles. She walked

_____ miles after lunch. How many _____ did Lucy

walk before lunch?

1. $199   stilts
    $ 16   tax

Remember to write the dollar sign.

2. 68   Nelson on stilts
    12   stilts

Nelson off stilts

Remember to write the units.

3. Round the answer from problem **1** to the **nearest hundred dollars.**

4. Write the answer from problem **1** using words.

_____

_____ dollars

Use work area.

5. Is 100 yards equal to 30 feet or 300 feet?

1 yard = 3 feet

Remember to write the units.

© Saxon

6. greater value

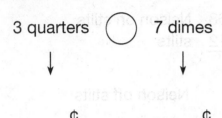

3 quarters ⬇ ◯ 7 dimes ⬇

_____ ¢   _____ ¢

7. Complete the table.

1 foot = 12 inches

Feet	1	2	3	4	5	6
Inches	12	24	36	48		

Use work area.

8. 14, 21, 28, _____, _____, _____, _____, ...

Use work area.

9. 8, 16, 24, _____, _____, _____, _____, ...

Use work area.

10. $987
    − $245

Remember to write the dollar sign.

11. $650
    + $250

12. $7.95
   + $1.50

Remember to write the decimal point.

13.   6
      6
      6
   + 6

14. Borrow across all zeros.

$$\begin{array}{r} \cancel{200} \\ - \ 122 \\ \hline \end{array}$$

15. $5.49
   + $0.86

Remember to write the decimal point.

16. m
   +   25
    100

$m =$ _____

17. six hundred three thousand, six hundred forty

_____ _____ _____ , _____ _____ _____

Use work area.

18. What fraction of a dollar is 3 quarters?

1 quarter $= \frac{1}{4}$ of a dollar

19. Do problem **19** on 📖 page 200.

Remember to write the units.

20. digits: _____ _____ , _____ _____ _____

words: _____

_____

Use work area.

© Saxon

Name _____

Teacher Note:
• Review "Length" on page 2 in the *Student Reference Guide*.

• Estimating Lengths and Distances

New Concept

• To **estimate** a distance, make a careful guess.

• One **inch** is about the distance across a **quarter.**

• One **foot** is about the length of a **regular step.**

• One **yard** is about the length of a **BIG step.**

Activity page 202

Estimating and Measuring Lengths

Materials needed:
• inch ruler
• yardstick

The chart below shows 6 objects to measure.

Before measuring each one, **estimate** a length.

For inches, you can think, "How many quarters long is it?"

For feet, think, "How many regular steps long is it?"

For yards, think, "How many BIG steps long is it?"

Fill in the chart by estimating and measuring each object.

Measure to the **closest** number of inches, feet, or yards.

Object to be Measured	Estimated Length	Measured Length
1. pencil	inches	inches
2. textbook	inches	inches
3. width of classroom door	feet	feet
4. your height	feet	feet
5. chalkboard	yards	yards
6. width of classroom	yards	yards

Lesson Practice

a. Estimate the **height** of your classroom in yards. _____ yards

Imagine taking BIG steps up the wall.

b. Use your answer to problem **a** to estimate the height of your classroom in feet.

_____ feet

1 yard = 3 feet

Written Practice

 page 203

1. half of a dollar = _____¢

$_____ + $_____ = t

salad

+___ sandwich

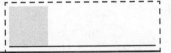

2. _____ mi + m = _____ mi

      morning

    +   afternoon

      altogether

Remember to write the units.

3.   costumes

    _____ tax

      total

4. Write the answer from problem **3** using words.

_____

_____ dollars

Use work area.

5. Write directions from school to Connie's house.

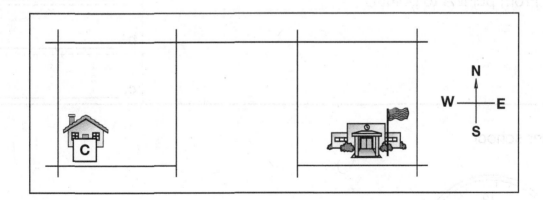

Walk _____ block north. Turn left and walk 3 blocks

_____. Turn left and walk 1 block _____.

Use work area.

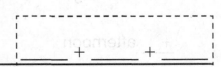

6. expanded form
5,280

_____ + _____ + _____

7. If it takes about 20 minutes to walk 1 mile, how long would it take to walk 2 miles?

Two miles is twice as far as _____ mile, so it should take about

twice as long: _____ minutes.

Use work area.

8. Measure each segment. Remember to write the units.

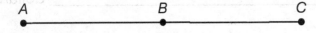

a. From point A to point B

b. From point B to point C

c. From point A to point C

a. _____

b. _____

c. _____

9. after school

_____ : _____

© Saxon

10. a. least to greatest

$116, $120, $110

_____, _____, _____
  least   greatest

b. Is $116 closer to $100 or $200?

_____

Round to the nearest hundred.

⌐ Use work area. ⌐

11. 9 dimes = _____¢

____ 83¢

What **coins** should she get back?

_____ nickel, _____ pennies

⌐ Use work area. ⌐

12. Complete the table.

1 week = 7 days

Weeks	1	2	3	4	5	6	7	8
Days	7	14	21					

⌐ Use work area. ⌐

13.

```
   4
   5
   6
 + 7
____
```

14. Borrow across all zeros.

```
  3̶0̶0̶
 − 95
____
```

15. $0.50
   $0.48
+ $0.92

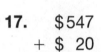

16. $360
− $150

17. $547
+ $ 20

18. $2.80
− $2.75

19. *m*
+ 25
___
100

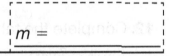

m =

20. Make a dot on the line for point *D* so that the distance from **point A to point D** is $3\frac{1}{4}$ inches.

Use work area.

Name _____

Teacher Notes:

• Review "Time" on page 2 in the *Student Reference Guide*.

• Use student clocks to enhance this lesson.

• Reading a Clock to the Nearest Minute

New Concept

• You already know how to read a clock to the nearest 5 minutes:

> The *short hand* shows **hours.**
>
> The *long hand* shows **minutes.**
>
> Each *number* around the clock is **5 minutes.**

• In between the numbers on a clock are marks. Each *mark* is **1 minute.**

• To read a clock to the nearest minute:

  1. Look at the short hand to tell the hours. If the short hand points between two numbers, use the smaller number.

  2. Look at the long hand. Count up by 5 on the numbers.

  3. Count up by 1 on the marks until you get to the long hand.

Example

It is afternoon. Write the time shown on the clock in digital form.

Math Language

We use **a.m.** to show the 12 hours *before* noon (morning).

We use **p.m.** to show the 12 hours *after* noon (afternoon and evening).

© Saxon

1. Read the hours on the short hand.
   It points between the 1 and the 2, so it is after 1 p.m.

2. Read the minutes on the long hand.
   The long hand points between the 4 and the 5.
   Count up by 5: 5, 10, 15, 20.

3. Count up by 1 on the marks until we get to
   the long hand: 21, 22, 23.

   The time is **1:23 p.m.**

Lesson Practice

If it is **morning,** what time is shown by each clock?

Use a student clock for help.

a.

_____ : _____

b.

_____ : _____

c.

_____ : _____

1. $\$\_\_\_\_\_ + m = \$\_\_\_\_\_$

_____ ticket

+ _____ snacks

_____ total

2. _____ sled

_____ tax

_____ total

3. Write the answer from problem **2** using words.

_____

_____ dollars

Use work area.

4. What fraction of a dollar is a 50¢ coin?

2 50¢ coins = 1 dollar

© Saxon

5. a. nearest **hundred** dollars

     $295 →

b. nearest **ten** dollars

     $93 →

a. _____

b. _____

6. Measure each segment. Remember to write the units.

     A   B   C

a. From point A to point B

b. From point B to point C

c. From point A to point C

a. _____

b. _____

c. _____

7. The length of your arm is nearly

A 2 inches.   **B** 2 feet.

C 2 yards.   **D** 2 miles.

_____

8. digits:

_____ _____ _____ , _____ _____ _____

words: _____

_____

Use work area.

© Saxon

9. 3 quarters + 1 nickel = _____ ¢

   − 78¢
   ‾‾‾‾‾‾

What **coins** should he get back?

_____ pennies

Use work area.

10. 8, 12, 16, _____, _____, _____, _____, …

Use work area.

11. 8, 16, 24, _____, _____, _____, _____, …

Use work area.

12. Complete the table.

Quarters	1	2	3	4	5	6
Value	$0.25	$0.50	$0.75	$1.00		

Use work area.

13. One bicycle tire costs $12.

   a. nearest **ten** dollars

      $12 →

   b. About how much would two tires cost?

     a. _____

     b. _____

14.   3
    3
    3
  + 3

_____

15.   200
  − 38

_____

16. Regroup.

   $0.75
 + $0.75

_____

17. $4.50
  − $0.25

_____

18. A table is **2 yards** long. How many **inches** is that?

1 yard = 3 feet

2 yards = _____ feet

1 foot = 12 inches

_____ feet = _____ inches

_____

19. sunrise

_____ : _____

20.

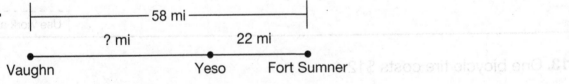

_____   Vaughn to Yeso

+ _____   Yeso to Fort Sumner

_____   Vaughn to Fort Sumner

Remember to write the units.

_____

© Saxon

Name _____

Teacher Note:

• Review "Word Problem Keywords" on page 6 in the *Student Reference Guide.*

• Stories About Comparing

New Concept

• Stories about comparing have a **subtraction** formula.

• For problems about **comparing two dates,** we subtract to find the number of years between the two dates.

Later − Earlier = Difference

Later
− Earlier
Difference

• Look for the comparing cue words **"before"** and **"after."**

Example

How many years were there from Charles Lindbergh's flight across the Atlantic Ocean in 1927 until Armstrong and Aldrin walked on the moon in 1969?

Subtract the earlier date from the later date.

Later	1969
− Earlier	− 1927
Difference	42

There were **42 years** between the two events.

• For problems about **comparing two amounts,** subtract the smaller amount from the bigger amount to find the difference.

Greater − Lesser = Difference

Greater
− Lesser
Difference

• Look for the comparing cue words **"more"** and **"less."**

© Saxon

Example

Frederick and his brother played a board game. Frederick scored 354 points. His brother scored 425 points. How many more points did Frederick's brother score than Frederick?

Subtract the smaller amount from the bigger amount.

$$
\begin{array}{r}
\overset{3}{4}\overset{1}{2}5 \\
-\ 3\ 5\ 4 \\
\hline
7\ 1
\end{array}
$$

Greater
− Lesser
Difference

Frederick's brother scored **71 more points** than Frederick.

Lesson Practice

Write Later − Earlier = Difference number sentences for problems **a** and **b**. Then answer each question.

a. The telephone was invented in 1876. This was how many years **after** the telegraph was invented in 1844?

_____ − _____ = d

The telephone was invented _____ years after the _____.

b. The bar code that is printed on products was invented in 1974. The laser that is used to read the bar codes was invented in 1960. The bar code was invented how many years **after** the laser?

_____ − _____ = d

The _____ was invented _____ years after

the laser.

© Saxon

Write a Greater – Lesser = Difference number sentence for problem **c.**
Then answer the questions.

c. Rose saved her money and bought a stereo that cost $238. Hans saved
his money and bought a stereo that cost $255. Whose stereo cost **more?**
How much **more?**

_____'s stereo cost more.

$_____ – $ _____ = d

Borrow.

_
_____

Hans's stereo cost $_____ more than _____'s
stereo.

(**Written Practice**) 📖 page 214

1.   milk shake

____   sandwich

      total

2. _____ + g = 28

      boys

+ g   girls

      total

3. $116

_____ dollars

Use work area.

4. nearest hundred dollars

$116 →

5.

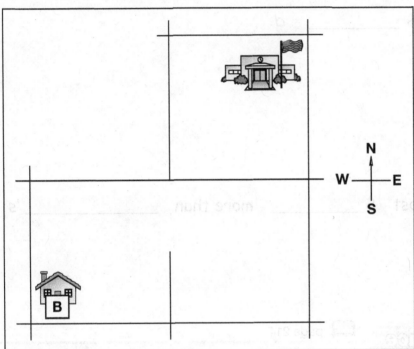

a. Bill lives **how many blocks** from school? _____ blocks

b. to Bill's house from school

Walk _____ blocks south. Turn right and

walk 2 blocks _____ .

Use work area.

6. Which **coin** is $\frac{1}{10}$ of a dollar?

7. Use a ruler to draw a line that is $2\frac{1}{2}$ inches long.

Use work area.

© Saxon

8. 150, 160, 170, _____, _____, _____, _____, ...

Use work area.

9. 3 quarters = _____ ¢

 – 64¢

What **coins** should he get back?

1 _____,

1 _____

Use work area.

10. a. **nearest ten** dollars

$38 →

b. **About** how much money would 2 tickets cost?

a. _____

b. _____

11. 5 quarters → $1.25

4 dimes →

3 nickels →

2 pennies → + _____

Use work area.

12. $284
 + $ 76

_____

13. Borrow.

 1̸0 0
 – 6 3

_____

14. $0.37
 $0.48
 + $1.00

_____

15. $8.50
 – $6.30

_____

16. Your classroom door is about how wide?

A 1 inch   **B** 1 foot

C 1 yard   **D** 1 mile

_____

17. least to greatest

$2, $0.08, 12¢

_____, _____, _____
   least   greatest

Use work area.

18. nine hundred thousand, three hundred thirty-two

_____ _____ _____ , _____ _____ _____

Use work area.

19. lunchtime

_____ : _____

20. Emma: 4 quarters + 3 dimes = $_____

Angela: 19 dimes = $_____

Which girl has **more** money? _____

$_____ − $_____ = d

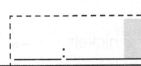

_____

Name _____

Teacher Notes:
- Review Hint #6 "Finding Missing Numbers."
- Review "Missing Numbers" on page 7 in the *Student Reference Guide*.
- For additional practice, students may complete Targeted Practice 40.

- **Missing Numbers in Subtraction**

- **Some Went Away Stories, Part 2**

New Concepts

- **Missing Numbers in Subtraction**

- Subtraction problems have three numbers:

Top number	15
− Bottom number	− 8
Difference	7

- When the *difference* is missing, **subtract** as usual.

- When the *top number* is missing, **add.**

Example

Find the missing number:

$$\begin{array}{r} m \\ -\ 13 \\ \hline 18 \end{array}$$

The *top number* is missing, so we **add up.**

$$\begin{array}{r} m \\ -\ 13 \\ \hline 18 \end{array} \quad \longrightarrow \quad \begin{array}{r} 18 \\ +\ 13 \\ \hline 31 \end{array}$$

The missing number is **31.**

- When the *bottom number* is missing, **subtract.**

© Saxon

Example

Find the missing number:

$$\begin{array}{r} 80 \\ - \square \\ \hline 45 \end{array}$$

The *bottom number* is missing, so we **subtract** the difference from the top number.

$$\begin{array}{r} 80 \\ - \square \\ \hline 45 \end{array} \quad \rightarrow \quad \begin{array}{r} 7 \\ \cancel{8}{}^{1}0 \\ - 4\ 5 \\ \hline 3\ 5 \end{array}$$

The missing number is **35.**

- **Some Went Away Stories, Part 2**

- Some went away stories have a subtraction formula.

$$\begin{array}{l} \text{Some} \\ - \text{ Some went away} \\ \hline \text{What is left} \end{array}$$

- Any number can be missing from the story.

- Read the story carefully and use the "Missing Numbers" chart on page 7 in the *Student Reference Guide* to solve the problems.

Lesson Practice

Find each missing number in problems **a–c.**

a. Top missing $\longrightarrow$ add

$$\begin{array}{r} \square \\ - 16 \\ \hline 16 \end{array} \quad \rightarrow \quad \begin{array}{r} 16 \\ + 16 \\ \hline \end{array}$$

b. Bottom missing $\longrightarrow$ subtract

$$\begin{array}{r} 66 \\ - m \\ \hline 24 \end{array} \quad \rightarrow \quad \begin{array}{r} 66 \\ - 24 \\ \hline \end{array}$$

c. Top missing ⟶ add

$$\begin{array}{r} \square \\ -\ 388 \\ \hline 125 \end{array} \quad \longrightarrow \quad \begin{array}{r} + \\ \hline \end{array}$$

d. Before the carnival, Angus had $21.50. He spent some money on rides and food. After the carnival, Angus had $9.00. How much did Angus spend at

the carnival? _____

Bottom missing ⟶ subtract

$$\begin{array}{r} \$21.50 \\ -\ s \\ \hline \$\ 9.00 \end{array} \quad \longrightarrow \quad \begin{array}{r} - \\ \hline \end{array}$$

Written Practice   📖 page 218

1.   gave

_____ cost

get back

2. Count up quarters by 25.

5 quarters ⟶

5 quarters ⟶ $\dfrac{+\ \_\_\_}{}$

3. two hundred eighty-nine dollars

How many hundreds? tens? ones?

4. Is the answer to problem **3** closer to $200 or $300?

5. from John's house to Mike's house
from Mike's house to school

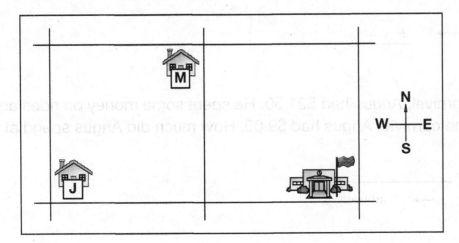

Walk _____ block east. Turn left and walk 1 block

_____ to Mike's house. Turn right and walk 1 block

_____. Turn _____ and walk 1 block

south to school.

Use work area.

6. If it takes 20 minutes to walk 1 mile, about how long would it take to walk **half** a mile?

Walking h_____ a mile should take about half as long,

so about _____ minutes.

Use work area.

7. Measure each segment. Remember to write the units.

A   B   C

a. From point A to point B

b. From point B to point C

c. From point A to point C

a. _____

b. _____

c. _____

8.   Denzel   What is the difference? _____ years

    _____ Angie   Who is older? _____

     difference

> Use work area.

9. 2 quarters + 1 dime = _____ ¢

     − 55¢

What **coin** should he get back?

1 _____

> Use work area.

10. 9, 18, _____, _____, _____,

     _____, _____, _____, _____,

     _____, 99

> Use work area.

11. Draw a dot at Jason's house on the map. Each mark is 1 block.

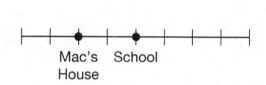

Mac's House   School

from Mac's house to Jason's house

Walk _____ blocks _____.

> Use work area.

12. Complete the table.

1 yard = 3 feet

Yards	1	2	3	4	5	6	7	8	9	10
Feet	3	6	9							

> Use work area.

13. $5.48
      + $3.27

14. $450
      − $150

15.   4
         4
         4
       + 4

16. 500
       − 75

17.   25
        + m
        ———
         75

m =

18.

90
85
80
75
70
°F

Remember to write °F or °C.

19. Use a ruler to draw a segment that is **1$\frac{1}{4}$ inches** long and another segment that is **1$\frac{3}{4}$ inches** long.

Use work area.

20. _____ − s = _____

Bottom missing → subtract

        35   35
      − s   →   − 29
      ———   ———
        29

© Saxon

page 221

Focus on
• Scale Maps

Teacher Notes:

• Introduce Hint #18 "Geometry Vocabulary."

• Refer students to "Angles" on page 15 and "Lines and Segments" on page 16 in the *Student Reference Guide*.

• A **scale** on a map tells what a distance on the map means in the real world.

• Find the scale on the map below:

1 in. = 1 mi

• The scale says that **1 inch on the map is 1 mile in the real world.**

Scale:
1 in. = 1 mi

Todd's House
Oak Ave.
1st St.
2nd St.
3rd St.
4th St.
Robin's House
Elm Ave.
School
Birch Ave.
Marcy's House

Math Language

A **line segment** is a part of a line with a beginning and an end. We can measure a line segment.

• Find Robin's house and the School on the map. The **line segment** from Robin's house to the School is **2 inches** long. So in the real world, the distance from Robin's house to the School is **2 miles.**

© Saxon

- Find Elm Ave. and Birch Ave. on the map. The distance between Elm Avenue and Birch Avenue is $\frac{1}{2}$ **inch.** So in the real world, the distance between Elm Avenue and Birch Avenue is $\frac{1}{2}$ **mile.**

- **Parallel** line segments do not cross. They stay the same distance apart, like railroad tracks.

  Elm Avenue and Birch Avenue are parallel streets.

- **Perpendicular** segments **intersect** (cross) and make square corners. Square corners are like the edge of your paper.

  Birch Avenue and 2nd Street are perpendicular streets.

Use a ruler and this map to answer problems **1–8.** Remember to write the units.

1. How far is it from **Todd's house to school** if he travels

   along the streets? _____

   Find Todd's house.
   Measure from Todd's house to 1st St.
   Measure down 1st St. to the School.
   Add the inches. Every inch shows 1 mile.

2. If Todd wants to take the shortest route to school,

   how many choices does he have? _____ choices

   How many different ways can Todd go to school in 3 miles?

3. How far does Todd ride his bike each day traveling **from**

   home to school and **back home?** _____

   The answer to problem **1** is the distance from Todd's home to school.
   The distance back home is the same.

4. How far is it from **Marcy's house to school?**

_____

Find Marcy's house.
Measure along Elm Ave. to the school.
Every inch is 1 mile. A $\frac{1}{2}$ inch is a $\frac{1}{2}$ mile.

5. How many miles is it from **Todd's house to Marcy's**

house along the roads? _____

Measure from Todd's house to 4th St.
Measure down 4th St. to Elm Ave.
Add the inches.

6. Todd rode his bike from school straight to Marcy's house. Then he rode home. How far did Todd ride?

_____

The distance from school to Marcy's house is the answer to problem **4**.
The distance from Marcy's house to Todd's house is the answer to problem **5**.
Add those answers.

7. Name two streets **parallel** to Oak Avenue.

_____ Ave. and _____ Ave.

Parallel is like railroad tracks.

8. Name two streets **perpendicular** to Oak Avenue.

_____ St. and _____ St.

Perpendicular makes square corners.

 page 222

Scale Map

Materials needed:

• ruler

Follow the instructions to complete the map. The scale is **1 inch equals 1 mile.**

*Jaime lives on the **northeast** corner of Maxwell St. and Grand Ave.*

• Find Jaime's house on the map.

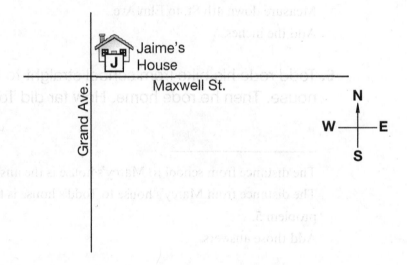

*On the way to school, Jaime rides **two miles east** on Maxwell.*

• Put the end of your ruler on the corner of Maxwell and Grand.

• Measure 2 inches (2 miles) **east** along Maxwell and make a dot.

*Then he turns **south** on Lime Ave. and rides **one mile** to Newton St.*

• Put the short end of your ruler along Maxwell with the edge of the ruler on the dot.

• Draw a line segment that goes 1 inch (1 mile) **south.**

• Write "Lime Ave." next to the line segment you drew.

*Newton St. is **parallel** to Maxwell. Newton and Grand **intersect**.*

- Draw a line segment that goes **west** from the end of Lime to Grand.

- Draw the line segment so it goes a little bit past Grand.

- Write "Newton St." next to this line segment.

*The school is on the **southwest** corner of Newton and Lime.*

- Find the place where Newton and Lime meet.

- Write "School" on the **southwest** corner.

Write directions for how Jaime can go **from school to home** along Newton St. and Grand Ave. Measure the distances. Every inch is one mile.

Go _____ miles west on Newton to Grand. Turn right and go

_____ mile _____ to the corner of Grand and

M_____.

LESSON 41

📖 page 223

• Modeling Fractions

Teacher Notes:
• Refer students to "Fraction Terms" on page 19 in the *Student Reference Guide.*
• Review "Spelling Numbers" on page 12 in the *Student Reference Guide.*

New Concept

- A **fraction** tells part of a whole.

- A fraction has two numbers:

  The **denominator** (bottom number) tells the number of *total parts.*

  The **numerator** (top number) tells the number of *shaded parts.*

numerator ⟶ $\frac{3}{4}$ is shaded.
denominator ⟶

✂ Activity 📖 page 224

Fraction Manipulatives
This activity is optional.

- To name a shaded part of a figure:

  1. Count the **total parts** (shaded and unshaded). This is the *denominator.*

  2. Count the **shaded parts.** This is the *numerator.*

  3. Write the fraction.

- Here are the names of some fractions:

$\frac{1}{2}$ one half $\frac{1}{3}$ one third

$\frac{1}{4}$ one fourth $\frac{1}{5}$ one fifth

$\frac{1}{6}$ one sixth $\frac{1}{8}$ one eighth

Example

Name the fraction shown.

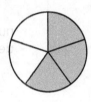

1. There are 5 total parts.

2. Three of the parts are shaded.

3. 3 **out of** 5 parts are shaded.

   The fraction is $\frac{3}{5}$.

   We read **"three fifths."**

Lesson Practice

a. What is the **denominator** of the fraction $\frac{4}{5}$? _____

b. What is the **numerator** of the fraction $\frac{2}{3}$? _____

Name each fraction using digits and words.

c.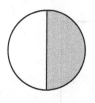

digits: _____

words: one _____

d.

digits: _____

words: _____ thirds

e.

digits: _____

words: _____

Written Practice 📖 page 226

1. Rosa's ticket

_____ brother's ticket

total

2. _____ + ☐ = _____   before dinner

+ ☐ after dinner

in all

3. 238

_____

_____

| Use work area. |

4. nearest **hundred**

2 ③ 8 →

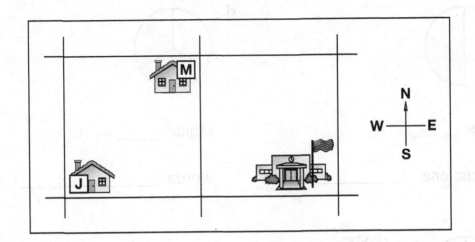

5. from Mike's house to John's house and from John's house to school

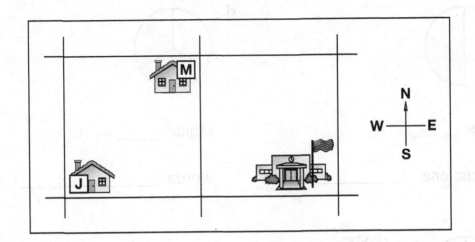

Walk _____ block west. Turn left and walk 1 block

_____ to John's house. Turn _____ and

walk 2 blocks _____ to school.

┌─────────────────┐
╎ Use work area. ╎
└─────────────────┘

6. Measure each distance to the nearest quarter inch. Remember to write the units.

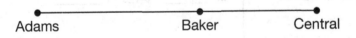

Adams   Baker   Central

a. From Adams to Baker

b. From Baker to Central

c. From Adams to Central

a. _____ b. _____ c. _____

7. 1 inch = 10 miles

Use your answer to part **c** of problem **6**.
Remember to write the units.

8.
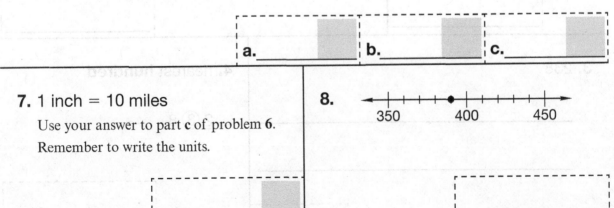

350   400   450

9. 3 quarters = _____ ¢

_– 65¢_

What **coin** should he get back?

1 _____

Use work area.

10. What is the eighth number in this sequence?

3, 6, 9, 12, _____, _____,

_____, ⊖

Use work area.

11. Complete the table.

Insects	1	2	3	4	5	6	7
Legs	6	12	18				

Use work area.

12. How many shaded?
How many total?

digits: _____

words: _____

_____

_____

Use work area.

13. Draw a line that is $3\frac{1}{4}$ inches long **perpendicular** to the line below.

Use work area.

14. 200
     300
   + 400

15. $5.25
     + $3.17

16. 45
      92
    + 11

17. $ 800
     − $225

18. Top missing ⟶ add

   □
  − 20 ⟶ ____
   55

  □ = _____

19. least to greatest value

   6 dimes = _____ ¢

   9 nickels = _____ ¢

   2 quarters = _____ ¢

   _____ ¢, _____ ¢, _____ ¢

   Use work area.

20. Draw dots for Bill's house and Ted's house on the map below.

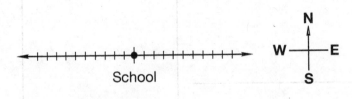

School

From Bill's house to Ted's house.

Ride _____ blocks _____.

Use work area.

Name _____

Teacher Note:
• Introduce Hint #20 "Drawing Fractional Parts."

• Drawing Fractions

New Concept

• Fractions show **equal** parts.

• The circle and the square below each show $\frac{1}{2}$.
The parts are **equal.**

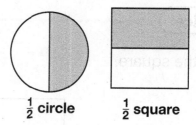

$\frac{1}{2}$ **circle** $\frac{1}{2}$ **square**

• The circle and the square below do **not** show $\frac{1}{2}$.
The parts are **not equal.**

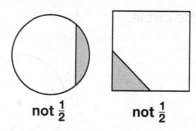

not $\frac{1}{2}$ **not** $\frac{1}{2}$

• To draw a picture of a fraction:

1. Draw the figure.

2. Divide it into **equal** parts.

3. Shade the correct number of parts.

© Saxon

Example

Draw and shade $\frac{1}{3}$ of a rectangle.

One third means **one part out of three** will be shaded.

1. Draw a rectangle.

2. Divide it into 3 **equal** parts.

3. Shade one of the parts.

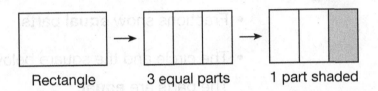

Rectangle   3 equal parts   1 part shaded

Lesson Practice

a. Shade $\frac{1}{2}$ of the square.

b. Shade $\frac{1}{4}$ of the circle.

c. Shade $\frac{2}{3}$ of the rectangle.

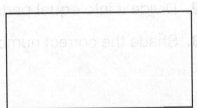

© Saxon

d. Is $\frac{1}{3}$ of the circle shaded? Why or why not?

_____, because the circle is divided into parts that

are not e _____.

Written Practice 📖 page 230

1. _____ mi − _____ mi = ☐

—
_____

Remember to write the units.

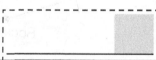

2.   keyboard

_____ tax

total

3. Round the answer to problem **2** to the **nearest hundred** dollars.

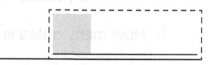

4.

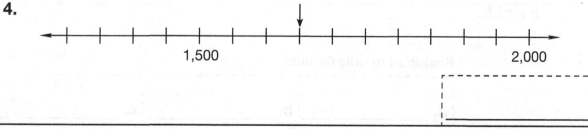

1,500   2,000

5. The number 5 in the fraction $\frac{2}{5}$ shows that there are _____ equal parts in the whole.

¦ Use work area. ¦

---

6. Complete the table.

1 yard = 3 feet

Yards	1	2	3	4
Feet	3	6		

¦ Use work area. ¦

7. Shade $\frac{1}{4}$ of the rectangle.

¦ Use work area. ¦

---

8. Use a ruler to measure from Banks to Cane and from Cane to Rockland. Label the distances on the map.

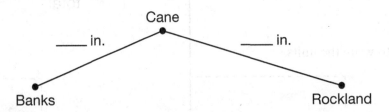

On the map, every quarter inch is 1 mile.

a. How many **miles** is it from **Rockland to Cane?**

b. How many **miles** is it from **Cane to Banks?**

c. To find the distance from Rockland to Banks, **add** your answers to **a** and **b**.

Remember to write the units.

a. _____ **b.** _____ **c.** _____

© Saxon

9. 800,744

_____ thousand,

_____

_____   ⌐ ‾ ‾ ‾ ‾ ‾ ‾ ‾ ¬
        ¦ Use work area. ¦
        ∟ _ _ _ _ _ _ _ ⌡

10. 1 quarter + 3 dimes + 1 nickel = _____ ¢

    − 59¢
    ‾‾‾‾‾‾‾‾‾

What coin should she get back?

    1 _____

_____   ⌐ ‾ ‾ ‾ ‾ ‾ ‾ ‾ ¬
        ¦ Use work area. ¦
        ∟ _ _ _ _ _ _ _ ⌡

11. 25,000

_____

_____   ⌐ ‾ ‾ ‾ ‾ ‾ ‾ ‾ ¬
        ¦ Use work area. ¦
        ∟ _ _ _ _ _ _ _ ⌡

12. What is the 12th number in this sequence?

4, 8, 12, 16, _____, _____, _____, _____, _____, _____, _____,

⌐ ‾ ‾ ‾ ‾ ‾ ‾ ‾ ‾ ¬
¦   ¦
∟ _____ ⌡

13. Count up by 12s. What is the 4th number?

12, _____, _____,

© Saxon

14. Bottom missing ⟶ subtract

$$\begin{array}{r} 100 \\ -\ \square \\ \hline 30 \end{array}$$

$\square =$ _____

15.
$$\begin{array}{r} 93 \\ 47 \\ +\ 58 \\ \hline \end{array}$$

_____

16.
$$\begin{array}{r} \$300 \\ -\ \$250 \\ \hline \end{array}$$

17.
$$\begin{array}{r} 400 \\ +\ 400 \\ \hline \end{array}$$

_____

18.
$$\begin{array}{r} \$\cancel{500} \\ -\ \$336 \\ \hline \end{array}$$

19. $\frac{1}{4}$ of a dollar plus $\frac{1}{10}$ of a dollar

_____ ¢ + _____ ¢ = _____ ¢

A 25¢   **B** 10¢

C 35¢   **D** 40¢

20. after dinner

Name _____

Teacher Notes:

• Review "Comparison Symbols" on page 12 in the *Student Reference Guide*.

• See Hint #19 "Fraction Manipulatives."

• For additional practice, students may complete Targeted Practice 43.

• Comparing Fractions, Part 1

New Concept

• We can **compare** fractions by drawing pictures.

Example

Compare $\frac{1}{2}$ and $\frac{1}{4}$.

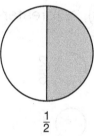   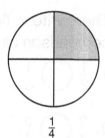

$\frac{1}{2}$ $\frac{1}{4}$

one half   one fourth

One half is greater than one fourth.

$$\frac{1}{2} > \frac{1}{4}$$

• Some fractions with different names are **equal.**

Example

Compare $\frac{1}{2}$ and $\frac{3}{6}$.

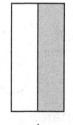   

$\frac{1}{2}$ $\frac{3}{6}$

one half   three sixths

One half is equal to three sixths.

$$\frac{1}{2} = \frac{3}{6}$$

- We can also compare fractions with fraction manipulatives.

 **Activity** 📖 page 234

Comparing Fractions

Materials needed:
- fraction manipulatives

Use fraction manipulatives to show each fraction.

Then write < (less than), > (greater than), or = (equal) in the comparison circle.

1. $\frac{1}{2}$ ◯ $\frac{1}{3}$ 2. $\frac{2}{3}$ ◯ $\frac{2}{5}$

3. $\frac{2}{3}$ ◯ $\frac{3}{4}$ 4. $\frac{1}{2}$ ◯ $\frac{2}{4}$

Lesson Practice

a. Shade each circle to show the fraction. Then compare the fractions.

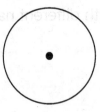   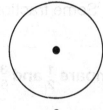

$\frac{1}{2}$ $\frac{2}{4}$

one half   two fourths

$\frac{1}{2}$ ◯ $\frac{2}{4}$

b. Use fraction pieces to compare:

$\frac{1}{4}$ ◯ $\frac{1}{5}$

© Saxon

c. Shade each rectangle to show the fraction. Then compare the fractions.

$\frac{1}{4}$

one fourth

$\frac{1}{2}$

one half

$\frac{1}{4}$ ◯ $\frac{1}{2}$

Written Practice 📖 page 236

1. _____ mi – _____ mi = /

_–____

2. $ 20
  $ 10 $ 28

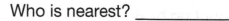

3. grandmother: 385 mi

cousin: 326 mi

brother: 410 mi

Who is nearest? _____

Compare hundreds.

Compare tens.

Who is farthest? _____

Compare hundreds.

⌐ ‾ ‾ ‾ ‾ ‾ ‾ ‾ ‾ ¬
¦ Use work area. ¦
∟ _ _ _ _ _ _ _ _ _ ⌟

4. 1995
    _1945_

5. **a.** digits: _____

   b. words: _____

   _____

   | Use work area. |

6. **three hundred eighty thousand dollars**

7. $s -$ _____ $=$ _____

   Top missing ⟶ add

   picked

   _____ gave

   left

   | Use work area. |

8. **Count up by 8.**

   8, _____, _____, 32, _____, _____, _____, 64, _____, _____, _____, 96

   | Use work area. |

9. Measure the distance from Leslie's house to Jenny's house along Jasper and Lincoln.

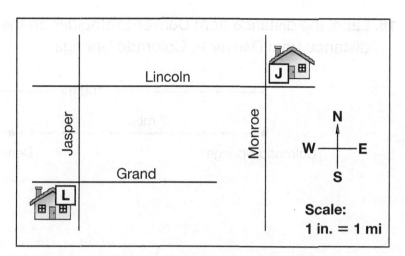

On the map, every inch is 1 mile. How far is it from Leslie's house to Jenny's house?

Remember to write the units.

---

10. from Leslie's house to Jenny's house

Drive 1 mile _____. Turn right and drive _____

miles _____.

Use work area.

---

11. parallel to Grand	**12.** $\begin{array}{r} 62 \\ 32 \\ +\ 22 \\ \hline \end{array}$	**13.** $\begin{array}{r} 650 \\ -\ 70 \\ \hline \end{array}$

14. $\begin{array}{r} \$8.45 \\ +\ \$0.70 \\ \hline \end{array}$	**15.** $\begin{array}{r} \$250 \\ -\ \$200 \\ \hline \end{array}$

16. Label the distance from Denver to Boulder on the map. Then find the distance from Denver to Colorado Springs.

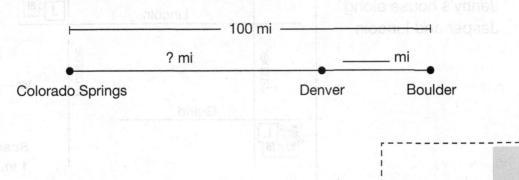

17. Shade $\frac{2}{3}$ of the circle.

Use work area.

18. Use fraction pieces to compare.

$\frac{2}{3} \bigcirc \frac{3}{4}$

Use work area.

19. Bottom missing → subtract

```
  175
-  □
─────
   32
```

$\square =$

20. What is the value of the 4 in 342,891?

expanded form

$300,000 + \underline{\hspace{2cm}} + 2,000 + 800 + 90 + 1$

© Saxon

Name _____

Teacher Notes:

• Review Hint #14 "Naming Fractions/Identifying Fractional Parts."

• Review "Fraction Terms" on page 19 in the *Student Reference Guide*.

• Fractions of a Group

New Concept

• Fractions can name parts of a whole figure.

• Fractions can also name parts of a **group.**

The **denominator** (bottom number) tells the *total number* of items in the group.

The **numerator** (top number) tells the number of items we are picking out of the group.

Example

What fraction of the marbles in the bag are striped?

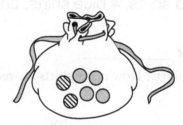

There are 6 total marbles in the bag.

2 out of 6 marbles are striped.

$\frac{2}{6}$ **(two sixths)** of the marbles are striped.

Lesson Practice

a. What fraction of the names of the days of the week **begin**

with the letter *S*? _____

How many total days? How many days begin with *S*?

© Saxon

Sunday

Monday

Tuesday

Wednesday

Thursday

Friday

Saturday

b. What fraction of the marbles in the bag are **striped?** _____

How many total marbles? How many marbles are striped?

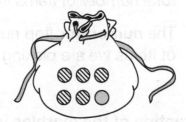

c. Brad has 3 red shirts, 4 blue shirts, and 1 green shirt. What fraction of his

shirts are **red?** _____

How many total shirts? How many shirts are red?

red

blue

+____ green

total

d. What fraction of the letters in the word SAXON are **vowels?** Use words
and digits to name the fraction.

How many total letters? How many letters are vowels?

words: _____

digits: _____

1. $\$\_\_\_\_\_ - \$\_\_\_\_\_ = I$

   regular price

   $-_____$ off

2. Use your answer from problem **1.**

   one pair

   $\_\_\_\_$ second pair

   total

3. $\$\_\_\_\_\_ - s = \$\_\_\_\_\_$

Bottom missing ⟶ subtract

   had

   $-\_\_\_\_$ gloves

   got back

4. a.

$$\begin{array}{r} \square \\ + 35 \\ \hline 149 \end{array}$$

b. Bottom missing ⟶ subtract

$$\begin{array}{r} 49 \\ - \square \\ \hline 28 \end{array}$$

c. Top missing ⟶ add

$$\begin{array}{r} m \\ - 200 \\ \hline 567 \end{array}$$

a. $\square =$ _____

b. $\square =$ _____

c. $m =$ _____

5. a. digits: _____

b. words: _____

_____

Use work area.

6. Shade $\frac{1}{2}$ of the square.

Use work area.

7.

A 7:45   **B** 7:15   **C** A quarter to 7   **D** A quarter after 7

8. How many total months? How many start with J?

See page 3 in the *Student Reference Guide*.

9. 2 quarters + 3 nickels = _____ ¢

$-$ 63¢

What **coins** should he get back?

10. sixteen thousand, four hundred sixty

11. Count up by 25.

25, _____, _____, _____, _____, 150, _____, _____, _____, 250

Use work area.

12.   41
            42
        + 43

13. $150
        − $ 90

14.   8
            8
            8
        +   8

15. $250
        − $237

16. Shade $\frac{1}{3}$ of the circle.

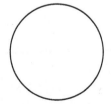

Use work area.

17. _____ − _____ = d

Room B

− _____ Room A

18. about

42 →

84 → $\underline{+}$

19. Draw a line $3\frac{1}{2}$ inches long.

Use work area.

20. What fraction of the students in Mrs. Levy's class have names that **begin with the letter M?**

How many total students? How many names start with M?

Mrs. Levy's Class	
Elliot	Lucy
Marquis	Conrad
Regina	Miller
Cali	Alex
Margot	Penny
Warren	Jill
Brandon	Mike
Jane	Aubree

• Probability, Part 1

New Concept

- **Probability** describes whether something is **more likely** or **less likely** to happen.

Example

When the arrow on this spinner is spun, which number is most likely? Which number is least likely?

The spinner is divided into 8 equal parts.

Five parts say "1."

Two parts say "2."

One part says "3."

"1" is most likely because there are *more parts* that say "1" than any other number.

"3" is least likely because there are *less parts* that say "3" than any other number.

 📖 page 245

Probability Demonstration

This activity is optional.

© Saxon

For problems **a** and **b** look at the picture of the bag and marbles.

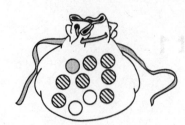

a. If one marble is taken from the bag, which color is **more likely** to be

picked, striped or white? _____

Are there more striped or white marbles?

b. If one marble is picked, is it *more likely* or *less likely* to be **gray?**

_____ likely

For problems **c** and **d** look at the picture of the spinner.

c. If Dwayne spins the spinner one time, which number is the spinner

less likely to stop on, 1 or 3? _____

Which part is smaller, 1 or 3?

d. If Isabel spins the spinner one time, what number is it **most likely** to

stop on? _____

Which part is biggest?

© Saxon

1. What is half of $60?

What amount is halfway between $0 and $60 on this number line?

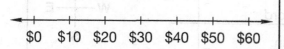

$0 $10 $20 $30 $40 $50 $60

2. _____ − s = _____

Bottom missing → subtract

in box

− _____ gave

left

3. a.   □
        + 206
        49

b. Bottom missing → subtract

        700
        − □
        280

a. □ = _____

b. □ = _____

4. What fraction is **gray?**

How many total stars? How many are gray?

☆ ☆ ☆ ☆ ☆ ★ ★ ★ ★ ★ ★ ★ ★

5. a. digits: _____

b. words: _____

_____

Use work area.

6. 10 dimes and 3 pennies

Are there more or less pennies?

_____ likely

© Saxon

7. Measure the distances from Tony's house to Andrew's house along the streets to the **nearest inch.**

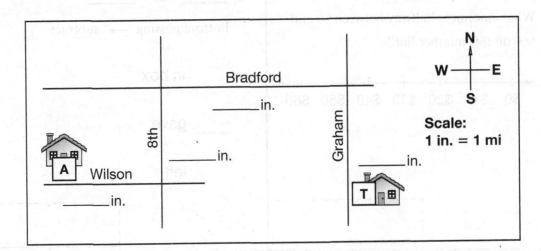

Add up the distances: _____ in.

On the map, every inch is 1 mile. How far is it from Tony's house to Andrew's house?

★ ★ ★ ★ ★ ★ ★ ★ ★ ★ ★ ★

8. from Tony's house to Andrew's house

Go 1 mile _____. Turn left and go _____ miles west.

Turn left and go 1 mile _____.

Turn _____ and go 1 mile _____.

Use work area.

9. perpendicular to Wilson

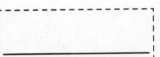

© Saxon

10. 412,600

_____

_____

‾‾‾‾‾‾‾‾‾‾‾‾‾‾‾‾‾‾‾‾‾‾‾‾‾‾‾‾‾‾‾‾‾‾ ⌐ ‾ ‾ ‾ ‾ ‾ ‾ ‾ ‾ ⌐
                                    ¦ Use work area. ¦
                                    ⌐ _ _ _ _ _ _ _ _ ⌐

11. Count up by 7.

7, _____, _____, _____, _____, 42, _____, _____, 63, _____, _____, _____

‾‾‾‾‾‾‾‾‾‾‾‾‾‾‾‾‾‾‾‾‾‾‾‾‾‾‾‾‾‾‾‾‾‾ ⌐ ‾ ‾ ‾ ‾ ‾ ‾ ‾ ‾ ⌐
                                    ¦ Use work area. ¦
                                    ⌐ _ _ _ _ _ _ _ _ ⌐

12. Shade $\frac{2}{4}$ of the circle.

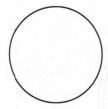

‾‾‾‾‾‾‾‾‾‾‾‾‾‾‾‾‾‾‾‾‾‾‾‾‾‾‾‾‾‾‾‾‾‾ ⌐ ‾ ‾ ‾ ‾ ‾ ‾ ‾ ‾ ⌐
                                    ¦ Use work area. ¦
                                    ⌐ _ _ _ _ _ _ _ _ ⌐

13. least to greatest

$\frac{1}{3}, \frac{1}{5}, \frac{1}{2}, \frac{1}{4}$

Use fraction pieces.

_____, _____, _____, _____

 least   greatest

‾‾‾‾‾‾‾‾‾‾‾‾‾‾‾‾‾‾‾‾‾‾‾‾‾‾‾‾‾‾‾‾‾‾ ⌐ ‾ ‾ ‾ ‾ ‾ ‾ ‾ ‾ ⌐
                                    ¦ Use work area. ¦
                                    ⌐ _ _ _ _ _ _ _ _ ⌐

14.   5
       8
       7
   + 4

15. $125
   − $100

16.   95
      76
   + 52

17. $350
   − $284

18. Bottom missing ⟶ subtract

     37
  − ▢
     18

▢ =

19. morning

20. 5 quarters and 7 pennies

What fraction is **pennies?**

How many total coins? How many pennies?

Name _____

Teacher Notes:

• Review "Fraction Terms" on page 19 in the *Student Reference Guide*.

• For additional practice, students may complete Targeted Practice 46.

• Fractions Equal to 1
• Mixed Numbers

New Concepts

• **Fractions Equal to 1**

• When the numerator (top number) and denominator (bottom number) are *equal*, **the fraction is equal to 1.**

Math Language

A **fraction** is a number that names part of a whole.

numerator ⟶ $\frac{2}{3}$
denominator ⟶

2 out of 3 parts

$\frac{2}{2} = 1$

2 out of 2 parts

$\frac{3}{3} = 1$

3 out of 3 parts

$\frac{4}{4} = 1$

4 out of 4 parts

Example

Write the fraction equal to 1 shown by the shaded figure.

The rectangle is divided into 6 parts. All 6 parts are shaded. Six out of 6 parts is $\frac{6}{6}$.

• **Mixed Numbers**

• A **mixed number** is a whole number and a fraction.

• Use the word "and" when naming mixed numbers.

3 whole circles

and $\frac{1}{2}$ circle

$= 3\frac{1}{2}$

↑ ↑
Whole Fraction
number

© Saxon

a. Which of these fractions **equals 1?** (Circle your answer.)

A $\frac{1}{2}$ **B** $\frac{2}{3}$ **C** $\frac{3}{4}$ **D** $\frac{5}{5}$

b. Shade the square to show the fraction $\frac{4}{4}$.

4 out of 4 parts

c. Compare: $\frac{3}{3}$ ◯ $\frac{4}{4}$

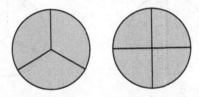

d. What fraction equal to 1 is represented by this shaded figure? _____

6 out of 6 parts

e. Write $5\frac{3}{10}$ using words.

_____ and _____ tenths

f. Shade the circles to show $2\frac{1}{2}$.

1. What fraction of a dollar is 10 dimes?

A dime is $\frac{1}{10}$ of a dollar.

2. Space Shuttle

$-$ _____ Sputnik

_____ years

3.

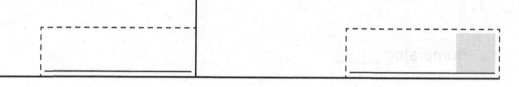

4. CD

$+$ _____ tax

_____ total

words: _____

Use work area.

5. 3 basketballs and 4 footballs

What fraction is **basketballs?**

How many total? How many basketballs?

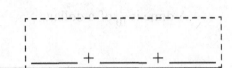

6. expanded form

1,440

_____ + _____ + _____

7. $\frac{8}{9}$

numerator: _____

denominator: _____

Use work area.

8. Draw a line $5\frac{1}{4}$ inches long.

Use work area.

9. Estimate and measure the height of your desk **in inches.**

estimate: _____

measure: _____

Use work area.

© Saxon

10.

_____ out of _____ are **not** gray.

_____

11. Complete the table.

Years	1	2	3	4	5	6	7	8	9
Months	12	24	36						

Use work area.

12. 976
      − 200

_____

13. 812
      + 30

_____

14. $4.38
      + $1.52

_____

15. 65
       48
      + 21

_____

© Saxon

16. Borrow across all zeros.

$$
\begin{array}{r}
2\cancel{0}0 \\
-\ 143 \\
\hline
\end{array}
$$

17.
$$
\begin{array}{r}
6 \\
7 \\
5 \\
+\ 4 \\
\hline
\end{array}
$$

18. $5 + 5 + 5 + 5 + 5 + 5 + 5 + 5 + 5 + 5 =$

Count up by 5 or find sets of ten.

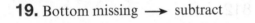

19. Bottom missing ⟶ subtract

$$
\begin{array}{r}
180 \\
-\ \square \\
\hline
50
\end{array}
$$

$\square =$

20. What fraction of the apples are **red?**

How many total apples? How many red?

$$
\begin{array}{r}
4 \quad \text{green} \\
+\ r \quad \text{red} \\
\hline
10 \quad \text{total}
\end{array}
$$

Name _____

Teacher Notes:

• Students will need their fraction manipulatives to complete the activity.

• For additional practice, students may complete Targeted Practice 47.

• Equivalent Fractions

New Concept

• Different fractions that name the same amount are called **equivalent fractions.**

• **Equivalent** is another way to say "equal."

• All the pictures below show fractions equivalent to $\frac{1}{2}$.

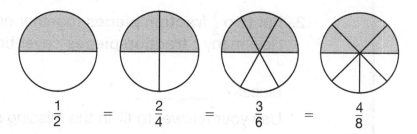

$$\frac{1}{2} = \frac{2}{4} = \frac{3}{6} = \frac{4}{8}$$

Example

What equivalent fractions are shown by these rectangles?

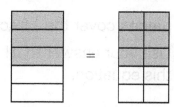

3 out of 5   6 out of 10

$\frac{3}{5}$ $\frac{6}{10}$

$$\frac{3}{5} = \frac{6}{10}$$

© Saxon

 page 255

Equivalent Fractions

Materials needed:
- fraction manipulatives

Use your fraction manipulatives to show equivalent fractions.

1. Put a $\frac{1}{3}$ **fraction piece** on your desk. How many $\frac{1}{6}$

   fraction pieces cover the $\frac{1}{3}$ fraction piece? _____

   Use your answer to fill in the missing number in this equation.

   $$\frac{1}{3} = \frac{\boxed{}}{6}$$

2. Put **two $\frac{1}{3}$ fraction pieces** together on your desk. How many $\frac{1}{6}$ **fraction pieces** cover both $\frac{1}{3}$ fraction

   pieces? _____

   Use your answer to fill in the missing number in this equation.

   $$\frac{2}{3} = \frac{\boxed{}}{6}$$

3. Put a $\frac{1}{4}$ **fraction piece** on your desk. How many $\frac{1}{8}$ **fraction**

   pieces cover the $\frac{1}{4}$ fraction piece? _____

   Use your answer to fill in the missing number in this equation.

   $$\frac{1}{4} = \frac{\boxed{}}{8}$$

4. Put **two $\frac{1}{4}$ fraction pieces** together on your desk. How many $\frac{1}{8}$ **fraction pieces** cover both $\frac{1}{4}$ fraction

   pieces? _____

   Use your answer to fill in the missing number in this equation.

   $$\frac{2}{4} = \frac{\boxed{}}{8}$$

a. Use your fraction pieces to find and name three fractions equivalent to $\frac{1}{2}$.

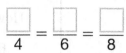

$$\frac{\boxed{}}{4} = \frac{\boxed{}}{6} = \frac{\boxed{}}{8}$$

b. **Two quarters** and **five dimes** both equal 50¢. Write two equivalent fractions of a dollar represented by these two sets of coins.

A quarter is $\frac{1}{4}$ of a dollar. A dime is $\frac{1}{10}$ of a dollar.

$$\frac{2}{\boxed{}} = \frac{5}{\boxed{}}$$

c. Show that one half is equivalent to two fourths. Shade **one half** of the square on the left. Shade **two fourths** of the square on the right.

$\frac{1}{2}$

$\frac{2}{4}$

d. Circle the shaded figure below that shows a **fraction equivalent to** $\frac{1}{2}$.

A $\frac{2}{3}$ B $\frac{3}{4}$ C $\frac{2}{6}$ D $\frac{5}{10}$

Written Practice 📖 page 257

1.   1968
    $\underline{-\ 1962}$

2.   meal

    tax

    tip

3. $m -$ _____ = _____

Top missing ⟶ add

m

$-$ _____ gave

_____ had

---

4. What fraction is white?

How many total? How many white?

6 white
5 black
$+ 3$ blue
_____ total

---

5. What fraction is NOT white?

How many total? How many **not** white?

---

6. Draw a $1\frac{3}{4}$ inch-long segment **parallel** to the segment below.

_____

Use work area.

---

7. two thousand, five hundred

_____ , _____ _____ _____

---

8. a. digits: _____ _____ , _____ _____ _____

b. words: _____

_____

Use work area.

9. Which fraction is **not** equal to 1?

A $\frac{2}{2}$ **B** $\frac{3}{3}$ **C** $\frac{4}{5}$ **D** $\frac{6}{6}$

10. Which fraction **equals** $\frac{1}{2}$? Use fraction pieces for help.

A $\frac{2}{5}$ **B** $\frac{2}{3}$ **C** $\frac{2}{4}$ **D** $\frac{2}{6}$

11. Which number in $\frac{4}{6}$ tells the number of **total parts** in the whole?

12.   800
    − 149
	13. 932
	    − 30

14. $5.76
   + $3.35
	15. $560
	   − $320

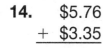

© Saxon

16. $0.84
         $0.96
      + $0.28

17. Top missing ⟶ add

$$\begin{array}{r} \square \\ -\ 35 \\ \hline 40 \end{array}$$

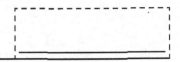
$\square$ =

18. How much money is $\frac{1}{4}$ of a dollar plus $\frac{3}{10}$ of a dollar?

_____¢ + _____¢ = _____¢

A 25¢   **B** 30¢   **C** 55¢   **D** 60¢

19. Complete the table.

Feet	1	2	3	4	5	6	7
Inches	12	24	36				

Use work area.

20.   Del Norte to Hooper

                        Hooper to Alamosa

                   _____   Alamosa to Del Norte

                        total

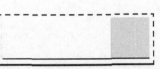

📖 page 260

Name _____

Finding Fractions and Mixed Numbers on a Number Line

Teacher Notes:

- Students will need a copy of **Lesson Activity 18** to complete this lesson.
- For additional practice, students may complete Targeted Practice 48.

New Concept

- **Whole numbers** are the numbers we use to count:

$$0, 1, 2, 3, 4, \ldots$$

Math Language

A **mixed number** is a number made up of a whole number and a fraction.

$$3\frac{2}{3}$$

- A number line can show fractions and mixed numbers between whole numbers.

Example

To what number is the arrow pointing?

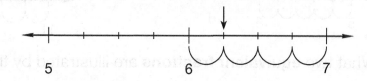

The whole number just before the arrow is **6.**

Count to the arrow to find the numerator: **1.**

Count the number of *parts* between 6 and 7: **4.**

The arrow is pointing to **$6\frac{1}{4}$.**

© Saxon

 page 263

Fractions on a Number Line

Materials needed:

• **Lesson Activity 18**

Name the fractions and mixed numbers shown on
Lesson Activity 18.

Lesson Practice

Name the fractions shown on these number lines.

a. _____

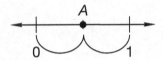

b. _____

c. _____

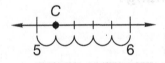

d. _____

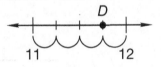

e. What two **equivalent fractions** are illustrated by this pair

of number lines? _____ and _____

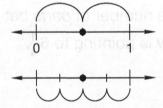

1. _____ hr – _____ hr = /

2. $_____ + m = $_____

       price

  + _m_   tax

       total

3. There are **11 girls** and **12 boys** in class.

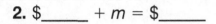

   11   girls
 + 12   boys

       total

What fraction of the students are **girls?** _____
How many total? How many girls?

What fraction of the students are **boys?** _____
How many total? How many boys?

Use work area.

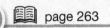

4. Is 28 seconds **more than** or **less than** half of a minute?

1 minute = 60 seconds

$\frac{1}{2}$ minute = _____ seconds

5.   Hawaii

_____ Arizona

6. $\frac{2}{5}$ ◯ $\frac{3}{4}$

Use fraction manipulatives for help.

7.

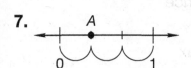

Use work area.

8. Find a fraction **equivalent to** $\frac{1}{4}$.

Use fraction manipulatives for help.

9. Write $4\frac{5}{6}$ using words.

_____ and _____

Use work area.

10. Bottom missing ⟶ subtract

$$\begin{array}{r} 77 \\ -\ \square \\ \hline 9 \end{array}$$

$\square =$ _____

11. Shade $\frac{1}{3}$ of the rectangle on the left.

Shade $\frac{2}{6}$ of the rectangle on the right.

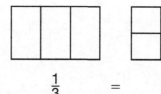

$$\frac{1}{3} \quad = \quad \frac{2}{6}$$

Use work area.

12.   966
  – 900
	13. 776
	  + 50

14. $625
 – $375
	15. $0.49
	    $0.94
	  + $0.55

16. 400 – 143	**17.** $4.56 + $5.00

18. Bottom missing ⟶ subtract

$$\begin{array}{r} 83 \\ -\ \square \\ \hline 46 \end{array}$$

$\square =$ ___

19. The number line goes from 600 to 700. Label 600 and 700. Then draw a dot at 620.

Use work area.

20. Read the problem and write the distances on the map.

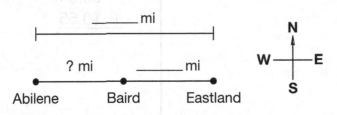

Abilene to Eastland

— ___ Baird to Eastland

Abilene to Baird

How many miles is it from Baird to Abilene? ___

What **direction** is it from Baird to Abilene? ___

Use work area.

Name _____

Teacher Note:

• Review "Comparison Symbols" on page 12 in *Student Reference Guide*.

• Comparing Fractions, Part 2

New Concept

• We can **compare** fractions using pictures or fraction manipulatives.

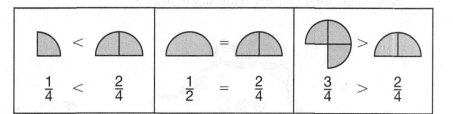

$$\frac{1}{4} < \frac{2}{4} \qquad \frac{1}{2} = \frac{2}{4} \qquad \frac{3}{4} > \frac{2}{4}$$

Lesson Practice

Use fraction manipulatives to compare.

a. Angela walks $\frac{3}{4}$ of a mile to school. Byron walks $\frac{3}{5}$ of a mile to school.

Who walks farther to school, Angela or Byron? _____

Compare $\frac{3}{4}$ and $\frac{3}{5}$.

b. What fraction of a dollar is 3 quarters? _____

1 quarter is $\frac{1}{4}$ of a dollar.

What fraction of a dollar is 7 dimes? _____

1 dime is $\frac{1}{10}$ of a dollar.

© Saxon

Compare the fractions by changing to cents.

3 quarters   7 dimes

↓   ◯   ↓

_____¢   _____¢

c. What fraction of the marbles **in the bag** are striped? _____

How many total marbles? How many striped?

What fraction of the marbles **in the box** are striped? _____

How many total marbles? How many striped?

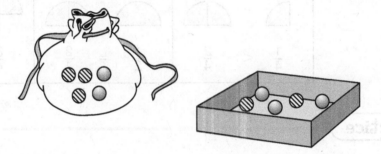

Does the bag or the box have a greater fraction of striped marbles?

_____

Use fraction manipulatives to compare the fractions.

d. Use fraction pieces to compare.

$\frac{2}{4}$ ◯ $\frac{2}{3}$

© Saxon

1. Who has more baseball cards?

_____

How many more? _____

_____ − _____ = d

−_____

2. $2.00 paper $2.95 price

+ _____ folder   _____ total

total   tax

3.   2 black
          3 white
        + 5 red

          total

What fraction of the cars are **not red?** _____

How many total? How many **not** red?

What fraction of the cars are **red?** _____

How many total? How many red?

Use fraction manipulatives to compare:

_____ ◯ _____
not red   red

4. Shade $\frac{3}{4}$ of this circle.

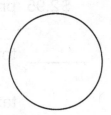

Use work area.

5. $\frac{1}{3}$ ◯ $\frac{2}{4}$

Use fraction pieces for help.

Use work area.

6. 3 quarters = _____ ¢

_____

What **coins** should he get back?

1 _____, 1 _____,

1 _____

Use work area.

7. Bottom missing ⟶ subtract

$$\begin{array}{r} 210 \\ -\ \square \\ \hline 99 \end{array}$$

$\square$ = _____

8. a.   video game

_____ roll-film camera

Remember to write the units.

b. Is 1948 **before** or **after** the first radio station?

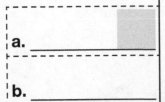

a. _____

b. _____

9. a. digits: _____

b. words: _____

_____

Use work area.

© Saxon

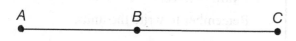

10. Measure to the nearest quarter inch.

Remember to write the units.

a. From point *A* to point *B*

b. From point *B* to point *C*

c. From point *A* to point *C*

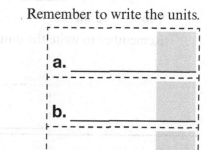

a. _____

b. _____

c. _____

11. 21, 28, _____, 42, 49, 56, ...

Use work area.

12.

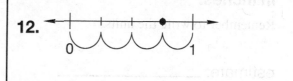

_____

13. What fraction of a dollar is 3 nickels? _____

1 nickel is $\frac{1}{20}$ of a dollar.

What fraction of a dollar is 7 pennies? _____

1 penny is $\frac{1}{100}$ of a dollar.

Compare the fractions by changing to cents.

3 nickels   7 pennies

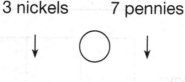

_____ ¢   _____ ¢

Use work area.

14.   9 8 9
      − 2 0 0

15. $0.38
          $0.84
       + $0.45

16. 1 ft − 1 in. = _____ in.

1 foot = 12 inches
Remember to write the units.

17. 1 yd − 1 ft = _____ ft

1 yard = 3 feet
Remember to write the units.

18. Estimate and measure the length of your textbook from top to bottom **in inches.**

Remember to write the units.

estimate: _____

measure: _____

Use work area.

19.

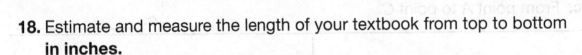

_____ Preston to Chauncey

_____ Chauncey to Milton

___ Milton to Preston

_____ total

20. How many $\frac{1}{6}$s equal $\frac{1}{3}$?

Tonya

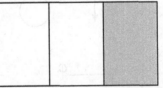

Sherri

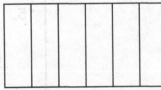

© Saxon

Name _____

📖 page 270

Teacher Note:
• For additional practice, students may complete Targeted Practice 50.

• Probability, Part 2

New Concept

• **Probability** describes whether something is **more likely, less likely,** or **equally likely** to happen.

• In the spinner below, the parts are the same size. So the arrow is *equally likely* to stop on 3 or 4.

Example

Is spinning 1 more likely or less likely than spinning 2?
Is spinning 2 more likely or less likely than spinning 3?

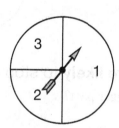

The part that says "1" is *bigger* than the part labeled "2."

The spinner is **more likely** to stop on 1 than 2.

The parts that say "2" and "3" are the *same* size.

The spinner is **equally likely** to stop on 2 and 3.

© Saxon

One marble will be picked from a bag with white, gray, black, and striped marbles. Look at the bag to answer questions **a–c.**

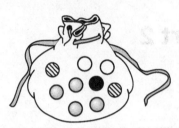

a. Which color marble is **least likely** to be picked? _____

Which color has the **least** marbles?

b. Which color is **most likely** to be picked? _____

Which color has the **most** marbles?

c. Which two colors are equally likely to be picked? _____

and _____

Which two colors have the same number of marbles?

The spinner will be spun once. Look at the spinner to answer questions **d–f.**

d. The spinner is **more likely** to stop on what color? _____

Which color has the **bigger** part?

e. The spinner is **less likely** to stop on what color? _____

Which color has the **smaller** part?

f. Circle the spinner below that is **equally likely** to stop on either color.

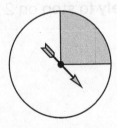 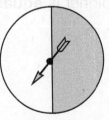 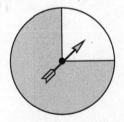

© Saxon

1. _____ − _____ = I

     began

  − _____ gone

2. $_____ + m = $_____

     has

  +   __m__ more

     costs

3.   white stripes
  + 7 red stripes
   13 total

What fraction of the stripes are white?

How many total? How many white?

4. Which fraction is **greater?**

$\frac{2}{3}$ or $\frac{1}{2}$

Use fraction pieces for help.

5. Which fraction is **smaller?**

$\frac{3}{4}$ or $\frac{3}{5}$

Use fraction pieces for help.

6.   1961 Roger Maris
   1927 Babe Ruth

7. a. Which point shows the number **6?**

b. Which points show numbers **less than 5?**

a. _____

b. _____ and _____

8. Draw point *T* on the number line at $7\frac{2}{3}$.

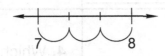

Use work area.

9. Use a ruler to measure from Monticello to Eatonton and from Eatonton to Sparta. Label the distances on the map.

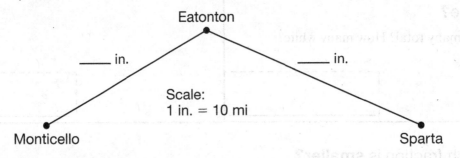

On the map, every inch is 10 miles.

a. How many **miles** is it from **Monticello to Eatonton?**

b. How many **miles** is it from **Eatonton to Sparta?**

c. To find the distance from Monticello to Sparta, **add** your answers to **a** and **b.**

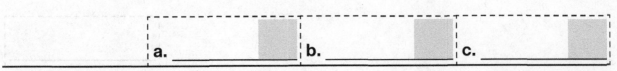

a. _____   b. _____   c. _____

© Saxon

10. Find a fraction **equivalent to** $\frac{2}{4}$.

Use fraction pieces for help.

_____

11. 1850 California
     1845 Texas
     _____

_____

12. What coin is half the value of a dime?

_____

13. 1980, 1990, 2000, _____,

_____, _____, ...

Use work area.

14. $0.99
      $0.62
   + $0.10

_____

15. $7.50
      − $2.50

_____

16.   ☐
       − 31
       ____
         17

☐ =

17. $140
       − $ 75

18. nearest hundred dollars

    a. $122   →

    b. $189   →

    c. Use your answers to **a** and **b** to estimate the **sum** of $122 and $189.

$$+ \underline{\hspace{2cm}}$$

  a. _____   **b.** _____   **c.** _____

19. a. What fraction of Greta's pencils are **sharpened?**

    How many total? How many sharpened?

  b. What fraction of Don's pencils are **sharpened?**

    How many total? How many sharpened?

  c. Use fraction manipulatives to compare:

$$\underline{\hspace{1.5cm}} \bigcirc \underline{\hspace{1.5cm}}$$
   Greta   Don

  a. _____   **b.** _____   **c.** _____

20. 4 blue and 7 white

Is Jodie **more likely** to pick blue or white?

Which color has more marbles?

Name _____

Teacher Notes:

• Students will need a dot cube to complete this investigation.

• This Investigation has been adapted for individual work. If students wish to play the games with a partner, they can follow the activity on 📖 pages 275–276 and **Lesson Activity 19.**

 page 275

Focus on
• Probability Games

• In this Investigation, you will help Anne and Bob play three probability games using a dot cube.

• A dot cube has six **faces.** Each face shows a number of dots: 1, 2, 3, 4, 5, or 6.

• When you roll a dot cube, the face on top tells the number.

 page 275

Probability Games

Materials needed:
• dot cube

Game 1

How to play

• Roll the dot cube. Count the number of dots on the top face.

• If the number of dots is 1 or 6, make an "X" in Anne's score chart.

• If the number of dots is 2, 3, 4, or 5, make an "X" in Bob's score chart.

- Keep rolling the dot cube until one of the score charts is full (10 points).

Anne's Score Chart (scores on 1 or 6)				

Bob's Score Chart (scores on 2, 3, 4, or 5)				

Game 2

How to play

- Roll the dot cube. Count the number of dots on the top face.
- If the number of dots is **even** (2, 4, or 6), make an "X" in Anne's score chart.
- If the number of dots is **odd** (1, 3, or 5), make an "X" in Bob's score chart.
- Keep rolling the dot cube until one of the score charts is full (10 points).

Anne's Score Chart (scores on 2, 4, or 6)				

Bob's Score Chart (scores on 1, 3, or 5)				

1. Which game is **fairer,** Game 1 or Game 2?

Game _____ is fairer because Anne and Bob can both score on three of the possible numbers.

© Saxon

Game 3

Now you will make up the rules to a **fair** game. In a **fair** game, both players will be equally likely of scoring.

How many different numbers of dots can you roll with

the dot cube? _____

For the game to be fair, each player should score on 3 out of the 6 numbers.

Complete the rules below. Then play the game.

How to play

- Roll the dot cube. Count the number of dots on the top face.

- If the number of dots is _____, _____, or _____, make an "X" in Anne's score chart.

- If the number of dots is _____, _____, or _____, make an "X" in Bob's score chart.

- Keep rolling the dot cube until one of the score charts is full (10 points).

Anne's Score Chart
(scores on _____, _____, or _____)

Bob's Score Chart
(scores on _____, _____, or _____)

2. In Game 1, which player is **more likely** to win, Anne or Bob? Why?

_____ is more likely to win because

Anne has _____ numbers that she scores

and Bob has _____ numbers that he scores.

3. In Game 2, which player is **more likely** to win, Anne or Bob? Why?

_____ and _____ are

e_____ likely to win because they both have 3 numbers that they score.

4. How did you design Game 3 so that the game was fair?

I wrote the rules so that Anne and Bob each score on

_____ numbers. That way the game is fair.

📖 page 277

Name _____

Teacher Notes:
- Refer students to "Quadrilaterals" on page 16 in the *Student Reference Guide.*
- Review Hint #18 "Geometry Vocabulary."

• Rectangles

New Concept

- A **rectangle** is a shape with **four sides.**

- A rectangle is a **flat** shape. A shoe box is not a rectangle because it is not flat.

- A rectangle has **four square corners** (right angles).

Rectangle   Not a rectangle

- The opposite sides of a rectangle are **parallel.** The sides that intersect are **perpendicular.**

- A **square** is a special type of rectangle with four **equal-length sides.**

 📖 page 278

Rectangle List

Materials needed:
- none

Look around your classroom to see an example of each object in the following list. Circle the ones that are rectangles.

© Saxon

door	clock
window	chalkboard
teacher	ruler

Complete the sentences below about rectangles.

- A rectangle has _____ sides.

- The opposite sides of a rectangle are _____.

- A rectangle has four _____ corners.

- A box is not a rectangle because it is not _____.

Lesson Practice

Circle the shapes below that are rectangles.

a.   b.   c.    d.

e. Draw a rectangle that is **not** a square.

f. Draw a rectangle that is a **square.**

© Saxon

1. $_____ – $_____ = p

       regular price

– ____   off

       sale price

The _____ price of the sofa was _____.

Use work area.

2.   aquarium

____   tax

      total

words: _____ dollars

Use work area.

3. One foot is what **fraction** of a yard?

See page 1 in the *Student Reference Guide.*

4. Shade $\frac{1}{3}$ of this circle.

Use work area.

© Saxon

5. 1799
 1732
_____

6. expanded form
 487
_____

7. Draw a rectangle.

A rectangle has _____ right angles.

8. Use an inch ruler to measure from Belmond to Dakota City along the roads. Label the distances on the map.

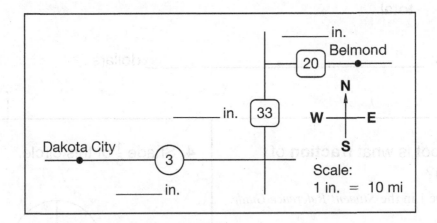

On the map, every inch is 10 miles. Write directions from Belmond to Dakota City.

Go _____ miles west from Belmond. Turn left and go 10 miles

_____. Turn right and go _____ miles _____

to Dakota City.

9. How many total miles is the drive from Belmond to Dakota City?

10. a. Which road on the map is **parallel** to Highway 3?

b. Which road is **perpendicular** to Highway 3?

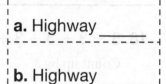

a. Highway _____

b. Highway _____

11. Find the next two numbers in this **doubling** sequence.

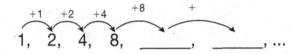

1, 2, 4, 8, _____, _____, ...

Use work area.

12. Which shape is **not** a rectangle? Why?

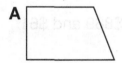

A   B   C

Shape _____ is not a rectangle because it does not have

four _____ corners.

Use work area.

13. _____ in. – _____ in. = d

_____
–

14. $3.00
           $0.48
        + $0.76

15. $5.00
  − $3.47

16. 562
  + 348

17. 460
  + 148

18. 3 + 3 + 3 + 3 + 3 + 3 + 3 + 3 + 3 + 3 =

Count up by 3.

19. a. nearest hundred dollars

$889 →

b. nearest ten dollars

$61 →

c. Use your answers to **a** and **b** to estimate the **sum** of $889 and $61.

  +

a.

b.

c.

20. Draw a line segment $2\frac{1}{2}$ inches long **parallel** to the line segment below.

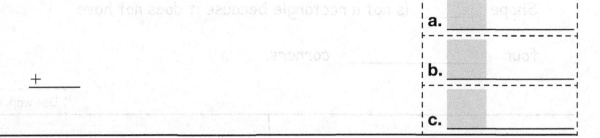

Use work area.

Name _____

 page 282

• Length and Width

Teacher Notes:

• Refer students to "Length and Width" on page 14 in the *Student Reference Guide*.

• Students will need a copy of **Lesson Activity 20** to complete this lesson.

 **New Concept**

• The **length** of a rectangle is the measure along the *long side*.

• The **width** of a rectangle is the measure along the *short side*.

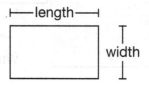

Activity page 284

Measuring Length and Width

Materials needed:
• **Lesson Activity 20**
• inch ruler

Measure the length and width of each rectangle on **Lesson Activity 20** to the nearest quarter inch.

Use a ruler to measure the length and width of each rectangle.

a.

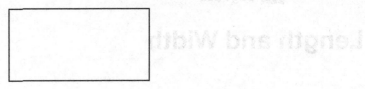

length: _____ width: _____

b.

length: _____ width: _____

c. Use a ruler to complete this rectangle that is $1\frac{1}{2}$ inches long and 1 inch wide.

d. Use a ruler to draw a rectangle with four sides that are 1 inch long.

What is the name of this special type of rectangle?

S_____

1. had

_____ earned

2. room A

_____ room B

altogether

3. One inch is what **fraction** of a foot?

4. Look at your answer to problem **3.**

What number is the **numerator?** _____

What number is the **denominator?** _____

Use work area.

5. this year

1840

6. Draw and label a dot on the number line at $\frac{3}{4}$.

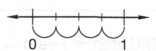

Use work area.

7.

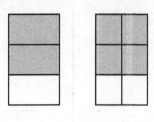

_____ = _____

8. from Julie's house to school

Go _____ blocks _____. Turn right and go _____

block _____.

Use work area.

9. a. digits: _____

b. words: _____

_____

Use work area.

10. 1 BIG step = 1 yard

10 BIG steps = _____ yards

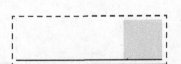

_____

© Saxon

11. Which shape is **not** a rectangle? Why?

A   ▢   B   ▭   C

Shape _____ is not a rectangle because it does not have _____ sides.

> Use work area.

12. Use a ruler to complete this rectangle that is 2 inches long and 1 inch wide.

> Use work area.

13. $5.90
     − $2.75

14. 1 ft − 2 in. = _____ in.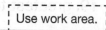

15.   450
    − 125

16.   87
     56
   + 36

17. $s - \underline{\hspace{1.5cm}} = \underline{\hspace{1.5cm}}$

s

$\underline{\hspace{1cm}}$

18. Use fraction pieces to write the fraction.

$1 = \dfrac{\square}{7}$

19. greatest to least miles

$\underline{\hspace{2cm}}$, $\underline{\hspace{2cm}}$, $\underline{\hspace{2cm}}$
greatest   least

Use work area.

20.

length: $\underline{\hspace{2cm}}$ width: $\underline{\hspace{2cm}}$

Use work area.

© Saxon

Name _____

Teacher Note:
• Review "Length and Width" on page 14 in the *Student Reference Guide*.

📖 page 287

• Rectangular Grid Patterns

New Concept

• **Grid paper** is special paper with perpendicular lines that make small squares.

• The distance between lines is called one **unit.** (On grid paper, we say *units* instead of *inches* or *feet.*)

• We can draw rectangles on grid paper.

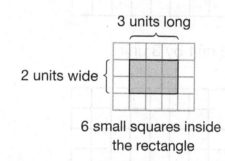

3 units long

2 units wide

6 small squares inside the rectangle

• A **column** is a line of squares going up and down.

• A **row** is a line of squares going across.

Activity  📖 page 289

Rectangular Patterns

Materials needed:

• none

Draw rectangles with the following lengths and widths on each grid. Then count the number of small squares inside each rectangle and write that number inside.

For instance, a 4 unit by 2 unit rectangle would look like this.

1. 5 unit by 4 unit

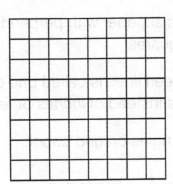

2. 3 unit by 3 unit

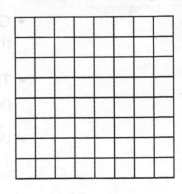

3. 6 unit by 3 unit

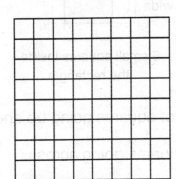

4. 7 unit by 4 unit

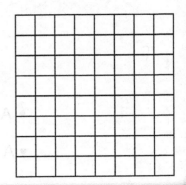

Find the number of small squares inside each rectangle. Write the length and width of each rectangle.

a. _____ small squares

length: _____ units   width: _____ units

b. _____ small squares

length: _____ units   width: _____ units

Draw each rectangle on the grid. Then find the number of small squares inside each rectangle.

c. 5 units by 2 units

_____ small squares

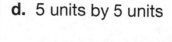

d. 5 units by 5 units

_____ small squares

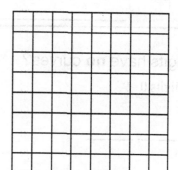

e. How many **columns** of squares are in this rectangle? _____

f. How many **rows** of squares are in this rectangle? _____

Written Practice

 page 290

1.   had

_____ read

2. _____ – _____ = d

Suzanne

_____ Vernon

more

3. Which digits have **no** curves?

Write the digits 0–9.

_____, _____, _____

What **fraction** of the digits have no curves? _____

How many total? How many without curves?

Use work area.

4. Draw a picture of $\frac{3}{5}$.

Use work area.

5.   1943
   1864

6. a. length

    b. width

      Remember to write "units."

    c. number of small squares

a. _____

b. _____

c. _____

7. Use a ruler to complete this rectangle that is $2\frac{1}{2}$ inches long and $1\frac{1}{4}$ inches wide.

Use work area.

8. Estimate and then measure the distance across your desk in inches.

estimate: _____

measure: _____

9. Find the 7th number in this sequence.

3, 6, 9, 12, _____, _____, ⊖, ...

Use work area.

10.   1920
   − 1620
_____

11.   72
     10
   + 28
_____

12. $5.00
   − $3.85
_____

13. $5.49
   + $3.94
_____

14. 1 yd – 12 in. = _____ in.

See page 1 in the *Student Reference Guide.*

15. 10 + 10 + 10 + 10 + 10 + 10 + 10 + 10 + 10 + 10 =

Count up by 10.

16. a. nearest ten dollars

$27 →

b. nearest hundred dollars

$367 →

c. Use your answers to **a** and **b** to estimate the **sum** of $27 and $367.

+ _____

Use work area.

17.   home to first

first to second

second to third

+ _____ third to home

18. Draw and label dots at $\frac{2}{5}$ and $\frac{3}{5}$ on the number line below.

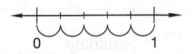

0   1

Use work area.

Use work area.

19. $\frac{2}{5}$ ◯ $\frac{3}{5}$

20. 2 red, 3 blue

Which color is **more likely** to be picked?

Which color has more marbles?

Use work area.

© Saxon

Name _____

 page 292

Teacher Note:
• Refer students to "Multiplication Table" on page 5 in the *Student Reference Guide.*

• Multiplication as Repeated Addition

New Concept

• We can **add** to find the total value of 6 nickels.

5¢ + 5¢ + 5¢ + 5¢ + 5¢ + 5¢ = **30¢**

• Think of each nickel as an **equal group** of 5 cents. Count up 6 groups of 5 cents.

5¢,   10¢,   15¢,   20¢,   25¢,   **30¢**

• Counting up equal groups is **multiplication**. The × is a multiplication sign.

6 × 5¢ = 30¢

6 times 5¢ equals 30¢.

Example

Write 4 × 7 as an addition problem and find the total.

4 × 7 means 4 groups of 7. Add four 7s.

7 + 7 + 7 + 7 = 28

To find the total, count up by 7 four times or use the multiplication table in the *Student Reference Guide.*

4 × 7 = 28

© Saxon

Write this addition as a multiplication and find the total.

$$3 + 3 + 3 + 3 + 3$$

We see 5 groups of 3. Count up by 3 to find the total.

$$5 \times 3 = 15$$

"Five times 3 is 15."

Example

Write the multiplication and total shown by this rectangle.

Count 4 columns and 4 rows.

There are 16 small squares in the rectangle.

$$4 \times 4 = 16$$

Lesson Practice

For problems **a–d,** write the multiplication as an addition, then write the total.

a. 3×5 _____ + _____ + _____ = _____

b. 4 times 6 _____ + _____ + _____ + _____ = _____

c. 2×8

d. 4×10

For problems **e** and **f,** write each addition as a multiplication, then write the total.

e. $2 + 2 + 2 + 2 + 2$ _____ $\times 2 =$ _____

© Saxon

f. $4 + 4 + 4$ _____ × _____ = _____

g. Write the multiplication and total shown by this rectangle.

_____ × _____ = _____

Written Practice

 page 294

1.

Park St.

300 yd

Greenleaf

200 yd

Whittier

Main St.

N
W —|— E
S

2. Add the distance along Main St. to your answer for problem **1.**

3. When Melody has gone around **2 out of 4 sides** of the park, what fraction of the distance around the park has she gone?

A $\frac{1}{2}$ **B** $\frac{2}{3}$ **C** $\frac{3}{4}$ **D** $\frac{3}{5}$

---

4. _____ $- s =$ _____

Bottom missing → subtract

$$-\quad s$$

---

5. Use a ruler to complete this rectangle that is $1\frac{1}{2}$ inches long and $1\frac{1}{2}$ inches wide.

What kind of rectangle is it?

a **S**_____

| Use work area.

6. Write as a multiplication problem.

$$4 + 4 + 4 + 4 + 4$$

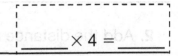

_____ $\times\ 4 =$ _____

---

7. Write the multiplication.

How many rows and columns?

_____ $\times$ _____ $=$ _____

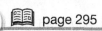
8. Write as an addition problem.

4×5

_____ + _____ + _____ + _____ = _____

Use work area.

9. Measure each distance to the nearest quarter inch.

Aubry   Reston   Hickory

a. From Aubry to Reston   **b.** From Reston to Hickory

c. From Aubry to Hickory

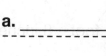

a. _____

b. _____

c. _____

10. How many different numbers can you roll with one dot cube? _____

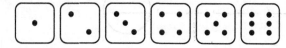

What **fraction** of those numbers are less than 3? _____

Use work area.

11. expanded form
276

12. _____ is more likely to score the point because Chad has

_____ ways to score a point and Vic has _____ ways

to score a point.

¦ Use work area. ¦

13. $6.45
     + $0.50

14. $3.65
      − $3.48

15.   24
        36
     + 64

16. 1 foot − 8 inches = _____ in.

17. 2 + 2 + 2 + 2 + 2 + 2 + 2 + 2 =
Count up by 2.

18. Find the **eighth** number in this sequence.

4, 8, 12, 16, _____, _____, _____, ⊖

¦ Use work area. ¦

19.   8
        6
        m
     + 5
     _____
       25

_m_ = _____

20.

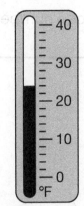

• Multiplication Table

Teacher Note:

• Review "Multiplication Table" on page 5 in the *Student Reference Guide.*

New Concept

• The numbers that are multiplied are called **factors.**

• The answer is called the **product.**

$$6 \quad \times \quad 5 \quad = \quad 30$$

factor × factor = product

• A **multiplication table** shows answers to many multiplication problems.

• To use a multiplication table:

1. Find one of the factors along the top of the table. Find the other factor along the left side of the table.

2. With a finger, trace *down* the column and *across* the row for the factors.

3. The product is the number where the column and row meet.

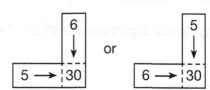

© Saxon

Activity page 299

Using a Multiplication Table

Materials needed:

- *Student Reference Guide*

Use the multiplication table on page 5 in the *Student Reference Guide* to find each product.

1. $6 \times 8 =$ _____

2. $8 \times 6 =$ _____

3. $9 \times 9 =$ _____

4. $7 \times 11 =$ _____

5. How many inches is 7 feet? $7 \times 12 =$ _____

6. How many feet is 8 yards? $8 \times 3 =$ _____

Lesson Practice

Use a multiplication table to find each product.

a. $4 \times 6 =$ _____

b. $6 \times 3 =$ _____

c. $8 \times 12 =$ _____

d. $9 \times 7 =$ _____

e. What is the value of 8 nickels?

   $8 \times$ _____ ¢ = _____ ¢

f. How many small squares are in an 8 unit by 4 unit rectangle?

   $8 \times 4 =$ _____

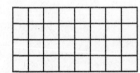

1. A side of each small square is 1 foot.

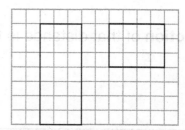

    a. How many feet **long** is the wall?

    b. How many feet **high** is the wall?

a. _____

b. _____

2. Write a multiplication problem for the **window.**

Use a multiplication table.

_____ × _____ = _____

3. 2007
   1999

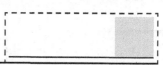

4. *School is 3 blocks **west** of Juan's home. Michael's **home** is 2 blocks north of school.*

Find and label the school and Michael's house on the map.

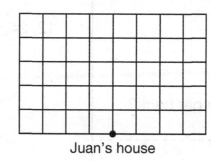

Juan's house

Use work area.

5. How many **blocks** is it from Juan's house to Michael's house? _____

What **fraction** of that distance is the walk to school? _____

Use work area.

---

6. addition: _____¢ + _____¢ + _____¢ + _____¢ = _____¢

multiplication: _____ × _____¢ = _____¢

Use work area.

---

7. Use a multiplication table.

7 × 9 =

8. 6 × 12 =

---

9. 8 × 8 =

10. 3 × 7 =

---

11. 5 dimes = _____¢

Count up dimes by 10.

– 45¢

What coin should he get back?

12. Find the **6th** number in this sequence.

12, 24, 36, 48, _____, ⊘

Use work area.

13. 360
   − 160

14. $4.58
   + $4.84

15.   75
     89
   + 98

16. $5.25
   − $2.75

17. 3 + 3 + 3 + 3 + 3 + 3 + 3 + 3 + 3 + 3 =

$$3 \times 10 =$$

18. 48
    − □
    ‾‾‾‾
     27

□ = _____

19. breakfast time

_____ : _____

20. 15 minutes is $\frac{15}{60}$ of an hour. Which fraction below is **equivalent** to $\frac{15}{60}$ of an hour?

A $\frac{1}{5}$ **B** $\frac{1}{4}$ **C** $\frac{1}{2}$ **D** $\frac{1}{10}$

_____

LESSON 56

📖 page 302

Name _____

Teacher Note:

• Review "Multiplication Table" on page 5 in the *Student Reference Guide*.

• Multiplication Facts: 0s, 1s, and 10s

New Concept

• When one of the factors is **zero,** the *product is zero.*

$$3 \times 0 = 0 \qquad\qquad 0 \times 8 = 0$$

Math Language

Factors are the numbers that are multiplied in a multiplication problem.

The **product** is the answer in a multiplication problem.

factor × factor = product

• When one of the factors is **one,** the product is the same as the *other factor.*

$$3 \times 1 = 3 \qquad\qquad 1 \times 8 = 8$$

• When one of the factors is **ten,** *put a zero on the other factor* to find the product.

$$3 \times 10 = 30 \qquad\qquad 10 \times 8 = 80$$

Activity 📖 page 304

Zeros, Ones, and Tens

This activity is optional.

Lesson Practice

Find each product. Use a multiplication table for help.

a. $5 \times 0 =$ _____   **b.** $9 \times 10 =$ _____   **c.** $4 \times 1 =$ _____

d. $10 \times 3 =$ _____   **e.** $6 \times 1 =$ _____   **f.** $0 \times 11 =$ _____

g. $1 \times 9 =$ _____   **h.** $12 \times 0 =$ _____   **i.** $7 \times 10 =$ _____

1. The **answer** when numbers are multiplied is called the

A sum.

B product.

C factor.

D difference.

2. How many cents is 2 quarters? _____¢

What **fraction** of a dollar is 2 quarters? _____

How many cents is 5 dimes? _____¢

What fraction of a dollar is 5 dimes? _____

Are the two fractions equivalent? Why?

The fractions are _e_____ because both amounts of money

are worth _____¢.

Use work area.

3. 169   multiplication facts
   69   facts with 1, 0, or 10

      other facts

4. 357

−

82

$\square$ =

5. Write the multiplication problem.

How many rows and columns?

_____ × _____ = _____

6. Write the multiplication problem.

_____ × _____ = _____

7. Write the multiplication problem.

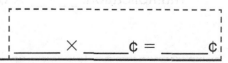
_____ × _____¢ = _____¢

8. Use a multiplication table for help.

   a. $1 \times 8 =$

   b. $5 \times 0 =$

   c. $0 \times 12 =$

a. _____

b. _____

c. _____

9. a. $1 \times 8 =$

   b. $9 \times 1 =$

   c. $1 \times 11 =$

a. _____

b. _____

c. _____

10. a. $10 \times 6 =$

   b. $4 \times 10 =$

   c. $10 \times 11 =$

a. _____

b. _____

c. _____

11. How many feet are in 2 yards?

See page 1 in the *Student Reference Guide.*

addition: _____ ft + _____ ft = _____ ft

multiplication: _____ $\times$ 3 ft = _____ ft

Use work area.

© Saxon

12. Complete this rectangle that is $1\frac{1}{4}$ inches long and $\frac{1}{2}$ inch wide.

Use work area.

Use a multiplication table to find the products in problems **13–15.**

13. $6 \times 7 =$

14. $9 \times 4 =$

15. $11 \times 11 =$

16.   440 yd
     $+$ 440 yd

17. $200
    – $125

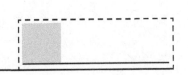

18. $9.90
    + $0.10

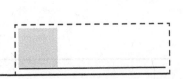

19. 1 yd – 1 in. = _____ in.

See page 1 in the *Student Reference Guide.*

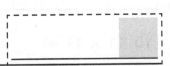

20. Which shape does **not** have four right angles?

A   B    C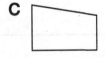

© Saxon

Name _____

📖 page 306

Teacher Note:
- Students will need coins, counters, or other small objects to complete the activity.

• Arrays

New Concept

- We have seen that a rectangle drawn on grid paper can show a multiplication fact.

Math Language

Factors are the numbers that are multiplied in a multiplication problem.

The **product** is the answer in a multiplication problem.

factor × factor = product

Column

Row {

$3 \times 2 = 6$

- The number of rows and columns are the **factors**, and the number of small squares inside the rectangle is the **product.**

- A rectangular pattern of items, called an **array,** can also show a multiplication fact.

Example

Write a multiplication fact for this rectangular array.

☆☆☆☆☆
☆☆☆☆☆
☆☆☆☆☆

Count 5 *columns* of 3 stars.

To find the product, count all the stars or use a multiplication table.

$$5 \times 3 = 15 \text{ or } 3 \times 5 = 15$$

 📖 page 308

Arrays

Materials needed:
• coins, counters, or small objects

Use counters or other objects to make a rectangular array on your desk for each multiplication problem shown below. Then find each product.

1. $5 \times 2 =$ _____   **2.** $6 \times 4 =$ _____

3. $7 \times 3 =$ _____   **4.** $3 \times 8 =$ _____

Lesson Practice

For problems **a** and **b,** write a multiplication fact illustrated by each array.

a. _____ $\times$ _____ = _____

X X X X X X X X X
X X X X X X X X X
X X X X X X X X X

b. _____ $\times$ _____ = _____

O O O O O O O O
O O O O O O O O
O O O O O O O O
O O O O O O O O

For **c** and **d,** draw a rectangular array of dots to represent each pair of factors. Then find each product.

c. $6 \times 2 =$ _____

d. $3 \times 9 =$ _____

Written Practice

 page 308

1. How many rectangles?

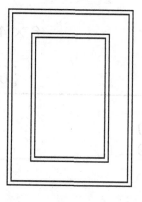

2. Measure the **smallest** rectangle in problem **1.**

  a. length

  b. width

  a. _____

  b. _____

3.   1959
 1912

_____

4. Write the multiplication fact.

How many rows and columns?

Use a multiplication table for help.

_____ × _____ = _____

5.   15 stars

−_____   13 stars

_____

6. Draw an array of dots with **6 columns** and **4 rows.** Then find the product.

Use a multiplication table for help.

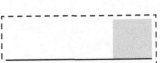

6 × 4 = _____

_____
| Use work area. |

7.   811
− _m_
 299

_m_ = _____

8. $50
 $39

_____

© Saxon

9. $6.10
$3.90

10. Write the multiplication fact.

How many rows and columns?
Use a multiplication table for help.

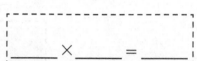

_____ × _____ = _____

11. a. $5 \times 1 =$

b. $7 \times 0 =$

c. $6 \times 10 =$

a. _____

b. _____

c. _____

Use a multiplication table to solve problems **12–14.**

12. $8 \times 7 =$

13. $6 \times 9 =$

14. $12 \times 12 =$

15.   880 yd
         +   88 yd

16. Borrow across all zeros.

$200
− $172

17. Write as a multiplication fact.

Use a multiplication table for help.

2 + 2 + 2 + 2 + 2 + 2 + 2

_____ × _____ = _____

18. Write as a multiplication fact.

5 + 5 + 5 + 5 + 5 + 5 + 5

_____ × _____ = _____

19. sunset

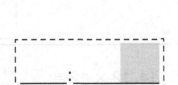

20. How many pennies equal 1 dime? _____ pennies

A penny is what **fraction** of a dime? _____

Use work area.

© Saxon

 page 311

Name _____

Teacher Note:

• Refer students to "Perimeter, Area, Volume" on page 17 in the *Student Reference Guide*.

• Perimeter

New Concept

• **Perimeter** is the distance around a shape.

• To find the perimeter, **add** the lengths of all sides.

• Remember that in a rectangle opposite sides have the same length.

Example

Math Language
A **rectangle** is a flat shape with four sides and four right angles.
Opposite sides of a rectangle are parallel and have the same length.

Find the perimeter of this rectangle.

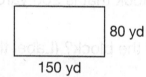

The length of the rectangle is 150 yd.
The top side of the rectangle is also 150 yd.

The width of the rectangle is 80 yd.
The left side is also 80 yd.

To find the perimeter of a rectangle, we add the lengths of four sides.

Imagine starting at one corner and walking around the rectangle.

$$
\begin{array}{r}
150 \text{ yd} \\
80 \text{ yd} \\
150 \text{ yd} \\
+ \quad 80 \text{ yd} \\
\hline
460 \text{ yd}
\end{array}
$$

The perimeter of the rectangle is **460 yd.**

© Saxon

Find the perimeter of each rectangle. Remember to write the units.

Perimeter → Add all sides.

a. _____

length

width

12 in.

[ ] 3 in.

length

+ ___ width

perimeter

b. _____

5 in.

[ ] 5 in.

c. Trinh lives on a block that is 200 yards long and 100 yards wide. What is

the **perimeter** of the block? (Label the drawing.) _____

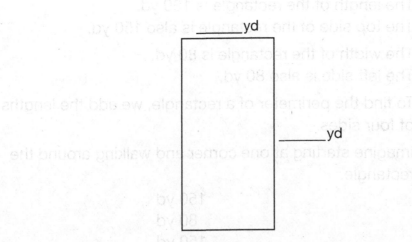

_____ yd

_____ yd

© Saxon

1. Perimeter ⟶ Add all sides.

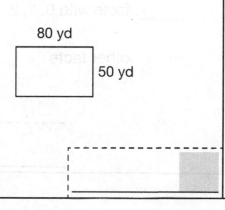

80 yd

50 yd

2.   one section

+ ____   another section

3. Write a multiplication fact for the picture in problem **3** on page 313.

How many rows and columns?

Use a multiplication table for help.

_____ × _____ = _____

4. Both girls are   r_____. Heidi is right because $\frac{5}{15}$ means

_____ out of _____ trees. Debbie is right because $\frac{1}{3}$ means

_____ out of _____ rows of trees.

Use work area.

5. Draw an array of dots to show 5 × 4.

Use work area.

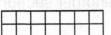

6. Write as a multiplication fact.

How many rows and columns?
Use a multiplication table for help.

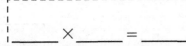

_____ × _____ = _____

7. all multiplication facts

_____ facts with 0, 1, 2, 5, and 10

_____ other facts

_____

See  page 314 for problems **8–11.**

8. a. parallel to 1st Street

   b. perpendicular to 1st Street

a. _____   b. _____

9. Each side of the park is 110 yd.

Perimeter ⟶ Add all sides.

_____

10. Is the park a **rectangle?**

_____ because it has _____ sides and _____ square corners.

Is the park a **square?**

_____ because it is a r_____ and all 4

s_____ have equal length.

_____
| Use work area. |

11. What **fraction** of the perimeter is one side?

Use a multiplication table for problems **12–17.**

12. $9 \times 8 =$

13. $9 \times 12 =$

14. $9 \times 11 =$

15. a. $7 \times 10 =$

  b. $7 \times 1 =$

  c. $7 \times 0 =$

a. _____

b. _____

c. _____

16. a. $7 \times 2 =$

  b. $2 \times 9 =$

  c. $8 \times 2 =$

a. _____

b. _____

c. _____

17. a. $4 \times 5 =$

b. $8 \times 5 =$

c. $5 \times 7 =$

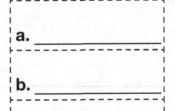

a. _____

b. _____

c. _____

18. Write as a multiplication fact.

$5 + 5 + 5 + 5 + 5$

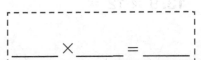

_____ $\times$ _____ $=$ _____

19. Write as an addition problem.

3×11

_____ $+$ _____ $+$ _____ $=$ _____

Use work area.

20. In $6 \times 7 = 42$, both 6 and 7 are

A addends.

B factors.

C products.

D sums.

_____

Name _____

Teacher Note:

• Review "Multiplication Table" on page 5 in the *Student Reference Guide.*

• Multiplication Facts: 2s and 5s

New Concept

• When one of the factors is **two,** *double* the other factor.

Math Language

Factors are the numbers that are multiplied in a multiplication problem.

The **product** is the answer in a multiplication problem.

$$4 \times 2 = 8 \qquad 2 \times 7 = 14$$
$$4 + 4 = 8 \qquad 7 + 7 = 14$$

• When one of the factors is **five,** the *product ends in 0 or in 5.* Count up by 5.

$$4 \times 5 = 20 \qquad 5 \times 7 = 35$$

5, 10, 15, 20   5, 10, 15, 20, 25, 30, 35

Lesson Practice

Find each product. Use a multiplication table for help.

a. $6 \times 5 =$ _____

b. $6 \times 2 =$ _____

c. $5 \times 5 =$ _____

d. $5 \times 2 =$ _____

e. $5 \times 8 =$ _____

f. $2 \times 8 =$ _____

g. $5 \times 9 =$ _____

h. $2 \times 9 =$ _____

© Saxon

1. The spinner is **most likely** to stop on which number?

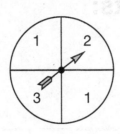

_____

2. The spinner is **equally likely** to stop on which two numbers?

_____ and _____

3. What fraction of the spinner is labeled 1? _____

How many total sections? How many labeled 1?

What fraction of the spinner is labeled 2? _____

How many total sections? How many labeled 2?

Compare the fractions:

| Use work area. |

4. What is the perimeter of the **whole shape?** _____

Perimeter ⟶ Add all sides.

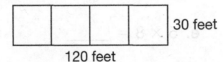

30 feet

120 feet

What is the perimeter of one **small square?** _____

All sides of a square are the same length.

| Use work area. |

© Saxon

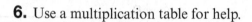

5.   half dollar

           quarter

           dime

    +   nickel

_____

6. Use a multiplication table for help.

a. $6 \times 5 =$

b. $6 \times 10 =$

c. $6 \times 2 =$

a. _____

b. _____

c. _____

_____

7. Write as a multiplication fact. Use a multiplication table for help.

$\$7 + \$7 + \$7 + \$7 + \$7 + \$7 + \$7 + \$7$

_____ $\times \$7 =$

_____

8.   1789
    1732

9. The sides of each tile are 1 inch long.

    a. length

    b. width

    c. How many tiles?

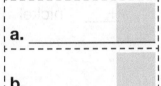

a. _____

b. _____

c. _____

10. Write the multiplication fact for the rectangle in problem **9.**

How many rows and columns?

Use a multiplication table for help.

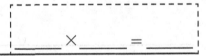

_____ $\times$ _____ = _____

11. Use a ruler to complete this rectangle that is $2\frac{1}{4}$ inches long and $1\frac{3}{4}$ inches wide.

┌ ─ ─ ─ ─ ─ ─ ─ ─ ┐
  Use work area.
└ ─ ─ ─ ─ ─ ─ ─ ─ ┘

12. Use a multiplication table.

a. $3 \times 6 =$

b. $7 \times 3 =$

c. $3 \times 9 =$

a. _____

b. _____

c. _____

13. a. $9 \times 1 =$

b. $9 \times 5 =$

c. $9 \times 0 =$

a. _____

b. _____

c. _____

14. $126
       $-$ $ 95

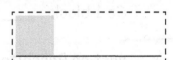

15. $4.58
       $+$ $4.60

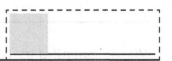

16.  950
            $-$ 150

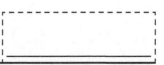

17.　$328
　　− $258

18.　　50
　　　25
　　　10
　　　　5
　　+ _m_
　　　100

_m_ =

19. from Braulio's house to school

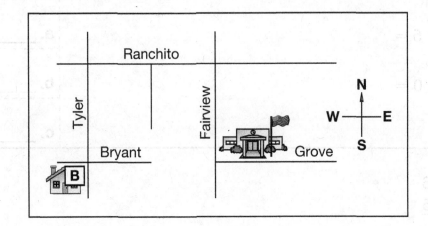

Go 1 block _____. Turn right and go _____ blocks

east on Ranchito. Turn right and go 1 block _____

on F_____.

Use work area.

20. a. parallel to Tyler

　　b. perpendicular to Bryant

a. _____

b. _____

Name _____

• Equal Groups Stories, Part One

New Concept

- **Equal groups** stories have a multiplication formula.

Math Language

The **product** is the answer in a multiplication problem.

> The teacher arranged the desks into **5 rows** with **6 desks in each row.** How many desks were there in all?
>
> number of groups × number **in each** group = total
> $$5 \times 6 = 30$$

- Five rows with 6 desks in each row makes **30** desks in all.

- To find a missing product in an equal groups story, **multiply.**

- Look for the equal groups story cue word *each*.

Example

There are 5 school days in each week. How many school days are in 7 weeks?

The word "each" tells us this is an equal groups story. We know to multiply.

There are 7 weeks and there are 5 school days in each week.

To find the product we can count up by 5 or use a multiplication table.

$$7 \times 5 = 35$$

There are **35 school days** in 7 weeks.

Write an equal groups (multiplication) number sentence for each story. Use a multiplication table for help finding the products. Remember to write the units.

a. There are 3 feet in **each** yard. How many feet long is a rope

5 yards long? _____

_____ × _____ = t

b. There are 12 eggs in **each** dozen. How may eggs is 2 dozen?

_____ × _____ = t

c. Cory earns $9 each hour for helping a painter. How much money does

Cory earn in 5 hours? _____

_____ × $_____ = t

page 323

1. _____ × _____ = t

Use a multiplication table for help.
Remember to write the units.

2. _____ × _____ = t

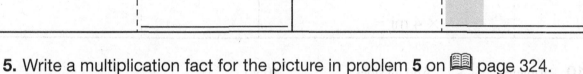
3. ____ × ____ = t

4. ____ × $\$$____ = t

5. Write a multiplication fact for the picture in problem **5** on page 324.

How many rows and columns?
Use a multiplication table for help.

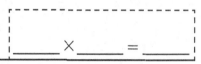

____ × ____ = ____

6. What is the value of the coins shown in problem **5?**

____ × 10¢ =

Use a multiplication table for help.

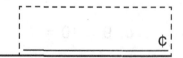

_____ ¢

7. Use a multiplication table.

a. 8 × 4 =

b. 4 × 6 =

c. 8 × 6 =

a. _____

b. _____

c. _____

8. Write as a multiplication fact.

4 mi + 4 mi + 4 mi + 4 mi + 4 mi + 4 mi

_____ × 4 mi = _____

9. What fraction of a dollar is $0.10?

1 dime is $\frac{1}{10}$ of a dollar.

_____

10. Perimeter ⟶ Add all sides.
Remember to write the units.

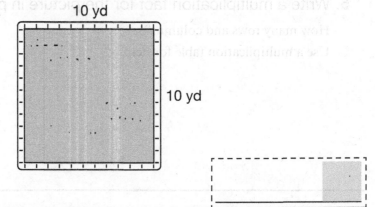

10 yd

10 yd

_____

11. Use a multiplication table.

a. 9 × 2 =

b. 9 × 5 =

c. 9 × 10 =

a. _____

b. _____

c. _____

12. Use a multiplication table.

a. 6 × 6 =

b. 7 × 7 =

c. 8 × 8 =

a. _____

b. _____

c. _____

© Saxon

13. $897
    + $ 75

14. 1 hour − 1 minute = _____ min

1 hour is 60 minutes.

Remember to write the units.

15. $0.56
    $0.48
    + $0.79

16. $6.50
    + $5.75

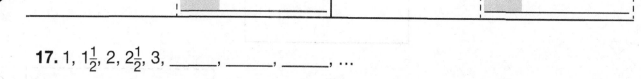

17. 1, $1\frac{1}{2}$, 2, $2\frac{1}{2}$, 3, _____, _____, _____, ...

| Use work area. |

18.   1
    2
    3
    4
    + m
    ___
    10

| m = |

19. 5 quarters   →

  6 dimes   →

  3 nickels   →

  4 pennies   →   + _____

---

20. Use a ruler to measure the length and width of the rectangle.

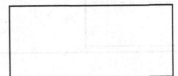

length: _____

width: _____

Teacher Notes:

• Students will need a copy of **Lesson Activity 22** to complete this investigation.

• This Investigation has been adapted for individual work.

 page 326

Focus on
• More About Bar Graphs

• Remember that a bar graph shows data with bars of different heights or lengths.

• The bars can be **vertical** (go up and down) or **horizontal** (go across).

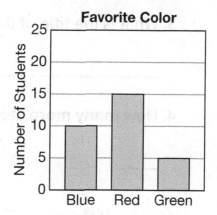

Vertical bar graph

Favorite Color

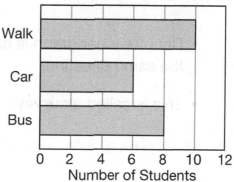

Horizontal bar graph

How Students Get to School

- The **title** on a bar graph tells what the graph is about.
- A **label** on the bottom or side tells what data is measured.
- The numbers along a bar graph are called the **scale.**

Look at the bar graphs to answer problems **1–4.**

1. What is the **title** of the *vertical* bar graph?

_____

2. How many students chose **red** as their favorite color?

_____

3. What is the **title** of the *horizontal* bar graph?

_____

4. How **many more** students ride the bus than ride in a car?

_____

bus

– _____ car

- Data for a bar graph is gathered by asking many people the same question.

- This is called a **survey.**

Maggie asked the students in her class this survey question:

"Siblings are brothers and sisters. How many siblings do you have?"

The tally chart below shows Maggie's data.

Number of Siblings

0	IIII
1	IIIII
2	IIIII
3	III
4	I

Follow the instructions below to make a horizontal bar graph of the data.

- Get a copy of **Lesson Activity 22.** The top bar graph is the horizontal bar graph.

- Write a **title** on the bar graph. The title can be the same as the title of the tally chart.

- Write a **label.** The label should be "Number of Students."

- The data in the tally chart are in five categories (the number of siblings). Write the number for each category in the blanks on the left side of the bar graph.

- The **scale** is along the bottom of the graph. Write the numbers 1, 2, 3, 4, and 5 along the scale.

- Graph the data from the tally chart.

Marcus asked the students in his class this survey question:

"Which of these fruits do you like best: apples, oranges, grapes, cherries, or bananas?"

The tally chart below shows Marcus's data.

Favorite Fruit

Apples	IIII
Oranges	~~IIII~~ I
Grapes	I
Cherries	III
Bananas	I

Follow the instructions below to make a vertical bar graph of the data.

- Use your copy of **Lesson Activity 22.** The bottom bar graph is the vertical bar graph.

- Write a **title** on the bar graph.

- Write a **label.**

- Write the names of the fruit in the blanks on the bottom of the bar graph.

- The **scale** is along the left side of the graph. Write numbers going up the scale.

- Graph the data from the tally chart.

Name _____

Teacher Notes:

• Introduce Hint #21 "Multiplication/ Division Fact Families."

• Review "Multiplication Table" on page 5 and "Quadrilaterals" on page 16 in the *Student Reference Guide*.

• Students will need color tiles to complete the activity.

• # Squares

• # Multiplication Facts: Square Numbers

New Concepts

• **Squares**

Math Language

A **rectangle** is a shape with four sides and four square corners (right angles).

• A **square** is a special type of rectangle with four sides of *equal length*.

• Squares can be arranged to make larger squares.

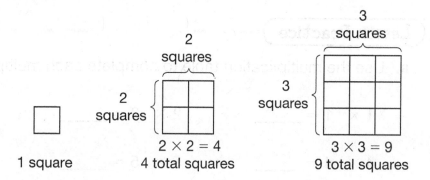

1 square

2 squares
2 squares
$2 \times 2 = 4$
4 total squares

3 squares
3 squares
$3 \times 3 = 9$
9 total squares

• **Multiplication Facts: Square Numbers**

• A **square number** is the product of two of the same factor.

• The squares above show the first three square numbers:

$$1 \times 1 = 1 \qquad 2 \times 2 = 4 \qquad 3 \times 3 = 9$$

• The circled numbers on the Multiplication Table in the *Student Reference Guide* are square numbers.

 page 330

Squares on a Grid

Materials needed:

- color tiles

Use square tiles to build **squares** that show the square numbers 1, 4, 9, 16, and 25. Complete the multiplication fact for each square number. Remember that both factors are the same.

_____ × _____ = 1   _____ × _____ = 4

_____ × _____ = 9   _____ × _____ = 16

_____ × _____ = 25

Lesson Practice

a. Use the multiplication table to complete each multiplication fact.

1 × 1 = _____   2 × 2 = _____   3 × 3 = _____

4 × 4 = _____   5 × 5 = _____   6 × 6 = _____

7 × 7 = _____   8 × 8 = _____   9 × 9 = _____

10 × 10 = _____   11 × 11 = _____   12 × 12 = _____

b. This square is made with **10 rows of 10 tiles.** How many tiles are in this square? _____

10×10

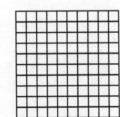

© Saxon

c. Here is a sequence of **square numbers.** What are the next three numbers in the sequence?

1, 4, 9, 16, _____, _____, _____, ...

Written Practice page 331

1. How many rows and columns? Use a multiplication table for help.

_____

2. Write a multiplication fact for the picture in problem **1.**

_____ × _____ = _____

3. _____ − _____ = d

4. _____ × 3 ft = t
   Use a multiplication table for help.

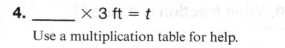

5. a. digits: _____ _____, _____ _____ _____

b. words: _____ thousand

_____

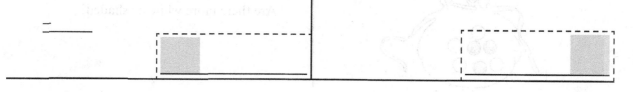

Use work area.

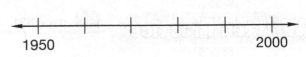

6. Which does **not** equal 16?

Use a multiplication table for help.

A 16 × 1

B 8 × 2

C 8 × 8

D 4 × 4

7. Label the tick marks on the timeline below. Then draw dots and label each date given below.

1976	1997
1969	1964

1950   2000

Use work area.

8. What number has **2** hundreds, **1** ten, and **3** ones?

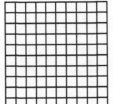 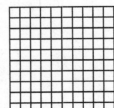 

9. What **fraction** is shaded?

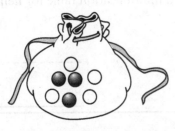

10. If one marble is picked from the bag in problem **9,** is white or shaded **more likely?**

Are there more white or shaded?

11. Compare:

$\frac{3}{7}$ ◯ $\frac{4}{7}$

Use work area.

© Saxon

12. Use a ruler to complete this rectangle that is 3 inches long and 2 inches wide.

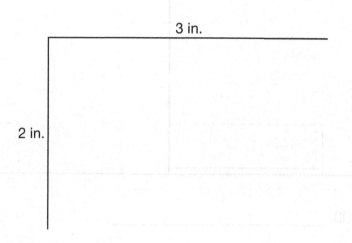

3 in.

2 in.

Find the **perimeter.**

Perimeter ⟶ Add all sides.

---

13. Use a multiplication table for help.

a. $9 \times 6 =$

b. $9 \times 5 =$

c. $7 \times 7 =$

a. _____

b. _____

c. _____

---

14. $0.38
       $0.75
     + $1.00

15. $450
       − $375

16. $463
      + $ 98

17. 11 × 11 =

Use a multiplication table for help.

18. 200, 400, 600, _____, _____, _____, _____, …

Use work area.

19. expanded form

73,492

_____ + _____ + _____ + _____ + _____

Use work area.

20. _____ − s = _____

_____

© Saxon

📖 page 334

Name _____

Teacher Notes:

• Introduce Hint #22 "Area and Perimeter Vocabulary."

• Review "Length and Width" on page 14 and "Perimeter, Area, Volume" on page 17 in the *Student Reference Guide*.

• Area, Part 1

New Concept

Math Language

The measure of the longer side of a rectangle is called the **length.**

The measure of the shorter side of a rectangle is called the **width.**

• **Perimeter** is the distance *around* a shape.

To measure perimeter, we add all the sides.

Perimeter ⟶ **Add all sides.**

Perimeter is measured in inches (in.), feet (ft), yards (yd), and miles (mi).

• **Area** is the amount of surface *inside* a shape.

To measure area, we **multiply** the length and the width.

Area = length × width

Area is measured in **squares** of different sizes: square inches (sq. in.), square feet (sq. ft), square yards (sq. yd), and square miles (sq. mi).

• The pictures below show the difference between perimeter and area.

perimeter   area

Activity 📖 page 336

Area

This activity is optional.

Example

Find the perimeter and area of a 5-inch by 7-inch rectangle.

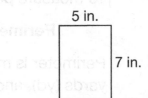

5 in.

7 in.

To find the perimeter, we **add** the measures of all the sides:

$$5 \text{ in.} + 7 \text{ in.} + 5 \text{ in.} + 7 \text{ in.} = 24 \text{ in.}$$

The perimeter is **24 inches.**

To find the area, we **multiply** the length and the width:

$$5 \text{ in.} \times 7 \text{ in.} = 35 \text{ sq. in.}$$

The area is **35 square inches.**

Lesson Practice

a. Circle the correct answer.

To measure **area,** we count

A segments.

B squares.

C circles.

D rectangles.

b. Stan covered the front cover of a journal with 1-inch stickers.

What was the area of the front cover? _____ sq. in.

Area = length × width

5 in.

6 in.

c. Silvia placed a stamp that was 1 square inch in the corner of a 3-inch by 5-inch envelope. Altogether, how many stamps would be needed to cover

the front of the envelope? _____ stamps

Area = length × width

5 in.

3 in.

d. What is the perimeter and area of a 6-inch by 4-inch rectangle?

6 in.

4 in.

perimeter: _____ in.

Perimeter ⟶ Add all sides.

area: _____ sq. in.

Area = length × width

1. _____ × $_____ = $_____

Use a multiplication table for help.

The cost of all _____ boxes was _____.

Use work area.

2. a. What fraction is shaded?

b. What fraction is **not** shaded?

a. _____

b. _____

3. Compare the fractions from problem **2.**

Use fraction manipulatives for help.

_____ ◯ _____

a.　　　　**b.**

Use work area.

4.

a. length

b. width

c. How many tiles?

d. area

Area = length × width

a. _____ b. _____ c. _____ d. _____

5. Find the perimeter of the rectangle in problem **4.**

Perimeter　⟶　Add all sides.

© Saxon

6. Which equals 10?

Use a multiplication table for help.

A 5 × 5 **B** 9 × 1

C 2 × 5 **D** 8 × 2

7. What number has **2** hundreds and **3** ones?

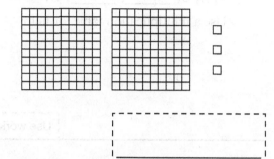

8. Use a multiplication table for help.

a. 10 × 6 =

b. 10 × 12 =

a. _____

b. _____

9. What is the **place value** of the 6?

825,630

See "Place Value" on page 13 in the
Student Reference Guide.

10.

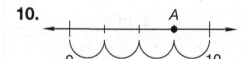

11. _____ − _____ = d

key rings

− _____ T-shirts

12. Which is the next item in this sequence?

 ☐, ⊞, ⊞, ...

 A

 B

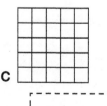 C

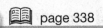

13. square numbers

1, 4, 9, _____, _____, ...

Use a multiplication table for help.

_____
¦ Use work area. ¦

14. Write the multiplication fact.

How many rows and columns?

```
x x x x x x
x x x x x x
x x x x x x
```

_____ × _____ = _____

15. $0.36
           $0.95
        + $2.00

16. $300
        − $104

17. $4\frac{1}{2}$

words: _____ and

_____

¦ Use work area. ¦

18. a.   10   **b.**   24
           + m   + n
           ----   ----
            25   34

¦ **a.** $m =$ _____ ¦

¦ **b.** $n =$ _____ ¦

19. expanded form

25,760

_____ + _____ + _____ + _____

¦ Use work area. ¦

20. Do problem **20** on
page 339.

📖 page 340

• Area, Part 2

Name _____

Teacher Notes:
- Review Hint #22 "Area and Perimeter Vocabulary."
- Review "Perimeter, Area, Volume" on page 17 in the *Student Reference Guide*.
- For additional practice, students may complete Targeted Practice 63.

New Concept

- **Area** is the amount of surface *inside* a shape.

- The area of small shapes is often measured in **square inches** (sq. in.).

- The square below is one square inch:

1 in.

1 in. | 1 sq. in.

- The area of larger shapes is often measured in **square feet** (sq. ft) and **square yards** (sq. yd).

- Remember that 3 feet equals 1 yard (3 ft = 1 yd).

📖 page 341

Estimate Area in Square Feet

This activity is optional.

Example

The picture shows a piece of carpet that is 3 yards long and 2 yards wide.

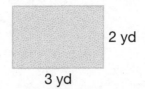

2 yd

3 yd

The carpet covers an area of how many square yards?

Multiply the length and the width.

3 yd × 2 yd = 6 sq. yd

The carpet covers an area of **6 square yards.**

The carpet covers an area of how many square feet?

One yard is 3 feet. Multiply the length and width by 3 to find the length and width in square feet.

length: 3 yd × 3 = 9 ft

width: 2 yd × 3 = 6 ft

Multiply the length and the width to find the area in square feet.

9 ft × 6 ft = 54 sq. ft

The carpet covers an area of **54 square feet.**

Lesson Practice

a. The floor of a small room is covered with one-foot square tiles. Bill counted 6 tiles along one wall and 8 tiles along a perpendicular wall.

How many **tiles** cover the whole floor? _____ tiles

How many rows and columns?

Use a multiplication table for help.

What is the **area** of the room? _____ sq. ft

Area = length × width

b. How many square yards of carpet are needed to cover the floor of a room

that is **4 yards** wide and **5 yards** long? _____ sq. yd

Area = length × width

c. One square yard is 9 square feet. Copy and complete the table below.

Use a multiplication table for help.

Square yards	1	2	3	4	5	6
Square feet	9	18				

Written Practice

📖 page 343

1. 1 big step = 3 ft

10 big steps = _____ ft

Multiply.

```
┌─────────────────────┐
│                   ▒ │
│  ─────────────────  │
└─────────────────────┘
```

2. _____ – _____ = d

_____
  –

Jimmy's _____ has been retired for _____ years.

```
┌ ─ ─ ─ ─ ─ ─ ─ ┐
│ Use work area. │
└ ─ ─ ─ ─ ─ ─ ─ ┘
```

3. Each square in the picture is 1 square foot.

a. length

b. width

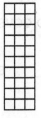

a. _____

b. _____

4. What is the **area** of the picture in problem **3**?

Area = length × width

Use a multiplication table for help.

_____ _____

5. Write a multiplication fact for the picture in problem **3**.

_____ × _____ = _____

6. Which equals 20?

Use a multiplication table for help.

A 2 × 10   **B** 19 × 1   **C** 5 × 5   **D** 10 × 10

_____

7. What number has **5 ones** and **6 hundreds**?

A 56   **B** 560   **C** 650   **D** 605

_____

8.
$$\begin{array}{r} \square \\ -\ 398 \\ \hline 245 \end{array}$$

$\square =$ _____

9. Use a multiplication table for help.

    a. $6 \times 10 =$ **b.** $16 \times 10 =$

a. _____

b. _____

---

10. What is the **place value** of the 4?

4̲12,576

See "Place Value" on page 13 in the *Student Reference Guide*.

_____

---

11. The picture shows 1 square yard.

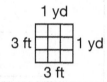

1 yd
3 ft ▢ 1 yd
3 ft

How many **square feet** is one square yard?

_____

12. Look at the picture in problem **11.**

  a. perimeter in **yards**

  b. perimeter in **feet**

    Perimeter ⟶ Add all sides.

a. _____

b. _____

---

13. Shade the circles to show the mixed number $2\frac{1}{3}$.

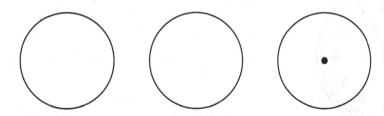

Use work area.

14. Write and compare the fractions shown by the shaded circles.

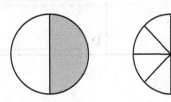

_____ ⬭ _____

Use work area.

15. Use a multiplication table.

    a. $4 \times 8 =$

    b. $3 \times 9 =$

    c. $7 \times 7 =$

a. _____

b. _____

c. _____

---

16. $498
  + $679

17. $0.87
     $0.75
  + $0.93

18. $5.00
  − $3.46

---

19. $323
  − $100

20. after lunch

_____ : _____

© Saxon

Name _____

Teacher Note:

• Review Hint #21 "Multiplication/
  Division Fact Families."

• **Multiplication Facts: 9s**

New Concept

• Multiplication facts for 9s have a special pattern.

• The **first** digit of the product is one less than the factor.

• The **two digits** of the product always add up to **9**.

Math Language

The numbers that are multiplied in a multiplication problem are called **factors**.

The answer in a multiplication problem is called the **product**.

factor × factor = product

Multiplication Facts for 9s

$9 \times \underline{2} = \underline{18}$	$(1 + 8 = 9)$
$9 \times \underline{3} = \underline{27}$	$(2 + 7 = 9)$
$9 \times \underline{4} = \underline{36}$	$(3 + 6 = 9)$
$9 \times \underline{5} = \underline{45}$	$(4 + 5 = 9)$
$9 \times \underline{6} = \underline{54}$	$(5 + 4 = 9)$
$9 \times \underline{7} = \underline{63}$	$(6 + 3 = 9)$
$9 \times \underline{8} = \underline{72}$	$(7 + 2 = 9)$
$9 \times \underline{9} = \underline{81}$	$(8 + 1 = 9)$
$9 \times \underline{10} = \underline{90}$	$(9 + 0 = 9)$

Lesson Practice

Find each product. Use a multiplication table for help. Remember, the **first digit is one less** than the number multiplied and the **two digits add up to nine.**

a. $9 \times 3 =$ _____

b. $9 \times 4 =$ _____

c. $9 \times 6 =$ _____

d. $9 \times 10 =$ _____

e. $9 \times 11 =$ _____

f. $9 \times 12 =$ _____

© Saxon

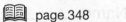
1. _____ × $_____ = $_____

Use a multiplication table for help.

The tickets cost $_____ .

2.

$20
+ $20 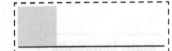 − _____

Use work area.

3. 9 tiles cover 1 square yard. How many tiles cover 3 square yards?

_____ × 9 tiles = _____ tiles

4. Use a ruler to draw a square with sides 3 inches long. Label the side lengths.

Use work area.

5. perimeter of the square in problem **4**

Perimeter ⟶ Add all sides.

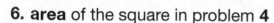

6. area of the square in problem **4**

Area = length × width

7. Shade $\frac{1}{2}$ of the rectangle on the left. Shade $\frac{1}{3}$ of the rectangle on the right.

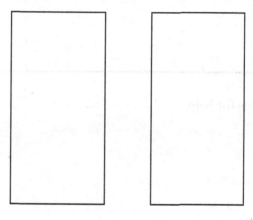

$\frac{1}{2}$ ◯ $\frac{1}{3}$

Use work area.

8. Write the multiplication fact for the picture on 📖 page 348.

_____ × _____ = _____

9. If one egg is removed from the 12 eggs in a carton, what **fraction** is left?

10. Complete the table.

Use a multiplication table for help.

Number of Dozen	1	2	3	4
Number of Eggs	12	24		

11. Use a multiplication table for help.

a. $9 \times 10 =$

b. $7 \times 9 =$

c. $9 \times 4 =$

a. _____

b. _____

c. _____

12. a. $9 \times 9 =$

b. $8 \times 8 =$

c. $7 \times 7 =$

a. _____

b. _____

c. _____

13. Which two numbers have a product of 77?

Use a multiplication table for help.

_____ × _____ = _____

14. Measure to the nearest quarter inch.

A   B

15. $999
        + $999

16. $100
        − $ 91

17. $9 + 9 + 9 + 9 + 9 + 9 =$

Multiply.

18. How many nickels equal 1 quarter? _____

A nickel is what **fraction** of a quarter? _____

Use work area.

19. The spinner is **least likely** to stop on which number?

20. _____ and _____ are both right because

_____ and _____ are equivalent f_____ .

Use work area.

© Saxon

Name _____

Teacher Notes:
- Refer students to "Angles" on page 15 in the *Student Reference Guide.*
- Review Hint #18 "Geometry Vocabulary."
- Students will need drinking straws to complete the activity.

• Angles

New Concept

• When two segments meet, they form an **angle.**

The **vertex** is where the two segments meet.

Angles

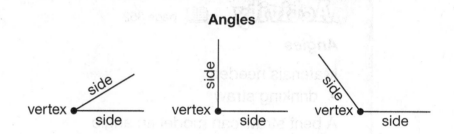

• A **right angle** is a square corner like the corner of a piece of paper.

A small square in the vertex shows a right angle.

• An **acute angle** is *smaller* than a right angle.

Acute Angles

• An **obtuse angle** is *larger* than a right angle.

Obtuse Angles

• A **straight angle** makes a line.

Activity 📖 page 352

Angles

Materials needed:
• drinking straw

A bent straw can model an angle.

For each angle below, bend your straw to fit the angle. Then write "acute," "right," or "obtuse" to describe the angle.

1. _____

2. _____

© Saxon

3. _____

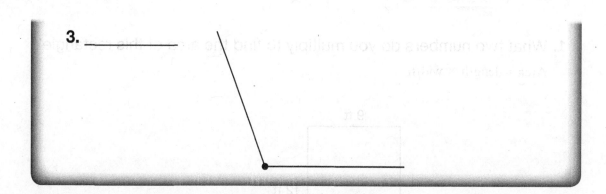

Lesson Practice

a. What is the name of the point where the sides of an angle meet?

V_____

b. What **kind** of angle is each angle of a rectangle? _____

Write "acute," "right," or "obtuse" to describe each angle below.

c. _____   **d.** _____   **e.** _____

© Saxon

1. What two numbers do you multiply to find the area of this rectangle?

Area = length × width

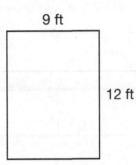

9 ft

12 ft

_____ and _____

2. **area** of the rectangle in problem **1**

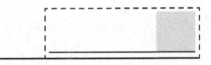

3.

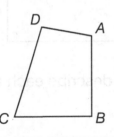

a. Which angle is **acute?**

b. Which angles are **obtuse?**

a. angle _____

b. angle _____

and angle _____

4. The shape _____ a rectangle because a rectangle

has 4 r_____ angles.

Use work area.

© Saxon

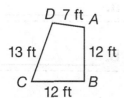

5. perimeter

Perimeter $\longrightarrow$ Add all sides.

6. There are 3 tiles in 1 foot. How many tiles are in 10 feet?

Multiply.

7. Do problem **7** on page 353.

8. 3 out of 7 are girls.

    a. What fraction are **girls?**

    b. What fraction are **boys?**

a. _____ b. _____

9. Compare the fractions from problem **8.**

____ ◯ ____

  a.   b.

Use work area.

10. How many minutes until 5:00?

11. a.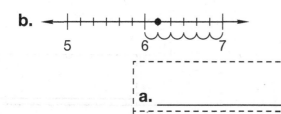

    b.

    a. _____

    b. _____

12.

13. Use a ruler to complete this rectangle $\frac{3}{4}$ inches long and $\frac{1}{2}$ inch wide.

_____

Use work area.

14. a. $3 \times 3 =$

b. $4 \times 4 =$ **a.** _____

c. $6 \times 6 =$ **b.** _____

c. _____

15. a. $3 \times 9 =$

b. $9 \times 4 =$ **a.** _____

c. $9 \times 8 =$ **b.** _____

c. _____

16. Bottom missing ⟶ subtract

$$\begin{array}{r} 81 \\ - \ \square \\ \hline 50 \end{array}$$

$\square =$ _____

17.
$$\begin{array}{r} 81 \\ + \ \square \\ \hline 150 \end{array}$$

$\square =$ _____

18. $9 + 9 + 9 + 9 + 9 + 9 + 9 + 9 =$

Multiply.

_____

19. Which does **not** equal 1?

A $\frac{2}{2}$ **B** $\frac{3}{3}$

C $\frac{10}{11}$ **D** $\frac{12}{12}$

_____

20.

_____

Name _____

Teacher Note:
• Review "Quadrilaterals" on page 16 and "Angles" on page 15 in the *Student Reference Guide*.

• Parallelograms

New Concept

Math Language

Parallel lines stay the same distance apart, like railroad tracks.

• A **parallelogram** is a four-sided flat shape with two pairs of parallel sides.

One pair of parallel sides

The other pair of parallel sides

• A rectangle is a parallelogram with four right angles.

Every rectangle is a parallelogram.

• A square is a parallelogram with four sides of equal length.

Every square is a rectangle *and* a parallelogram.

Example

Find the perimeter of this parallelogram.

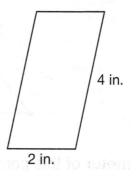

4 in.

2 in.

Add all the sides. The parallel sides of a parallelogram have the same measure.

2 in. + 4 in. + 2 in. + 4 in. = 12 in.

The perimeter of the parallelogram is **12 inches.**

- We name an **angle** of a parallelogram by the letter at the corner (vertex) of the angle.

- We name a **side** by the letters at the end of the side.

Example

Which angles of this parallelogram are acute and which are obtuse?

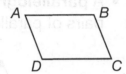

Acute angles are smaller than a right angle (square corner). **Angle A** and **angle C** are acute angles.

Obtuse angles are larger than a right angle. **Angle B** and **angle D** are obtuse angles.

Which side is parallel to side AB?

Parallel sides are across from each other. The side across from side *AB* is **side DC.**

Lesson Practice

a. Complete this parallelogram that does **not** have right angles. Remember that opposite sides of a parallelogram have the same measures. You may use a ruler.

b. What is the **perimeter** of this parallelogram? _____

Perimeter ⟶ Add all sides.

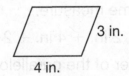

3 in.

4 in.

c. Circle the shape that is **not** a parallelogram.

A   **B** 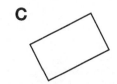 **C** **D**

d. Which shapes in problem **c** are **rectangles**?

_____ and _____

e. Which angles in this parallelogram are **obtuse**?

angle _____ and angle _____

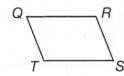

f. Which side of the parallelogram in **e** is **parallel to side QT?** side _____

Written Practice 📖 page 358

1. _____ + _____ + _____ = _____

      1 box

      1 box

+__ 1 box

Use work area.

2. Do problem **2** on 📖 page 358.

© Saxon

3. 7, 8, 15

fact family

+_____   +_____   -_____   -_____

Use work area.

4. Which is **not** a parallelogram?

A   B   C   D

---

5. One square yard is 9 square feet. How many square feet is 9 square yards?

_____ × 9 sq. ft = _____ sq. ft

6. Name the shape of the park.

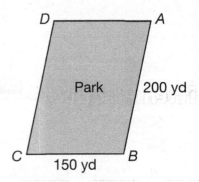

p

7. Use the picture in problem **6.**

a. **acute** angles

b. **obtuse** angles

a. angle _____ and angle _____

b. angle _____ and angle _____

8. Use the picture in problem **6.**

perimeter

Perimeter ⟶ Add all sides.

_____

9. Use the picture in problem **6.**

side **parallel to side _AB_**

side _____

10.

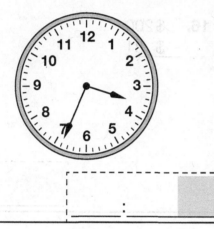

_____ : _____

11.   40
         28
       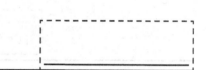

_____

12. Measure to the nearest quarter inch.

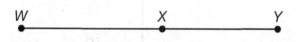

W _____ X _____ Y

a. segment _WX_

b. segment _XY_

c. segment _WY_

a. _____

b. _____

c. _____

13. least likely color

Marbles in Bag

Color	Number
red	2
blue	3
green	5

_____

14. Use the table from problem **13.**

    a. number of **total** marbles

    b. **fraction** that is blue

a. _____ b. _____

---

15. $3.75
    + $4.29

16. $200
    − $ 81

---

17. $9 + 9 + 9 + 9 + 9 + 9 + 9 =$

Multiply.

18. Write a **fraction equal to 1** that has a denominator of 10.

$$\frac{\square}{10}$$

---

19. Which does **not** equal $\frac{1}{2}$?

  A $\frac{2}{4}$ **B** $\frac{3}{6}$

  C $\frac{4}{7}$ **D** $\frac{5}{10}$

20.

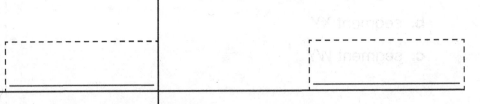

Teacher Note:
- Refer students to "Polygons" on page 14 in the *Student Reference Guide.*

• Polygons

New Concept

- A **polygon** is a closed, flat shape with *straight* sides.

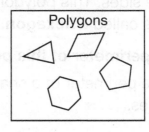
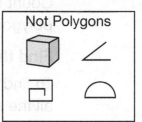

- A **circle** is not a polygon because it does not have straight sides.

- Polygons are named by their **number of sides.**

Polygons

Name	Example	Number of sides
Triangle	△	3
Quadrilateral	▭	4
Pentagon	⬠	5
Hexagon	⬡	6
Octagon	⯃	8

- Parallelograms, rectangles, and squares are all **quadrilaterals** because they all have four sides.

Example

What kind of polygon is this shape?

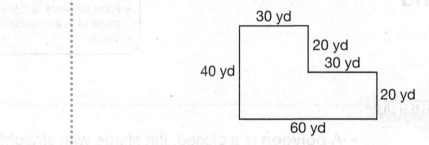

Count the sides. This polygon has 6 sides. A six-sided polygon is called a **hexagon.**

Find the perimeter of this polygon.

To find the perimeter of a shape, we add the measures of all the sides.

$$
\begin{array}{r}
30 \ \text{yd} \\
20 \ \text{yd} \\
30 \ \text{yd} \\
20 \ \text{yd} \\
60 \ \text{yd} \\
+\ 40 \ \text{yd} \\
\hline
200 \ \text{yd}
\end{array}
$$

The perimeter of the hexagon is **200 yards.**

Lesson Practice

a. Miguel arranged two kinds of polygons to make this pattern. Name the two types of polygons.

Count the sides.

S _____ and O _____

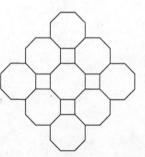

b. Draw a 3-sided polygon. What is the name for a 3-sided polygon?

†_____

c. Circle the shape that is a polygon.

 A B C D

d. Each side of the hexagon is 12 in. What is its perimeter? _____

Every side is 12 in. and there are 6 sides.

12 in.

e. What is the perimeter of the quadrilateral?

_____

Perimeter → Add all sides.

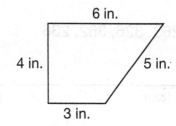
6 in.
4 in.   5 in.
3 in.

Written Practice   page 365

1.

2nd job

_____ 1st job

_ _ _ _ _ _ _
Use work area.

2.

2nd job

_____ 1st job

_ _ _ _ _ _ _
Use work area.

3. Estimate the total.

$590 $\rightarrow$ _____

$285 $\rightarrow$ $+$ _____

4.   2008
        1998
        ‾‾‾‾‾‾

5. a. How much money did Gabe get back?

2 quarters $\rightarrow$ _____

2 dimes $\rightarrow$ _____

3 pennies $\rightarrow$ $+$ _____

b. How much did the postcard cost?

$1.00

$-$ _____
‾‾‾‾‾‾‾‾

a. _____

b. _____

6. 263, 326, 362, 236

_____, _____, _____, _____
least   greatest

Use work area.

7. Do problem 7 on 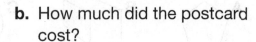 page 366.

8. a. What **fraction** of an hour is 15 minutes?

b. How many **minutes** is $\frac{3}{4}$ of an hour?

a. _____

b. _____

9. $\frac{3}{4}$

a. numerator

b. denominator

a. _____

b. _____

10. Write a multiplication fact for the groups of squares.

$3 \times$ _____ = _____

---

11. 3,000 + 400 + 5 =

A 3,450

B 3,405

C 3,045

D 30,405

12. 9, 18, 27, 36, 45, _____, _____,

_____, ...

Use work area.

---

13. Write a multiplication fact for the array.

```
XXXXXXX
XXXXXXX
XXXXXXX
XXXXXXX
```

_____ × _____ = _____

14. $0.32
         $0.58
       + $0.25

---

15. $360
        − $296

16. Which polygon is next?

Count the sides of the polygons.

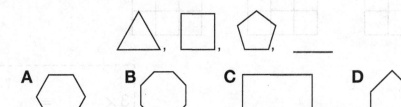

17. Write this addition as a multiplication. Find the total.

$8 + 8 + 8 + 8 + 8 + 8 + 8 =$

_____ × _____ = _____

18. Which point shows **16?**

19. Measure the length to the nearest quarter inch.

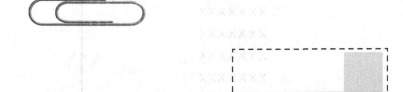

20. The figure is a square.

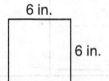

6 in.

6 in.

a. perimeter

Perimeter ⟶ Add all sides.

b. area

Area = length × width

a. _____

b. _____

© Saxon

📖 page 368

• Congruent Shapes

New Concept

• **Congruent** figures have the *same size **and** shape*.

Congruent Triangles   Not Congruent Triangles

          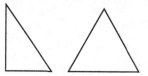

• The three triangles below are all congruent.

Activity 📖 page 370

Congruent Shapes
This activity is optional.

Lesson Practice

a. Complete the definition of congruent figures.

Congruent figures have the same _____ and

_____ .

b. Draw a triangle that is congruent to this triangle. Because congruent figures have the same size and shape, use a ruler to measure the sides of the triangle first.

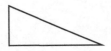

c. Circle the triangle that is **congruent** to the triangle in problem **b.**

Congruent means same size and shape.

A 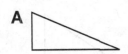 B   C   D

d. Circle the pair of figures that is **not congruent.**

A  B

C 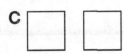 D

1.

red bush

_____ yellow bush

2.

yellow bush

_____ tax

3. What **coins** would Mary get back? Use your answer to problem **2.**

$9.00

_____

_____ quarters, _____ nickel, _____ penny

Use work area.

4. perimeter of the square garden

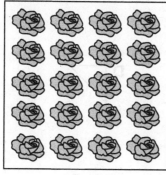

7 yd

5. area of the garden in problem **4**

Area = length × width

6. Write a multiplication fact for the rose bushes in problem **4.**

_____ × _____ = _____

7. What fraction is **yellow?**

Red	Pink	Yellow	White	Peach
6	5	3	2	4

6 red
5 pink
3 yellow
2 white
+ 4 peach

total

8. Use the table from problem **7.**
Compare the **fraction that is
red** to the **fraction that is pink.**

___ ◯ ___
red   pink

Use work area.

9.

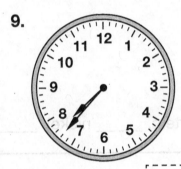

10. Which is **not** a polygon?

A   **B**   **C** ▢   **D**

11. Do problem **11** on  page 372.

12. What kind of polygon is this?

Count the sides.

†

13. What kind of polygon is this?

Count the sides. Do not count the line inside the shape.

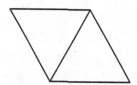

q

14. Write a **fraction equal to 1** that has a denominator of 8.

15. a. 5 × 0 =

b. 5 × 7 =

c. 7 × 10 =

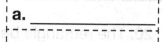

a. _____

b. _____

c. _____

16. Write this addition as a multiplication. Find the total.

7 + 7 + 7 + 7 + 7 + 7 + 7 =

_____ × _____ = _____

17.
```
   78
   78
+  78
```

18.
```
   500
-  234
```

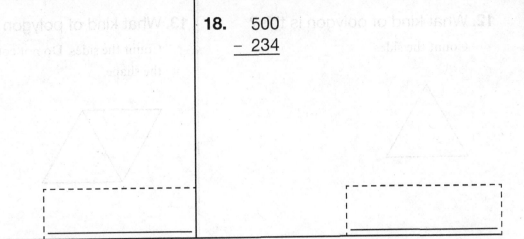

19. Use a ruler to draw a rectangle that is $1\frac{1}{2}$ inches long and $\frac{3}{4}$ inches wide.

Use work area.

20. The rectangle below is congruent to the rectangle you drew in problem **19.** Shade $\frac{2}{3}$ of the rectangle.

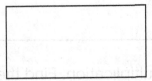

Use work area.

© Saxon

📖 page 373

Name _____

Teacher Notes:

• Refer students to "Triangles" on page 15 in the *Student Reference Guide.*

• Review "Angles" on page 15 in the *Student Reference Guide.*

• Students will need a copy of **Lesson Activity 24** to complete the activity.

• Triangles

New Concept

• A **triangle** is a polygon with three sides.

• Some triangles have special names because of the lengths of their sides or the types of angles.

Types of Triangles

Name	Example	Characteristic
Equilateral	△	three equal sides
Isosceles	△	two equal sides
Right	◺	one right angle
Scalene	◺	all sides different lengths

Activity 📖 page 375

Make Equilateral and Right Triangles

Materials needed:
• **Lesson Activity 24**

Follow the instructions on **Lesson Activity 24** to complete this activity.

a. Kristin fit triangular pattern blocks together to make a hexagon.

How many triangles are in the figure? _____

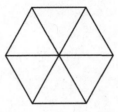

b. What type of triangles did Kristin use to make the hexagon above? Choose one type of triangle from the chart of special triangles.

<u>e</u>_____

c. Draw a right angle by tracing the corner of your textbook. Then make a **right triangle** by drawing one more side.

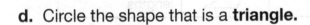

d. Circle the shape that is a **triangle.**

A   B   C   D

1. 1 day = 7 hours

5 days = _____ hours

Multiply.

A 28 hrs

B 35 hrs

C 42 hrs

D 56 hrs

2. a.

b.

a. _____

b. _____

3. Do problem **3** on 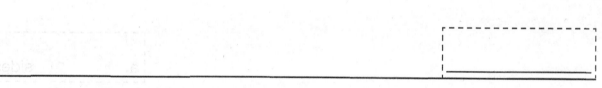 page 376.

Congruent means same size and shape.

_____

4.

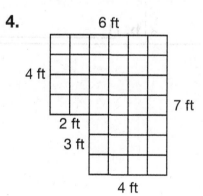

perimeter of the figure

© Saxon

5. a. Count the squares in the figure in problem **4.** _____ squares

    b. What is the **area** of the figure?
Every square is 1 square foot.

Every square is _____ square foot and there are

_____ squares.

So the area must be _____ s_____

f_____.

Use work area.

6. a. Count the sides of the shape in problem **4.**

    b. What is the **name** of this polygon?

a. _____ sides

b. h_____

7. What fraction is **gray?**

4   blue
3   white
+ 3   gray

total

Marbles in Bag

Color	Number
Blue	4
White	3
Gray	3

© Saxon

8. Compare the **fraction that is white** to the **fraction that is blue.**

_____ ◯ _____
white   blue

> Use work area.

9. Is gray, white, or blue **most likely** to be picked?

> _____

10. Which two colors are **equally likely** to be picked?

_____ and _____

11. 25,000

words: _____

_____

> Use work area.

12. What is the **place value** of the 2?
25,000

See "Place Value" on page 13 in the _Student Reference Guide._

> _____

13. What **fraction** is shaded?

> _____

14. Shade $\frac{7}{8}$ of the circle.

> Use work area.

15. Write a **fraction equal to 1** that has a denominator of 9.

$\frac{\square}{9}$

> _____

16. a. $6 \times 6 =$

b. $7 \times 7 =$

c. $8 \times 8 =$

17. a. $9 \times 5 =$

b. $9 \times 10 =$

c. $9 \times 8 =$

a. _____

b. _____

c. _____

a. _____

b. _____

c. _____

18. perimeter of parallelogram

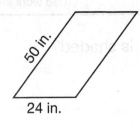
50 in.
24 in.

_____

19. perimeter of triangle

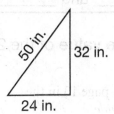
50 in. 32 in.
24 in.

_____

20.

_____ parallelogram

_____ triangle

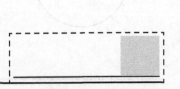

© Saxon

Name _____

Teacher Note:
• Review Hint #21 "Multiplication/
  Division Fact Families."

• Multiplication Facts: Memory Group

New Concept

Math Language

The numbers that are multiplied in a multiplication problem are called **factors**.

The answer in a multiplication problem is called the **product.**

factor × factor = product

• In multiplication, the **product will be the same** for any order of the same factors.

• When you learn one multiplication fact, you also know another fact.

• Here are the last facts to learn. Each pair of facts uses the same three numbers.

$$3 \times 4 = 12 \quad \longrightarrow \quad 4 \times 3 = 12$$

$$3 \times 6 = 18 \quad \longrightarrow \quad 6 \times 3 = 18$$

$$3 \times 7 = 21 \quad \longrightarrow \quad 7 \times 3 = 21$$

$$3 \times 8 = 24 \quad \longrightarrow \quad 8 \times 3 = 24$$

$$4 \times 6 = 24 \quad \longrightarrow \quad 6 \times 4 = 24$$

$$4 \times 7 = 28 \quad \longrightarrow \quad 7 \times 4 = 28$$

$$4 \times 8 = 32 \quad \longrightarrow \quad 8 \times 4 = 32$$

$$6 \times 7 = 42 \quad \longrightarrow \quad 7 \times 6 = 42$$

$$6 \times 8 = 48 \quad \longrightarrow \quad 8 \times 6 = 48$$

$$7 \times 8 = 56 \quad \longrightarrow \quad 8 \times 7 = 56$$

• **Practice all the multiplication facts every day.**

 page 379

Flash Cards

This activity is optional.

Lesson Practice

Find each product. Use a multiplication table for help.

a.   3
    × 4

b.   4
    × 6

c.   6
    × 7

d.   3
    × 7

e.   6
    × 8

f.   4
    × 8

g.   3
    × 6

h.   4
    × 7

i.   7
    × 8

j.   3
    × 8

1. Write a multiplication fact for the figure.

Use a multiplication table for help.

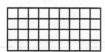

_____ × _____ = _____

2. 1 ft = 12 in.

8 ft = _____ in.

Multiply.

_____

3. Name each polygon.

Count the sides.

a. **b.** **c.**

a. _____

b. _____

c. _____

4. Do problem **4** on 📖 page 380.

_____

5. a. 1 yd = _____ ft

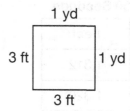

1 yd

3 ft   1 yd

3 ft

b. 1 sq. yd = _____ sq. ft

What is the area of the figure in square feet?

a. _____

b. _____

© Saxon

6. Do problem **6** on 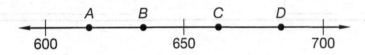 page 380.

Congruent means same size and shape.

- - - - - - - - - -

7. nearest ten

89 →

8. Which point shows **662?**

```
        A    B      C      D
   ←————+————+——————+——————+————→
   600         650         700
```

9. nearest hundred

662 →

10.
$$831 - \square = 294$$

$\square =$ _____

11. Distance in 60 Seconds

Attempt	Feet
1st try	1,312
2nd try	1,320
3rd try	1,303
4th try	1,332

_____, _____, _____, _____

least   greatest

Use work area.

12. after dinner

13. Complete problem **13** on 📖 page 381.

Use fraction pieces for help.

14. $\frac{1}{2}$ ◯ $\frac{3}{8}$

15. Use a multiplication table for help.

   a. $3 \times 4 =$

   b. $3 \times 6 =$

   c. $3 \times 7 =$

16. a. $6 \times 4 =$

   b. $6 \times 7 =$

   c. $6 \times 8 =$

a. _____

b. _____

c. _____

a. _____

b. _____

c. _____

© Saxon

17. a. $7 \times 4 =$

    b. $7 \times 8 =$

    c. $3 \times 8 =$

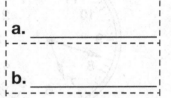

a. _____

b. _____

c. _____

---

18. $\$1.98$
  $+\ \$3.65$

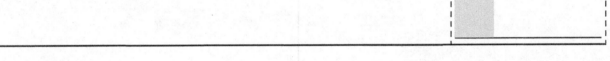

---

19. $\$603$
  $-\ \$476$

---

20. Which point shows $2\frac{1}{2}$?

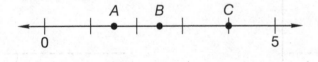

Teacher Note:
* Students need color tiles to complete this Investigation.

 page 383

Focus on
• Symmetry, Part 1

* The wings on the butterfly below are mirror images of each other.

* This kind of mirror image is called **symmetry.**

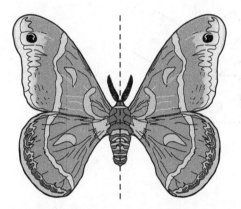

Math Language

A **vertical** line goes up and down.

A **horizontal** line goes across.

* The vertical line across the butterfly shows the two equal halves. This line is called a **line of symmetry.**

* The tile pattern below has a *horizontal* line of symmetry.

The parts above and below the line are mirror images.

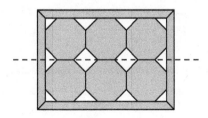

Find another line of symmetry in the tile pattern. Use a ruler to draw the line.

The line of symmetry is vertical.

© Saxon

 page 383

Symmetry, Part 1

Materials needed:
- color tiles

Use four or six color tiles to make a pattern with **symmetry.** Place the tiles on *both sides* of the line of symmetry. Make sure the sides match.

When your pattern is done, trace the pattern on the paper.

Here is an example:

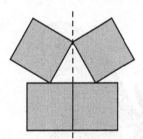

line of symmetry

page 385

Name _____

Teacher Notes:

• Introduce Hint #23 "Geometric Solids."

• Refer students to "Geometric Solids" on page 17 in the *Student Reference Guide.*

• Use Geosolids to enhance this lesson.

• Rectangular Prisms

New Concept

• Rectangles are *flat* shapes that you can draw on paper.

• A **rectangular prism** has the shape of a shoe box or cereal box. It is **not** flat.

• Rectangular prisms have **faces** that are shaped like rectangles.

• Two faces meet at an **edge.**

• Two edges meet at a **vertex** (corner). More than one vertex are *vertices.*

Rectangular Prism

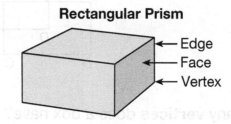

← Edge
— Face
← Vertex

• Even though a rectangular prism is not flat, you can draw a picture of a box on paper.

   1. First, draw two **congruent** rectangles.

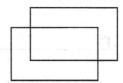

2. Then connect the corners with lines.

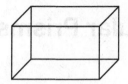

- A **cube** is a special type of rectangular prism. Every face is a square and all the edges are the same length.

Cube

Lesson Practice

a. Draw lines between corners with the same letter to complete this picture of a transparent box.

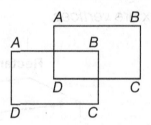

b. How many **vertices** does a box have? _____

Use a manipulative for help.

c. How many **edges** does a box have? _____

d. Complete this definition of a **cube.**

A cube is a r_____ prism that has a square for every

f_____ and e_____ with the same length.

1.

        engines

   + 1 caboose

103 – _____ = /

There were _____ cars, not counting the engines and caboose.

Use work area.

2.

        1st ticket

  + _____ 2nd ticket

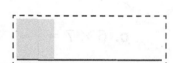

---

3. $20.00

   – _____

4. Do problem **4** on  page 388.

---

5. morning

_____ : _____

---

6. Are train tracks **parallel** or **perpendicular?**

See the *Student Reference Guide.*

7. $17\frac{3}{10}$

words: _____

_____

Use work area.

8. a. $8 \times 7 =$

b. $4 \times 7 =$

c. $6 \times 7 =$

a. _____

b. _____

c. _____

9. a. $3 \times 8 =$

b. $4 \times 8 =$

c. $6 \times 8 =$

a. _____

b. _____

c. _____

10. a. $9 \times 4 =$

b. $9 \times 6 =$

c. $9 \times 8 =$

a. _____

b. _____

c. _____

11. Complete the **rectangular prism.**

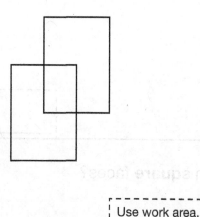

12. A rectangular prism has how many **faces?**

Use a manipulative for help.

- - - - - - - - - - - - - - - - - -
¦ Use work area. ¦
- - - - - - - - - - - - - - - - - -

13. Measure the sides of the right triangle to the nearest quarter inch.

a. side *AB*

b. side *BC*

c. side *CA*

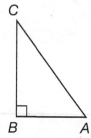

a. _____ **b.** _____ **c.** _____

14. Use a ruler to complete a triangle congruent to the right triangle in problem **13.**

Congruent means same size and shape.

B   *A*

- - - - - - - - - - - - - - - - - -
¦ Use work area. ¦
- - - - - - - - - - - - - - - - - -

15. Do problem **15** on 📖 page 389.

16. What **fraction** of a dollar is 3 quarters?

17. What solid is a rectangular prism with **square** faces?

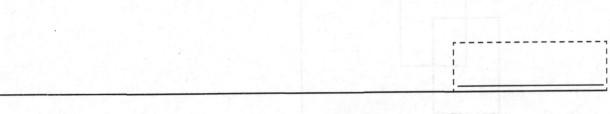

C

18. $ 32
    $ 68
  + $124

19. $206
  − $ 78

20.

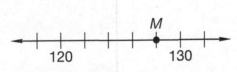

M

120   130

© Saxon

📖 page 390

Teacher Notes:
• Introduce Hint #24 "Volume."
• Students will need color cubes to complete this activity.

Name _____

• Counting Cubes

Math Language

A **rectangular prism** is a solid that has the shape of a box.

A **cube** is a special type of rectangular prism that has square faces and edges of equal length.

• A rectangular prism can be built from cubes.

• The prism will have several *layers* of the same size stacked on top of each other.

The prism below has three layers.

• Every layer in the prism has 3 rows of 3 cubes. Multiply to find the number of cubes in each layer.

3 rows × 3 cubes = 9 cubes

• Then multiply to find the total number of cubes in the prism.

3 layers × 9 cubes = 27 cubes

 📖 page 391

Counting Cubes

Materials needed:
• cubes

Use cubes to build the stack shown in each picture. Then answer the questions about each stack of cubes.

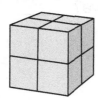

1. How many cubes are in one layer? _____

2. How many layers are there? _____

3. How many cubes are there in all? _____
Multiply.

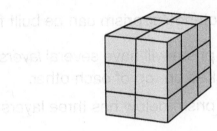

4. How many cubes are in one layer? _____

5. How many layers are there? _____

6. How many cubes are there in all? _____
Multiply.

Lesson Practice

A prism is made of layers of cubes, as shown.

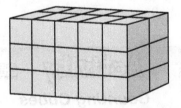

a. How many cubes are in each layer? _____

b. How many layers are there? _____

c. How many cubes are there? _____
Multiply.

1.   480
   256

2.

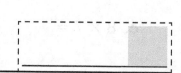

185 mi

Elam   Junction City

Elam to Junction City

$+$____ Junction City to Elam

3. Use a ruler to measure the distance from Denver to Chicago on page 392.

_____ in.

Every inch is 200 miles. What is the distance from Denver to Chicago?

4. morning

5. a. $7 \times 2 =$

b. $7 \times 5 =$

c. $7 \times 9 =$

a. _____

b. _____

c. _____

6. a. $8 \times 4 =$

a. _____

b. $8 \times 6 =$

b. _____

c. $8 \times 7 =$

c. _____

7. a. $6 \times 3 =$

a. _____

b. $6 \times 4 =$

b. _____

c. $6 \times 7 =$

c. _____

8. a. $9 \times 3 =$

a. _____

b. $9 \times 7 =$

b. _____

c. $9 \times 9 =$

c. _____

9. Complete the **cube.**

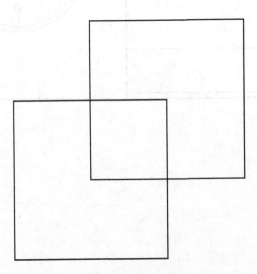

Use work area.

10. What shape is every face of a cube?

s _____

11. A rectangular prism has how many **edges?**

Use a manipulative for help.

_____

12. Do problem **12** on 📖 page 393.

_____

13. How many small cubes make the larger cube?

How many in one layer? How many layers?

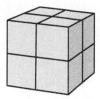

_____

14. a. side length

b. perimeter

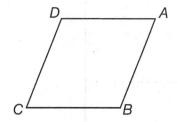

a. _____

b. _____

15. What shape is the polygon in problem **14?**

p _____

16. Use the shape in problem **14.**

   a. obtuse angles

   b. acute angles

> **a.** angle _____ and angle _____
>
> **b.** angle _____ and angle _____

17. See the multiplication table in the *Student Reference Guide*.

   0, 1, 4, 9, 16, 25, _____, _____, _____, …

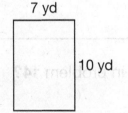

> Use work area.

18.	**19.**
$0.36	$2.00
$0.74	− $1.26
+ $2.00	

---

20. area

7 yd

10 yd

© Saxon

 page 394

Name _____

Teacher Notes:
- Review Hint #24 "Volume."
- Review "Perimeter, Area, Volume" on page 17 in the *Student Reference Guide*.

• Volume

New Concept

- **Volume** is the amount of space an object occupies.

- Volume is measured in *cubes* of different sizes: **cubic inches** (cu. in.), **cubic feet** (cu. ft), and **cubic yards** (cu. yd).

- A cube with one-inch-long edges has a volume of *one cubic inch.*

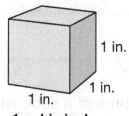

1 in.
1 in.
1 in.

1 cubic inch

Math Language

A **rectangular prism** is a solid that has the shape of a box.

- To find the volume of a rectangular prism:

  1. Count the cubes in one layer.
  2. Multiply that number by the number of layers.

Example

Find the volume of this rectangular prism. Each cube in the prism is 1 cubic inch.

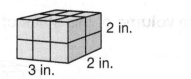

2 in.
3 in.   2 in.

1. Find the number of cubes in one layer.
   The top layer has 3 rows of 2 cubes each.

© Saxon

So the number of cubes in one layer is:

3 rows × 2 cubes = 6 cubes

2. Multiply by the number of layers.

Count 2 layers in the prism.

2 layers × 6 cubes = 12 cubes

Every cube is 1 cubic inch, so the volume of the rectangular prism is **12 cubic inches.**

Activity   page 395

Volume

This activity is optional.

Lesson Practice

a. What is the volume of a cube with one-foot-long edges?

_____ C _____ foot

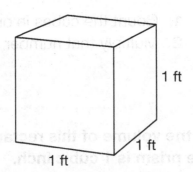

1 ft

1 ft

1 ft

b. What is the **volume** of this stack of boxes? _____ cu. ft

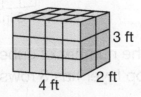

3 ft

4 ft   2 ft

How many in one layer? How many layers?

1. $\$98 + m = \$149$

2.   days in 1 year

$$-\ 181$$

3. _____ × _____ = t

4. morning

5.

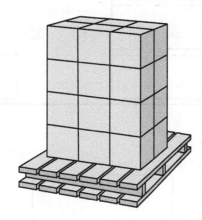

a. How many boxes in one layer?

b. How many layers?

c. How many total boxes?

a. _____

b. _____

c. _____

6. If each box in problem **5** is **1 cubic foot** (1 cu. ft), what is the volume of the stack of boxes?

7. a. $3 \times 6 =$

b. $3 \times 8 =$

c. $3 \times 7 =$

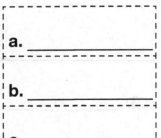

a. _____

b. _____

c. _____

8. a. $5 \times 9 =$

b. $9 \times 2 =$

c. $9 \times 9 =$

a. _____

b. _____

c. _____

9. Write this addition as a multiplication fact. Find the total.

$$\$5 + \$5 + \$5 + \$5 + \$5 + \$5$$

_____ $\times$ _____ = _____

10. Complete this **cube.**

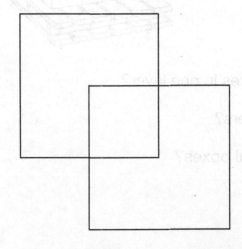

¡ Use work area. ¡

11. A cube has how many **vertices?**
Use a manipulative for help.

12. Do problem **12** on 📖 page 398.

13. 14, 21, 28, 35, _____, _____, _____, ...

Use work area.

14. a. $6 \times 7 =$

b. $7 \times 7 =$

c. $8 \times 7 =$

a. _____   **b.** _____   **c.** _____

15. $800
       − $724

16. $6.49
       + $5.52

17. $9 + 9 + 9 + 9 + 9 + 9 + 9 + 9 + 9 =$
Multiply.

18. Write each fraction or mixed number in words.

a. $\frac{3}{7}$ _____

b. $3\frac{1}{2}$ _____ and _____

c. $\frac{9}{10}$ _____

d. $2\frac{3}{4}$ _____ and _____

| Use work area. |

19.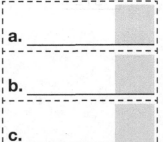

4 in.
10 in.
6 in.

a. length

b. width

c. height

a. _____

b. _____

c. _____

20. area of the top of the box in problem **19**

© Saxon

Name _____

Teacher Notes:

• Review "Equivalence Table for Units" on page 1 in the *Student Reference Guide*.

• Students need an ounce/pound scale to complete this activity.

• Weight: Ounces, Pounds, and Tons

New Concept

• **Weight** is how heavy an object is.

• **Pounds** (lb) are a common unit of weight. A playground ball weighs about one pound.

• Very light objects are measured in **ounces** (oz). A metal spoon weighs about one ounce.

• Very heavy objects are measured in **tons.** A small car weighs about a ton.

Metal spoon   Playground ball   Small automobile

1 ounce   1 pound   1 ton

• One pound equals 16 ounces.

• One ton equals 2,000 pounds.

Units of Weight

1 pound = 16 ounces
1 ton = 2,000 pounds

© Saxon

Example

If a large car weighs about two tons, then it weighs about how many pounds?

One ton is 2,000 pounds.

Two tons is 2,000 lb + 2,000 lb = 4,000 lb.

The large car weighs about **4,000 pounds.**

 Activity 📖 page 401

Weighing Objects

Materials needed:
- scale

The chart below lists several classroom objects. Use a scale to weigh each object. Your teacher can help you read the scale. Write the weights of the objects in the chart.

Weights of Objects

Name of Object	Weight
Textbook	
Box of crayons	
Ruler	
Stapler	

1. Which object weighs the most? _____

2. Which object weighs the least? _____

Lesson Practice

a. Would you describe the weight of a large dog in ounces, pounds, or tons?

_____

b. Circle the object that weighs about an ounce.

A Birthday card   **B** Box of cereal   **C** Brick wall

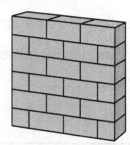

c. The kitten weighed about two pounds. About how many **ounces** did the

kitten weigh? _____ oz

1 pound = 16 ounces

d. The horse weighed about **one half of a ton.** About how many pounds did
the horse weigh? (Circle the correct answer.)

1 ton = 2,000 pounds

A 500 pounds   **B** 1,000 pounds

C 1,500 pounds   **D** 2,000 pounds

Written Practice   page 402

1.   coal cars

____ box cars

altogether

2. _____ + m = _____

morning

$+ \; m$ more

nightfall

3. Use a ruler to measure the distance in problem **3** on 📖 page 402.

Jonestown to Seagraves: _____ in.

Every inch is 50 miles. What is the distance from Jonestown to Seagraves?

---

4. noon

5. Are the stripes on a United States flag parallel or perpendicular?

---

6. $16,000

words: _____

Use work area.

---

7. 1 lb = _____ oz
See the *Student Reference Guide.*

8. four tenths

---

9.   current year

   − 1869

10. a. $6 \times 2 =$

b. $8 \times 5 =$

c. $5 \times 6 =$

a. _____

b. _____

c. _____

---

11. Write as a multiplication problem. Find the total.

3 ft + 3 ft + 3 ft + 3 ft

_____ × _____ = _____

12. a. 1 ton = _____ lb

See the *Student Reference Guide.*

b. 2 tons = _____ lb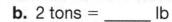

a. _____

b. _____

13. a. $6 \times 7 =$

b. $7 \times 8 =$

c. $6 \times 8 =$

a. _____

b. _____

c. _____

14. $6.75
− $4.48

_____

15. $1.00
− $0.01

_____

16. 10
20
+ *m*
_____
100

m = _____

17. a. How many 1-inch cubes are in this prism?

b. What is the **volume** in cu. in.?

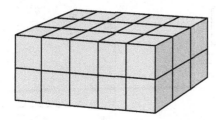

How many in one layer? How many layers?

a. _____   **b.** _____

18. Use a ruler to measure each distance in problem **18.**

Every **quarter inch** on the map is 10 miles.

a. Calmer to Seaton: _____ in.

b. Calmer to Bayview: _____ in.

c. Bayview to Seaton: _____ in.

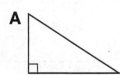 **a.** _____

 **b.** _____

 c. _____

19. Which does **not** have a right angle? How can you tell?

A   B   C   D

A small **s**_____ in an angle shows a **r**_____ angle.

So Figure _____ does not have any right angles.

Use work area.

20. a. How many **sides** does choice **D** have in problem 19?

b. What is the **name** of this polygon?

See the *Student Reference Guide.*

a. _____

b. _____

📖 page 404

Name _____

Teacher Notes:

• Review Hint #23 "Geometric Solids."

• Review "Geometric Solids" on page 17 in the *Student Reference Guide*.

• Use Relational Geosolids to enhance this lesson.

• Geometric Solids

New Concept

• Shapes like circles and rectangles are **flat.** They can be drawn on a piece of paper.

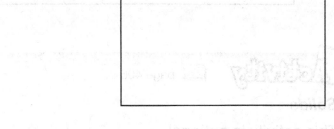

• Shapes that take up space are called **geometric solids.** Many objects in the real world have the shape of a geometric solid.

• The chart on the next page shows pictures and names of some geometric solids.

Geometric Solids

Shape	Name
	Cube
	Rectangular prism
	Triangular prism
	Pyramid
	Cylinder
	Cone
	Sphere

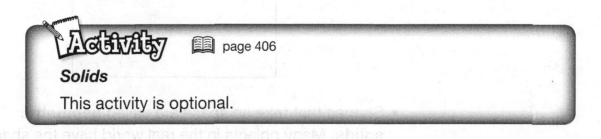

Activity 📖 page 406

Solids

This activity is optional.

Write the geometric name for the shape of each figure below. Use the chart in this lesson.

a. t _____ p _____

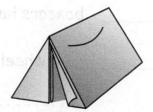

b. S _____

c. C _____

d. r _____ p _____

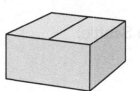

e. C _____

f. p _____

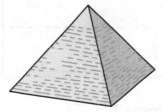

Written Practice 📖 page 407

1. Read the scale on 📖 page 407.　　　　100

_____ lb　　　　　　　　　　　　 — _____

2. $7.75   1st ticket
$\underline{\$7.75}$ 2nd ticket

total

_____

3. 7 boxcars with 8 wheels each

_____ × _____ = _____

All _____ boxcars have a

total of _____ wheels.

Use work area.

4. Use a ruler to measure the distance in problem **4** on 📖 page 407.

San Francisco to Seattle:

_____ in.

Every inch is 200 miles. What is the distance from San Francisco to Seattle?

_____

5. afternoon

_____:_____

6.   Shade $1\frac{1}{4}$.   Shade $1\frac{3}{8}$.

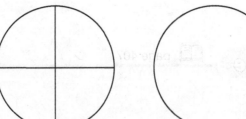

$1\frac{1}{4}$ ◯ $1\frac{3}{8}$

Use work area.

7. a. $9 \times 5 =$

   b. $7 \times 9 =$

   c. $2 \times 9 =$

> a. _____
>
> b. _____
>
> c. _____

8. a. $5 \times 0 =$

   b. $9 \times 1 =$

   c. $10 \times 8 =$

> a. _____
>
> b. _____
>
> c. _____

9. Do problem **9** on 📖 page 408.

> _____

10. $\$1.00$
     $-\ \$0.22$

What **coins** should she get back?

_____ quarters and _____ pennies

> Use work area.

11. a. 2 tons = _____ lb

   b. 4 tons = _____ lb

   See the *Student Reference Guide.*

> a. _____
>
> b. _____

12. a. $6 \times 3 =$

   b. $7 \times 6 =$

   c. $8 \times 7 =$

> a. _____
>
> b. _____
>
> c. _____

13. $\$472$
     $-\ \$396$

> _____

14. $354
$263
+ $ 50

15. 5 + 5 + 5 + 5 + 5 + 5 + 5 + 5 + 5 + 5 =

Multiply.

16. 12
a
+ 16
36

a =

17. a. How many 1-cubic-foot boxes are in this prism?

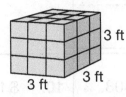

3 ft

3 ft   3 ft

How many in one layer?
How many layers?

b. What is the **volume** in cu. ft?

a. _____

b. _____

18. Choose an **ounce,** a **pound,** or a **ton** for each picture in problem **18** on 📖 page 408.

a. _____

b. _____

c. _____

19. Name each solid in problem **19** on 📖 page 409.

See the *Student Reference Guide.*

a. C _____

b. p _____

c. S _____

20. Do problem **20** on 📖 page 409.

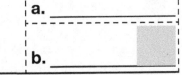

Teacher Notes:
- Review Hint #21 "Multiplication/ Division Fact Families."
- Review "Multiplication Table" on page 5 in the *Student Reference Guide*.

Name _____

• Multiplication Facts: 11s and 12s

New Concept

Math Language

Factors are the numbers that are multiplied in a multiplication problem.

The **product** is the answer in a multiplication problem.

factor × factor = product

- In multiplication, the **product will be the same** for any order of the same factors. When you learn one multiplication fact, you also know another fact.

- Most of the 11s facts have a pattern. The product is the factor written *twice*.

$$11 \times 3 = 33 \rightarrow 3 \times 11 = 33$$
$$11 \times 4 = 44 \rightarrow 4 \times 11 = 44$$
$$11 \times 6 = 66 \rightarrow 6 \times 11 = 66$$
$$11 \times 7 = 77 \rightarrow 7 \times 11 = 77$$
$$11 \times 8 = 88 \rightarrow 8 \times 11 = 88$$
$$11 \times 12 = 132 \rightarrow 12 \times 11 = 132$$

- To learn the 12s facts, practice them every day. Use the multiplication table until you know them.

$$12 \times 3 = 36 \rightarrow 3 \times 12 = 36$$
$$12 \times 4 = 48 \rightarrow 4 \times 12 = 48$$
$$12 \times 6 = 72 \rightarrow 6 \times 12 = 72$$
$$12 \times 7 = 84 \rightarrow 7 \times 12 = 84$$
$$12 \times 8 = 96 \rightarrow 8 \times 12 = 96$$

 page 411

Modeling 11s and 12s

This activity is optional.

Find each product. Use a multiplication table for help.

a. 11 × 11 = _____   **b.** 11 × 12 = _____   **c.** 12 × 5 = _____

d. 12 × 6 = _____   **e.** 7 × 12 = _____   **f.** 8 × 12 = _____

g. 9 × 12 = _____   **h.** 12 × 10 = _____   **i.** 12 × 12 = _____

j. The word **"dozen" means 12.** John raises chickens and puts eggs in cartons. Each carton contains a dozen eggs. Complete the table to show the number of eggs in one through 12 cartons.

Number of Cartons	1	2	3	4	5	6	7	8	9	10	11	12
Number of Eggs	12	24										

How many eggs are in 9 cartons? _____ eggs

How many eggs are in 12 cartons? _____ eggs

Written Practice   📖 page 413

1. 1 big step = 3 ft

  9 big steps = _____ ft

2. 1869 1st railroad
    1849 Gold Rush

3. Use a ruler to measure the distance in problem **3** on 📖 page 414.

Plains to Westcott: _____ in.

Every inch is 100 miles. What is the distance from Plains to Westcott?

---

4. Name each solid in problem **4** on 📖 page 414.

See the *Student Reference Guide*.

a. C _____

b. C _____

c. S _____

---

5. a. $9 \times 6 =$

b. $4 \times 9 =$

c. $9 \times 9 =$

a. _____

b. _____

c. _____

---

6. Are the stripes across the circle parallel or perpendicular?

---

7. $48,000

words: _____

_____ dollars

Use work area.

8. Write as a multiplication problem.
Find the total.

12 + 12 + 12 + 12 + 12 + 12

_____ × _____ = _____

9. a. 3 tons = _____ lb

b. 4 tons = _____ lb

See the *Student Reference Guide.*

a. _____

b. _____

10. Write **three tenths** as a fraction.

_____

11. a. 8 × 7 =

b. 4 × 6 =

c. 6 × 7 =

a. _____

b. _____

c. _____

12. $ 0.85
$ 0.76
+ $10.00

13. $5.00
− $3.29

14. 1 ft = 12 in.

12 ft = _____ in.

15. a. 11 × 11 =

b. 11 × 12 =

c. 9 × 12 =

a. _____

b. _____

c. _____

16. a. How many boxes are in this prism?

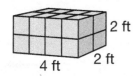

2 ft

4 ft   2 ft

How many in one layer? How many layers?

a. _____

b. What is the **volume** in cu. ft?

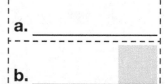

b. _____

17. Write a multiplication fact for this array.

How many rows and columns?

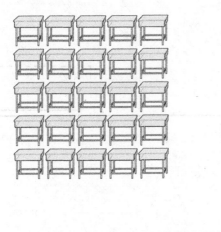

_____ × _____ = _____

18. Write the two fractions shown by these shaded squares. Then compare the two fractions.

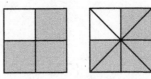

_____ ◯ _____

Use work area.

19. Use a ruler to measure each distance in problem **19** on 📖 page 415.

a. Granville to Lexington

b. Lexington to Hampshire

c. Granville to Hampshire through Lexington

a. _____

b. _____

c. _____

20. On the map in problem **19**, every $\frac{1}{4}$ inch is 10 miles.

How far is it from Lexington to Hampshire?

📖 page 416

Name _____

Teacher Notes:

- Review "Perimeter, Area, Volume" on page 17 in the *Student Reference Guide.*
- Students will need color cubes to complete this activity.
- For additional practice, students may complete Targeted Practice 77.

• Multiplying Three Numbers

New Concept

Math Language

Factors are the numbers that are multiplied in a multiplication problem.

The **product** is the answer in a multiplication problem.

- To multiply three factors:

  1. Multiply two of the factors and write the product.
  2. Multiply the product and the third factor to find the answer.

Example

Multiply: $4 \times 2 \times 7$

1. Multiply the first two factors.

$$4 \times 2 = 8$$

2. Multiply that product by the third factor.

$$8 \times 7 = 56$$

The product of all three factors is **56.**

- To find the **volume of a rectangular prism,** multiply the three factors.

Volume = length × width × height

© Saxon

Activity 📖 page 417

Multiplying to Find Volume

Materials needed:

• cubes

One way to find the volume of a box is to count the number of cubes in one layer and multiply by the number of layers.

Another way to find the volume of a box is to multiply three numbers: length, width, and height.

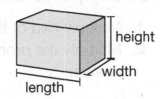

Use cubes to build the rectangular prism shown below.
The prism is 3 cubes long, 2 cubes wide, and 2 cubes high.

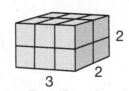

1. Count the cubes you used to build the rectangular

prism. How many cubes are there in all? _____ cubes

2. Every cube is 1 cubic inch. What is the volume of the

prism? _____ cu. in.

3. What are the length, width, and height of the prism in inches?

length: _____ in.   width: _____ in.   height: _____ in.

4. What is the product when you multiply 3 × 2 × 2? _____

© Saxon

Find each product in **a–d**. Use a multiplication table for help.

a. $2 \times 2 \times 2 = \underline{\hspace{1cm}}$

b. $3 \times 3 \times 4 = \underline{\hspace{1cm}}$

c. $1 \times 2 \times 11 = \underline{\hspace{1cm}}$

d. $6 \times 2 \times 5 = \underline{\hspace{1cm}}$

e. What is the length, width, and height of this figure?

length: _____ units   width: _____ units   height: _____ units

f. Find the volume of the figure by multiplying the length, width, and height.

_____ $\times$ _____ $\times$ _____ = _____ cubic units

Written Practice   page 418

1. _____ $+ m = $ _____ $-$ _____

The boxcar can carry _____ tons of additional cargo.

Use work area.

2. 4 tables with 8 chairs each

_____ $\times$ _____ = _____

3. a. Complete this picture of a **cube.**

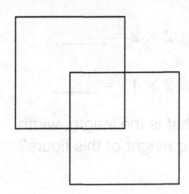

b. How many **faces?** _____

Use a manipulative for help.

c. How many **vertices?** _____.

¦ Use work area. ¦

4. Use a ruler to draw a **rectangle** that is 4 inches long and 1 inch wide.

¦ Use work area. ¦

5. a. perimeter of the rectangle in problem **4**

Perimeter ⟶ Add all sides.

b. area

Area = length × width

a. _____   **b.** _____

6. a. 1 ton = _____ lb

b. 2 tons = _____ lb

c. 3 tons = _____ lb

¦ Use work area. ¦

7. Shade this rectangle to show $\frac{3}{7}$.

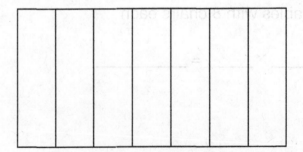

¦ Use work area. ¦

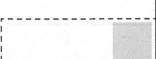

8. $\frac{1}{2}$ ton = _____ lb

See the *Student Reference Guide*.

9. Write **eight tenths** as a fraction.

10. Each box is **1 cubic foot.**

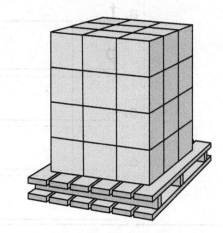

a. How many layers? _____

b. How many boxes in each layer? _____

c. How many total boxes? _____

d. What is the volume? _____

Use work area.

11. Draw an **obtuse** angle.

See the *Student Reference Guide*.

Use work area.

12. 107,400

words: _____

_____

Use work area.

13. The date 7-57 shows a month and a year.

What is the 7th month? _____

See the *Student Reference Guide*.

Write the full 4-digit year for "57". _____

Use work area.

14. $684
   + $286

15. $7.50
    − $7.29

16. $2 \times 3 \times 4 =$ _____

17. a. Name this shape.

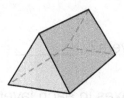

b. How many **triangular faces?**
Use a manipulative for help.

c. How many **rectangular faces?**

d. How many **total faces?**

a. † _____

p _____

b. _____

c. _____

d. _____

18. a. $8 \times 12 =$

b. $9 \times 12 =$

c. $11 \times 12 =$

a. _____

b. _____

c. _____

19. Do problem **19** on 📖 420.
Congruent means same size
and shape.

_____

20. a. fraction shaded
How many parts? How many shaded?

b. Is the arrow **more likely** to stop on shaded
or unshaded?
Are there more shaded or unshaded?

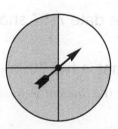

a. _____   b. _____

Name _____

Teacher Note:

• Review the "Multiplication Table" on page 5 in the *Student Reference Guide.*

• Multiplying Multiples of Ten

New Concept

Math Language

Digits are the numbers 0, 1, 2, 3, 4, 5, 6, 7, 8, and 9. Larger numbers use more than one digit.

• The **multiples of ten** are the numbers we say when we count up by 10.

10,   20,   30,   40,   50, ...

• To multiply multiples of ten:

  1. Multiply the digit that is not zero.
  2. Write a zero on the end of the product.

Example

Multiply: 4 × 30

1. Multiply the digit that is not zero.

$$4 \times 3 = 12$$

2. Write a zero on the end of that product.

$$12 \longrightarrow 120$$

The product of 4 and 30 is **120.**

Example

Diana has seven $20 bills. How much money is that?

Multiply to find the total amount of money.

$$7 \times \$20$$

1. Multiply the digit that is not zero.

$$7 \times \$2 = \$14$$

© Saxon

2. Write a zero on the end of that product.

$$\$14 \quad \rightarrow \quad \$140$$

Diana has **$140.**

Lesson Practice

a. How much money is eight $20 bills?

$8 \times \$20 = \$$ _____

b. If 5 classrooms each have 30 students, then how many students are in all 5 classrooms?

5×30 students = _____ students

Find each product for problems **c–f.**

c. $4 \times 60 =$ _____

d. $7 \times 30 =$ _____

e. $8 \times 40 =$ _____

f. $3 \times 80 =$ _____

Written Practice

📖 page 423

1. _____ $\times$ $_____ = $_____

Use work area.

2.
$$\begin{array}{r} 190 \\ + \; m \\ \hline 240 \end{array}$$

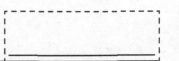

3.

$10
+ $10   − $14.75

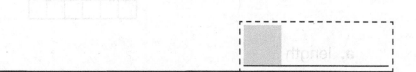

---

4. Name the solid.

See the *Student Reference Guide*.

---

5. a. Complete this drawing of a **rectangular prism**.

b. How many **vertices?** _____
Use a manipulative for help.

c. How many **edges?** _____

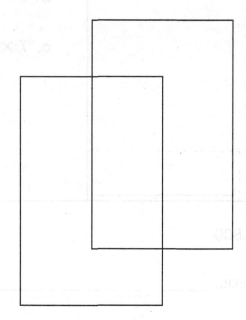

⌐ Use work area. ¬

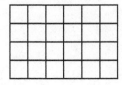

6. The side of each tile is one inch long.

    a. length

    b. width

    c. total tiles

    d. area

a. _____

b. _____

c. _____

d. _____

7. perimeter of the rectangle in problem **6**

8. a. $7 \times 0 =$

    b. $7 \times 5 =$

    c. $7 \times 9 =$

a. _____

b. _____

c. _____

9. 52,800

words: _____

_____

Use work area.

10. a. $5 \times 12 =$

   b. $6 \times 12 =$

   c. $7 \times 12 =$

a. _____

b. _____

c. _____

11. a. $6 \times 7 =$

   b. $6 \times 8 =$

   c. $6 \times 9 =$

a. _____

b. _____

c. _____

12. a. $3 \times 20 =$

   b. $6 \times 30 =$

   c. $4 \times 40 =$

a. _____

b. _____

c. _____

13. $676
   + $234

14. $1.00
   − $0.73

15. $3 \times 3 \times 3 =$

16. $7 \times 50 =$

17. A full-grown cat could weigh

   A 8 ounces.

   B 8 pounds.

   C 8 tons.

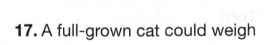

18. a. 1 lb = _____ oz

See the *Student Reference Guide.*

b. An ounce is what **fraction** of a pound?

a. _____ b. _____

19. Name two roads **perpendicular** to Wildrose.

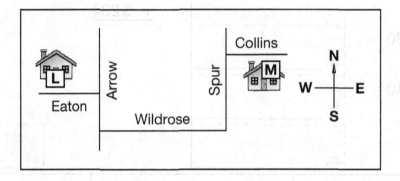

_____ and _____

Use work area.

20. Write directions **from Monica's home to Leslie's home** on the map in problem **19.**

Go _____ to Spur Street. Turn left and go

_____ to Wildrose Street. Turn _____

and go west to _____ Street. Turn right and go

_____ to _____ Street. Turn left and go

_____ to Leslie's home.

Use work area.

Name _____

Teacher Notes:
- Review Hint #16 "Measuring."
- Review "Equivalence Table for Units" on page 1 in the *Student Reference Guide*.
- Students will need a centimeter ruler and a meterstick to complete this activity.

• Length: Centimeters, Meters, and Kilometers

New Concept

- In the United States, we usually measure length in inches (in.), feet (ft), yards (yd), and miles (mi).

- Most of the rest of the world uses the **metric system** of measurement.

- A **centimeter** (cm) is about the width of a finger or half an inch.

- A **meter** (m) is about the length of one BIG step or one yard.

- A **kilometer** (km) is about half a mile.

Metric Units of Length

Unit	Abbreviation	Reference
centimeter	cm	width of a finger
meter	m	one BIG step
kilometer	km	$\frac{6}{10}$ mile
1 meter = 100 centimeters		
1 kilometer = 1000 meters		

Example

Which length could be the length of a pencil?

A 15 centimeters   **B** 15 meters

C 15 kilometers   **D** 15 feet

A centimeter is about half an inch, so answer **A** could be right.

A meter is one BIG step. 15 BIG steps is too long, so the answer is not **B**.

A kilometer is about half a mile. Answer **C** is too long.

Answer **D,** 15 feet, is too long.

The best answer is answer **A,** 15 centimeters.

• Measure centimeters with a centimeter ruler.

• To measure an object in centimeters:

1. Put the "0" mark of the centimeter ruler on the left end of the object.
2. Read the number that is closest to the other end of the object.
3. Write the units: *centimeters* or *cm*.

 **Activity** 📖 page 426

Metric Units of Length

Materials needed:

• centimeter ruler

• meterstick

Find the centimeter side of your ruler. Use it to measure each item to the nearest centimeter.

1. width of your paper: _____ cm

2. length of your paper: _____ cm

3. length of your pencil: _____ cm

4. length of the segment below: _____ cm

_____

Now get a meterstick. Use it to measure each item to the nearest meter.

5. width of the classroom door: _____ m

6. height of the classroom door: _____ m

7. length of the chalkboard: _____ m

8. width of your classroom: _____ m

Lesson Practice

a. The segment below is 2 inches long. Measure the segment to the nearest

centimeter. _____ cm   _____

b. Measure the length of your math book to the nearest centimeter. _____ cm

c. A meter is how many centimeters? _____ cm

d. How many meters is a kilometer? _____ m

Refer to this rectangle
to answer problems **e–h.**

e. How long is the rectangle in centimeters? _____ cm

f. How wide is the rectangle in centimeters? _____ cm

g. How many centimeters is the **perimeter** of the rectangle? _____ cm

h. How many square centimeters is the **area** of the rectangle? _____ sq. cm

1. 9 rows of 4 passengers each

2. days in 1 year

$$- \quad 90$$

3. 6 days of 4 miles each

4. a. Complete this drawing of a **cube.**

b. How many **faces?** _____
Use a manipulative for help.

c. How many **edges?** _____

d. How many **vertices?** _____

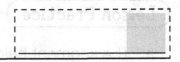

Use work area.

5. a. How many total cubes? _____   **b.** volume _____
Volume = length × width × height

Use work area.

6. Draw a rectangle that is 5 cm long and 2 cm wide.

Use work area.

7. a. perimeter of the rectangle in problem **6**

   b. area

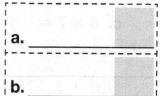

a. _____

b. _____

8. Do problem **8** on 📖 page 429.

a. _____

b. _____

9. a. Complete this triangle congruent to the triangle in problem **8**.

b. perimeter of the triangle: _____

Use work area.

10. a. $9 \times 7 =$

   b. $6 \times 9 =$

   c. $4 \times 9 =$

a. _____

b. _____

c. _____

11. a. $2 \times 40 =$

   b. $3 \times 70 =$

   c. $4 \times 50 =$

a. _____

b. _____

c. _____

12. Write as a multiplication problem. Find the total.

7 days + 7 days + 7 days + 7 days + 7 days

_____ × _____ = _____

13. _____ lb = 1 ton

See the *Student Reference Guide.*

4,000 lb = _____ tons

_____

14. a. $8 \times 4 =$

   b. $8 \times 6 =$

   c. $8 \times 7 =$

a. _____

b. _____

c. _____

15. $7.60
      $8.70
    + $3.70

16. $7.50
      − $3.75

17. 1, $1\frac{1}{4}$, $1\frac{1}{2}$, $1\frac{3}{4}$, 2, _____, _____, _____, _____, ...

Use work area.

18. Do problem **18** on page 430.

_____ °F

_____ °C

19.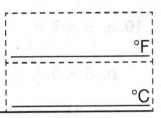
3 in.   8 in.

4 in.

   a. length

   b. width

   c. height

a. _____

b. _____

c. _____

20. Find the **area of the top** of the rectangular prism in problem **19.**

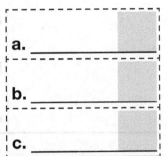

© Saxon

📖 page 431

Name _____

Teacher Notes:
- Introduce Hint #25 "Gram/Kilogram Manipulatives."
- Review "Equivalence Table for Units" on page 1 in the *Student Reference Guide*.
- Students will need a gram mass (a large paper clip) and a kilogram mass (a basketball or 2-pound book) to complete this activity.

• Mass: Grams and Kilograms

New Concept

- In the United States, we usually measure weight in ounces (oz), pounds (lb), and tons.

- The metric system measures **mass** (weight) in grams and kilograms.

- A **gram** (g) is about as heavy as a dollar bill or a large paper clip.

- A **kilogram** (kg) is about as heavy as your math textbook.

Metric Units of Mass

Unit	Abbreviation	Reference
gram	g	dollar bill or large paper clip
kilogram	kg	basketball
1 kilogram = 1,000 grams		

Example

Which is the best estimate for the mass of a pencil?

12 grams   12 kilograms

One gram is about the weight of a large paper clip. Twelve paper clips might be as heavy as a pencil.

One kilogram is about the weight of a basketball. Twelve basketballs are much heavier than a pencil.

The best estimate for the mass of a pencil is **12 grams.**

 page 432

Metric Units of Mass

Materials needed:

- gram-mass equivalent (e.g., a large paper clip)

- kilogram-mass equivalent (e.g., a basketball, student textbook)

Get two objects from your teacher. One will have the mass of a gram and one will have the mass of a kilogram. The kilogram is heavier.

Compare each item in the list below to your gram and kilogram masses. Then write each item in the correct column on the table.

worksheet	desk	tape dispenser
dot cube	pair of shoes	stick of gum
chalkboard eraser	computer	bicycle

Mass of Objects

Close to a gram	More than a gram, less then a kilogram	More than a kilogram

Lesson Practice

a. The mass of a dollar bill is about a gram. A kilogram of dollar bills would be about how many dollar bills?

_____ dollar bills $1,000 \text{ g} = 1 \text{ kg}$

b. Circle the better estimate for the mass of a month-old baby.

5 grams   5 kilograms

c. Arrange these objects in order from **least mass to greatest mass:**

your math book

your desk

a pencil

an eyelash

a paper clip

_____, _____, _____,
      least

_____, _____
        greatest

Written Practice page 433

1. The game _____ fair because Rick scores on _____

different numbers and Antonia scores on _____ different

numbers. So _____ is more likely to score.

> Use work area.

2. Complete the table.

Hours	1	2	3	4	5
Miles	40	80			

> Use work area.

3. _____ lb = 1 ton

See the *Student Reference Guide.*

4,000 lb = _____ tons

4. parallelogram with four right angles

5. Write the fractions shaded. Then compare the fractions.

Use work area.

6. Which does **not** equal 12?

A 1 × 12

B 2 × 6

C 3 × 4

D 6 × 6

7. 4 quarters ⟶ _____

8 nickels ⟶ _____

2 dimes ⟶ _____

1 penny ⟶ _+_____

8. a. digits: _____

b. words: _____

_____

Use work area.

© Saxon

9. Name each figure.

See the *Student Reference Guide.*

a. **b.**  **c.** **d.**

a. _____ b. _____

c. _____ d. _____

10. Complete this picture of a **cube.**

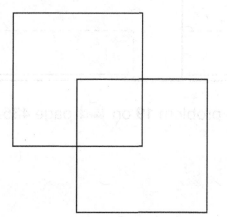

How many **edges?** _____

Use a manipulative for help.

Use work area.

11. Each square is 1 square centimeter.

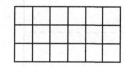

a. length   **b.** width

c. total tiles   **d.** area

a. _____ b. _____

c. _____ d. _____

12. Write as a multiplication problem. Find the total.

12 in. + 12 in. + 12 in. + 12 in. + 12 in. + 12 in.

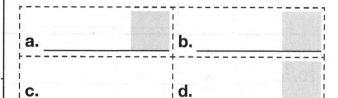

_____ × _____ = _____

13. a. $8 \times 7 =$

  b. $7 \times 6 =$

  a. _____

  c. $3 \times 7 =$

  b. _____

  c. _____

14. a. $4 \times 30 =$

  b. $6 \times 30 =$

  a. _____

  c. $8 \times 30 =$

  b. _____

  c. _____

15. 1 m = 100 cm

  2 m = _____ cm

16. $\begin{array}{r} \$587 \\ - \$295 \\ \hline \end{array}$

17. $\begin{array}{r} \$5.45 \\ + \$3.57 \\ \hline \end{array}$

18. What is the best estimate of the mass of a full-grown cat?

  4 kilograms   4 grams

19. Do problem **19** on 📖 page 435.

20. a. _____ × _____ × _____ = _____

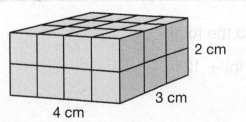

4 cm   3 cm   2 cm

  b. volume: _____

  Volume = length × width × height

  Use work area.

page 436

Focus on
- ## More About Geometric Solids

Teacher Notes:
- Review "Geometric Solids" on page 17 in the *Student Reference Guide*.
- Students need Geosolids to complete this Investigation.

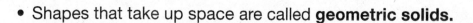

- Shapes that take up space are called **geometric solids.**

- Many solids have **faces, edges,** and **vertices.**

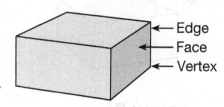

←— Edge
←— Face
←— Vertex

- A **face** is the flat side of a solid.

- An **edge** is where two or more faces meet.

- A **vertex** is where two or more edges meet.

Give the geometric name for each solid in problems **1–4.**
Tell the number and shape of the faces. Count the numbers of edges and vertices. Use the Geosolids to help you answer the questions.

1.

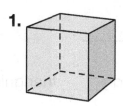

name: C_____

_____ square faces

_____ edges   _____ vertices

© Saxon

2.

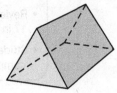

name: t_____ p_____

_____ rectangular faces and _____ triangular faces

_____ edges _____ vertices

3.

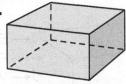

name: r_____ p_____

_____ rectangular faces

_____ edges _____ vertices

4.

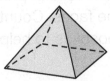

name: p_____

_____ square face and _____ triangular faces

_____ edges _____ vertices

© Saxon

• Some solids have *curved* surfaces instead of flat faces.

Give the geometric name for each solid in problems **5–7.**

5.

1 curved surface
2 flat surfaces shaped like circles

name: **C**_____

6.

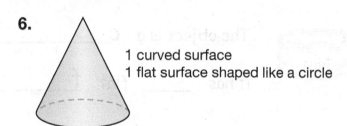

1 curved surface
1 flat surface shaped like a circle

name: **C**_____

7.

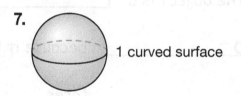

1 curved surface

name: **S**_____

 📖 page 437

Classifying Solids
Materials needed:
• none
Many real-world objects have the shape of geometric solids.

For each object shown below, write its geometric name and explain how you know that name is correct.

A

The object is a C_____ because it has ____ square f_____.

B

The object is a S_____ because

it has ____ curved surface and no flat surfaces.

C

Tuna

The object is a C_____ because

it has ____ flat f_____ and

____ curved surface.

D

Crackers

The object is a r_____

p_____ because it has ____

r_____ faces

E

The object is a t_____

p_____ because it has

3 r_____ faces and

2 t_____ faces.

© Saxon

F   The object is a C_____ because

it has 1 f_____ face and

1 c_____ surface.

Use the *Student Reference Guide* and manipulatives to help answer problems **8–12.**

8. Which geometric solid shown below does **not** belong with the others? How do you know?

A 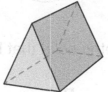   B

C    D

Figure _____ is different because it has no

_____ surfaces.

9. Circle the object that best represents a **triangular prism.**

A    B

C    D

10. Circle the geometric solid that has **two flat surfaces** and **one curved surface.**

A   B

C   D

11. Circle the geometric solid that has **eight vertices.**

A 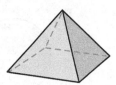   B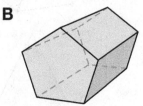

C 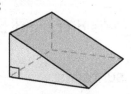   D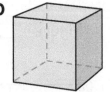

12. Circle the geometric name for this solid.

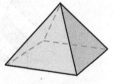

A pyramid   **B** rectangular prism

C triangular prism   **D** cube

Name _____

┌─────────────────────────────────────┐
│ **Teacher Note:**   │
│ • Introduce Hint #26 "Multiplication │
│   (Carrying on Fingers)."   │
└─────────────────────────────────────┘

• Multiplying Two-Digit Numbers, Part 1

New Concept

- Multiplying by 2 is **doubling.**
  The product is the same as adding twice.

$$
\begin{array}{r}
24 \\
\times\ \ 2 \\
\hline
48
\end{array}
\qquad
\begin{array}{r}
24 \\
+\ 24 \\
\hline
48
\end{array}
$$

- Here are the doubles facts:

$2 \times 0 = 0$	$2 \times 1 = 2$
$2 \times 2 = 4$	$2 \times 3 = 6$
$2 \times 4 = 8$	$2 \times 5 = 10$
$2 \times 6 = 12$	$2 \times 7 = 14$
$2 \times 8 = 16$	$2 \times 9 = 18$

- To double a two-digit number:

  1. Multiply the ones.

  Write the last digit of the product.
  If necessary, *carry the first digit on your fingers.*

  2. Multiply the tens.

  Add the carried digit to that product.
  Write the sum.

© Saxon

 page 441

Doubling Money

- This activity is optional.

Example

A ticket to the amusement park costs $34. How much would two tickets cost?

Multiply $34 by 2 to find the answer.

1. Multiply the ones digit: $4 \times 2 = 8$.

$$\begin{array}{r} \$3\boxed{4} \\ \times \quad \boxed{2} \\ \hline \$ \quad 8 \end{array}$$

2. Multiply the tens digit: $3 \times 2 = 6$.

$$\begin{array}{r} \$\boxed{3}\;4 \\ \times \quad \boxed{2} \\ \hline \$ 6\;8 \end{array}$$

Two tickets to the amusement park would cost **$68.**

Example

One yard is 36 inches. How many inches is two yards?

Multiply 36 inches by 2 to find the answer.

1. Multiply the ones digit: $6 \times 2 = 12$.
Write the 2 and *carry the 1* on a finger.

$$\begin{array}{r} 3\boxed{6} \\ \times \quad \boxed{2} \\ \hline 2 \end{array}$$

2. Multiply the tens digit: $3 \times 2 = 6$.
Add the carried 1 to 6 ($6 + 1 = 7$) and write the sum.

$$\begin{array}{r} \boxed{3}\;6 \\ \times \quad \boxed{2} \\ \hline 7\;2 \end{array}$$

Two yards is **72 inches.**

Find each product. Carry on your fingers.

a. $14
   ×   2

b.   43
   ×   2

c. $27
   ×   2

d.   39
   ×   2

e. July and August each have 31 days.

Altogether, how many days are

in July and August? _____

   31
   ×   2

f. One pair of shoes costs $45.

What would two pairs of shoes cost? _____

   $45
   ×   2

Written Practice   📖 page 442

1. 1 m = _____ cm

    3 m = _____ cm
    See the *Student Reference Guide.*

2.   100
     _73_

3. 2,000, 4,000, 6,000, _____, _____, _____, …

¦ Use work area. ¦

4. lunch time

_____:_____

5. Circle every multiplication fact that equals 24.

Use a multiplication table for help.

A 3×6

B 2×12

C 1×24

D 4×6

---

6. 5 quarters → _____

5 dimes → _____

5 nickels → _____

5 pennies → + _____

7. 3 tens and 4 thousands

A 34,000

B 4,003

C 4,030

D 30,004

---

8. $1 \text{ m} = $ _____ cm

$\frac{1}{2} \text{ m} = $ _____ cm

9. Carry on your fingers.

Use a multiplication table for help.

a. $\begin{array}{r} 24 \\ \times\ 2 \\ \hline \end{array}$ **b.** $\begin{array}{r} 48 \\ \times\ 2 \\ \hline \end{array}$

a. _____

b. _____

10. Each cube is 1 cubic inch.

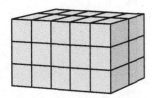

   a. cubes in each layer _____

   b. number of layers _____

   c. total number of cubes _____

   d. volume _____

      ⌐ Use work area. ¬

---

11. Write a fraction **equal to 1.**

   □
   —
   5

Write the mixed number

one and one fifth. _____

Which number is greater? _____

      ⌐ Use work area. ¬

12. Use a multiplication table for help.

   a. $9 \times 8 =$

   b. $7 \times 8 =$

   c. $3 \times 7 =$

   a. _____

   b. _____

   c. _____

---

13. See problem **13** on page 444.

   a. length

   b. width

   c. height

   d. name of the solid

      See the *Student Reference Guide.*

   a. _____

   b. _____

   c. _____

   d. _____

---

14. area of the top of the shape in problem **13**

15. Do problem **15** on  page 444.

16. Use a multiplication table for help.

a. $2 \times 5 \times 4 =$

b. $6 \times 50 =$

17. a. $4 \times 70 =$

b. $6 \times 60 =$

c. $9 \times 40 =$

a. _____

b. _____

c. _____

a. _____

b. _____

18. $ 10.00
     $\underline{-\ \$\ \ 5.60}$

19. $95
      $85
     $\underline{+\ \$75}$

20. a. least likely number

b. most likely number

c. fraction of the face with the number 2

a. _____ b. _____ c. _____

LESSON

82

📖 page 445

Name _____

Teacher Notes:

• Introduce Hint #27 "Ways to Show Division."

• Refer students to "Division" on page 8 in the *Student Reference Guide*.

• Students will need counters or tiles to complete the activity.

• Fair Share

New Concept

• Separating a group into smaller *equal* groups is **division.**

• To separate groups into 2 equal groups, **divide by 2.**

• To write a division, use a **division symbol** ÷ or a **division box** ⟍ .

• **Read the largest number first.**

24 ÷ 2 = 12 "24 divided by 2 equals 12."

$$2)\overline{24} \quad \overset{12}{} $$

"24 divided by 2 equals 12."

• Use a picture or manipulatives to divide a group by 2.

Example

Eighteen students line up in 2 equal rows. How many students are in each row? Use digits and symbols to show two different ways to write the division of 18 into 2 equal groups.

Draw a picture to solve the problem.

Draw a total of 18 circles in two equal rows. Each circle shows a student.

Each row is equal. Each row has 9 circles. There are **9 students** in each row.

Write the division with a division symbol and a division box.

$$18 \div 2 = 9 \qquad 2\overline{)18}^{\,9}$$

 page 446

Fair Share

Materials needed:

• counters or tiles

Use your textbook to complete this activity.

• To use a multiplication table to divide by 2:

    1. Find the **row** that starts with 2.

    2. Go to the right until you find the number you are dividing.

    3. Go up to the top of the column. The number at the top is the answer.

Example

Eighteen students line up in 2 equal rows. How many students are in each row? Use a multiplication table to find the answer.

1. Find the row that starts with 2.

2. Go to the right until you get to 18.

3. Go up to the top. The answer is 9.

	0	1	2	3	4	5	6	7	8	⑨
0	0	0	0	0	0	0	0	0	0	0
1	0	1	2	3	4	5	6	7	8	9
②	0	2	4	6	8	10	12	14	16	⑱

There are **9 students** in each row.

a. We find half of a number by dividing by 2. We can use all the fingers on both hands to show 10 divided by 2. Open both your hands. There are 10 fingers. Now close one hand. How many fingers do you count on your

open hand? _____ fingers

b. Use the picture to find half of 12. _____

c. Draw a total of 8 Xs on your paper arranged in 2 equal rows.

How many Xs are in each row? _____

Show two ways to write the division of 8 into 2 parts.

$8 \div$ _____ $=$ _____

d. Twenty students lined up in 2 equal rows. How many students were

in each row? _____ students

Use a multiplication table to divide.

📖 page 448

1. 1 km = _____ m

5 km = _____ m

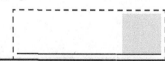

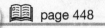

2. $189.00
    $ 13.23

3. twice as many as Monday
Carry on your fingers.

$$\begin{array}{r} 15 \\ \times\ \ 2 \\ \hline \end{array}$$

4. Which does **not** equal 18?

A 3×6 **B** 9×9

C 18×1 **D** 2×9

5. Bobby is five years old. Which of these could be his height?

A 100 m   **B** 100 cm   **C** 100 km

6. 1 hundred and 3 tens

7. What is **half** of 16?

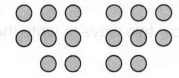

8. Draw a square with 5 cm sides.

Use work area.

© Saxon

9. a. perimeter of the square

    b. area of the square

10. a. $5 \times 4 \times 3 =$

    b. Carry on your fingers.

$$\begin{array}{r} 25 \\ \times\ \ 2 \\ \hline \end{array}$$

a. _____

b. _____

a. _____

b. _____

11. place value of the 2

751,<u>2</u>83

_____

12. Each cube is 1 cubic centimeter.

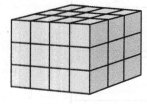

    a. cubes in each layer

    b. number of layers

    c. total number of cubes

    d. volume

a. _____

b. _____

c. _____

d. _____

13. a. $6 \times 7 =$

    b. $7 \times 80 =$

    c. $8 \times 90 =$

a. _____

b. _____

c. _____

14. $4.58
         + $8.97

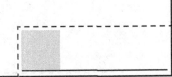

15. $800
         – $735

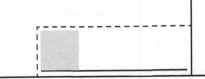

16.   24
         + _m_
         ———
         100

_m =_ _____

17. expanded form

57,240

_____ + _____ + _____ + _____

Use work area.

18. Name each polygon in problem **18** on page 449.

Count the sides.

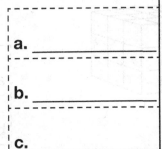

a. _____

b. _____

c. _____

19. Name each solid in problem **19** on page 449.

See the _Student Reference Guide._

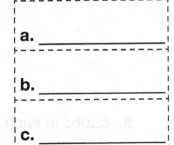

a. _____

b. _____

c. _____

20. Which is reasonable for the mass of a grape?

6 grams   6 kilograms

© Saxon

Name _____

📖 page 450

Teacher Notes:
- Review Hint #27 "Ways to Show Division."
- For additional practice, students may complete Targeted Practice 83.

• Finding Half of a Number

New Concept

- **Half** means *divide by 2*.

- Use a multiplication table to divide by 2.

  1. Find the **row** that starts with 2.

  2. **Go to the right** until you find the number you are dividing.

  3. **Go up** to the top of the column. The number at the top is the answer.

Example

Use a multiplication table to find half of 22.

1. Find the row that starts with 2.
2. Go to the right until you get to 22.
3. Go up to the top. The answer is 11.

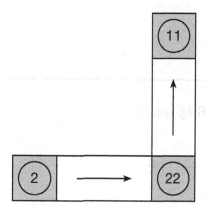

Half of 22 is **11**.

$$22 \div 2 = 11 \qquad 2\overline{)22} \;\; ^{11}$$

Use a multiplication table to divide by 2.

a. One day is 24 hours. How many hours is **half** of a day?

_____

b. Sixteen ounces equals a pound. How many ounces is **half** of a pound?

_____

c. $2\overline{)14}$ **d.** $8 \div 2 =$ _____

Written Practice page 452

1. $8.95
     $2.00

2. 10 pens for 89¢ each

    $10 \times 89¢ =$ _____ ¢

Write the product with a dollar
sign and decimal point.

3. What is **half** of 12?

Use a multiplication table to divide.

A $\frac{1}{2}$ **B** 6

C 2   **D** 12

4. Use a ruler to measure the distance in problem **4** on 📖 page 452.

Fortner to Mesa: _____ in.
Every inch is 100 miles. What is the distance from Fortner to Mesa?

---

5. morning

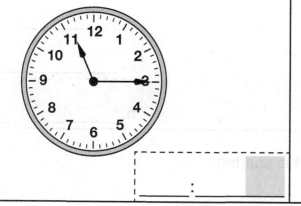

6. Write two different multiplication facts that have a **product** of 6.

_____ × _____ = 6

_____ × _____ = 6

Use work area.

7. expanded form

560

_____ + _____

8. a. 10 × 25¢ =

Write the product with a dollar sign and decimal point.

b. 7 × 40 =

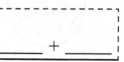

a.

b.

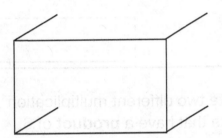

9. Which is a likely distance for the length of a race?

A 100 m   **B** 100 cm   **C** 100 km

10. Do problem **10** on page 453.

11. Complete this drawing of a rectangular prism.

a. number of **faces**

b. number of **vertices**

a. _____

b. _____

12. Write the fraction of each circle that is shaded.

_____   _____   _____   _____

Now write the fractions from **least to greatest.**

Use fraction pieces for help.

_____, _____, _____, _____

least   greatest

⌐ ‾ ‾ ‾ ‾ ‾ ‾ ‾ ‾ ⌐
  Use work area.
∟ _ _ _ _ _ _ _ _ ∟

532

© Saxon

13. Each square is 1 square foot.

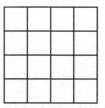

a. length

b. width

c. area

d. What special kind of rectangle is it?

a. _____

b. _____

c. _____

d. _____

---

14. Write as a multiplication problem. Find the total.

10 cm + 10 cm + 10 cm + 10 cm + 10 cm

_____ × _____ = _____

15. a. 4 × 80 =

b. 3 × 90 =

c. 6 × 70 =

a. _____

b. _____

c. _____

16.
```
  $ 35
  $ 47
+ $176
```

17.
```
  $12.48
− $ 6.97
```

18. Carry on your fingers.

$$\begin{array}{r} 57 \\ \times\ \ 2 \\ \hline \end{array}$$

---

19. $3 \times 4 \times 5 =$

---

20. Use a centimeter ruler to measure each distance in problem **20** on page 454.

   a. point A to point B

   b. point B to point C

   c. Add your answers to **a** and **b** to find the distance from point A to point C.

$$\begin{array}{r} + \\ \hline \end{array}$$

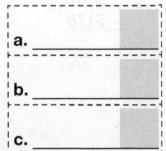

a. _____

b. _____

c. _____

Name _____

Teacher Note:
• Review Hint #26 "Multiplication (Carrying on Fingers)."

• Multiplying Two-Digit Numbers, Part 2

New Concept

• To multiply a two-digit number:

1. Multiply the ones.

2. Write the last digit of the product.

3. If necessary, *carry the first digit* on your fingers.

4. Multiply the tens.

5. *Add* the carried digit to that product.

Example

Find the product: 5 × 26

1. Multiply the ones: 6 × 5 = 30.

2. Write the 0.

3. *Carry the 3* on your fingers.

$$\begin{array}{r} 2\,6 \\ \times\ \ 5 \\ \hline 0 \end{array}$$

4. Multiply the tens: 2 × 5 = 10.

5. *Add* the carried 3 to 10 (3 + 10 = 13) and write the sum.

$$\begin{array}{r} 2\,6 \\ \times\ \ 5 \\ \hline 130 \end{array}$$

The product of 5 and 26 is **130.**

Find each product. Carry on your fingers.

a.   12
      $\times$ 4

b.   21
      $\times$ 5

c.   15
      $\times$ 4

d.   35
      $\times$ 3

e. A foot is 12 inches. The ceiling is 8 feet high. How many inches high

is the ceiling? _____

    12
  $\times$ 8

f. A pound is 16 ounces. Leon weighed 7 pounds when he was born.

How many ounces is 7 pounds? _____

    16
  $\times$ 7

Written Practice   📖 page 458

1. 7 classrooms with 30 students each

Carry on your fingers.

    30
  $\times$ 7

2.   72
        64

3. 10 stamps for 42¢ each

10 × 42¢ = _____ ¢

Write the product with a dollar
sign and decimal point.

4. 1 ton = _____ lb

7 tons = _____ lb

See the *Student Reference Guide.*

5. a.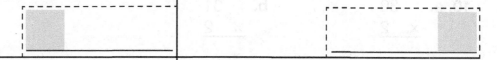
0   1

b.
6   7   8

a. _____

b. _____

6. 1 lb = 16 oz

half a pound = _____ oz

Use a multiplication table to divide.

7. Write three different multiplication
facts that equal 18.

1 × _____ = 18

2 × _____ = 18

3 × _____ = 18

8. In one hour, how far could they
have traveled along the open
highway?

A 100 m   **B** 100 cm   **C** 100 km

Use work area.

9. Do problem **9** on 📖 page 458.

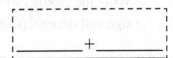

10. a. 30
　　　　 × 2

b. 31
　　 × 2

a. _____

b. _____

11. a. 31
　　　　 × 3

b. 31
　　 × 4

a. _____

b. _____

12. Each cube is 1 cubic inch.

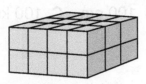

a. length

b. width

c. height

d. volume

　　Volume = length × width × height

a. _____

b. _____

c. _____

d. _____

© Saxon

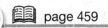

13. a.   80
        × 7

b.   60
        × 8

c.   60
        × 7

a. _____

b. _____

c. _____

14. $20.00
       − $12.87

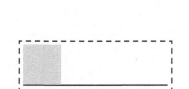

15. $0.96
       $0.87
     + $0.79

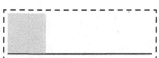

16. Carry on your fingers.

       $24
     ×   3

17. a. fraction name for 1

b. Shade the circle to show $\frac{4}{4}$.

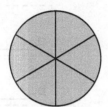

_____

┌─────────────┐
│ Use work area. │
└─────────────┘

18. dinner time

19. Do problem **19** on 📖 page 459.

20. Which best names the shape of the Earth?

See the *Student Reference Guide.*

A circle   **B** sphere

C rectangle   **D** cylinder

📖 page 460

Name _____

Using Manipulatives to Divide by a One-Digit Number

Teacher Notes:
- Introduce Hint #28 "Word Problem Cues, Part 2."
- Review Hint #27 "Ways to Show Division."
- Review "Word Problem Keywords" on page 6 and "Division" on page 8 in the *Student Reference Guide*.
- Students will need counters or tiles to complete the lesson.

New Concept

- Separating a group into smaller *equal* groups is **division.**

- Use a picture or manipulatives to divide a group into smaller equal groups.

Example

Fifteen students lined up in 3 equal rows. How many students were in each row? Use digits and symbols to show two different ways to write the division of 15 into 3 equal groups.

Draw a picture to solve the problem.

Draw a total of 15 circles in three equal rows. Each circle shows a student.

○ ○ ○ ○ ○
○ ○ ○ ○ ○
○ ○ ○ ○ ○

Each row is equal. Each row has 5 circles. There are **5 students** in each row.

Now write the division with a division symbol and a division box.

$$15 \div 3 = 5 \qquad 3\overline{)15}^{\,5}$$

 page 461

Equal Groups

Materials needed:
• counters or tiles

Use your textbook to complete this activity.

• To use a multiplication table to divide:

1. Find the **row** that starts with the *smaller* number (the number you are dividing by).

2. **Go to the right** until you find the *larger* number (the number you are dividing).

3. **Go up** to the top of the column. The number at the top is the answer.

Example

Fifteen students lined up in 3 equal rows. How many students were in each row? Use a multiplication table to find the answer.

1. Find the row that starts with the smaller number, 3.

2. Go to the right until you get to the larger number, 15.

3. Go up to the top. The answer is 5.

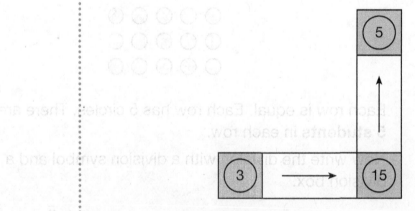

There are **5 students** in each row.

a. Eighteen books were stacked in **three equal piles.**

How many books were in each pile? _____

Show two ways to write the division.

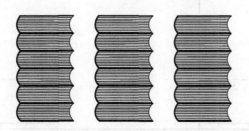

$18 \div 3 =$ _____

$3\overline{)18}$

b. Eighteen books were put in stacks with **3 books in each stack.**

How many stacks of books were there? _____

Draw stacks of 3 books until you get to 18 total books. Then show two ways to write the division.

$18 \div$ _____ $= 3$

$\overline{)18}^{3}$

Divide on a multiplication table to find each answer. Then show two ways to write the division.

c. Todd has 20 quarters. He puts 4 quarters in each stack.

How many stacks did he make? _____

$20 \div$ _____ $=$ _____

$\overline{)20}$

d. Becki cuts a 12-inch long ribbon into 4 equal pieces.

How long was each piece of ribbon? _____

$12 \div$ _____ $=$ _____

$\overline{)12}$

1. half of 18 cm

Use a multiplication table to divide.

2. $17.27

     $ 1.22

3. What **coins** should he get back?

     $1.00

   − $0.42

_____ quarters, _____ nickel, and _____ pennies

Use work area.

4. Double the rectangle in problem 4 on 📖 page 463.

   10

× _____

5. half of $14

Use a multiplication table to divide.

6. a.

    $23

  ×   3

b. Carry on your fingers.

    $23

  ×   4

7. 24 books in 3 equal stacks

Use a multiplication table to divide.

Use work area.

8. 24 books into stacks of 6

Use a multiplication table to divide.

9. Do problem **9** on  page 463.

_____ + _____

10. Each cube is 1 cubic inch.

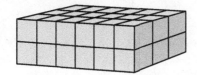

a. cubes in each layer

b. number of layers

c. total number of cubes

d. volume

a. _____   **b.** _____   **c.** _____   **d.** _____

11. a.
$$\begin{array}{r} 15 \\ + m \\ \hline 25 \end{array}$$

b.
$$\begin{array}{r} n \\ + 12 \\ \hline 20 \end{array}$$

a. $m =$ _____

b. $n =$ _____

12. a.
$$\begin{array}{r} 90 \\ \times 9 \\ \hline \end{array}$$

b.
$$\begin{array}{r} 80 \\ \times 8 \\ \hline \end{array}$$

c.
$$\begin{array}{r} 70 \\ \times 7 \\ \hline \end{array}$$

a. _____

b. _____

c. _____

13.
$$\begin{array}{r} \$786 \\ - \$694 \\ \hline \end{array}$$

14.
$$\begin{array}{r} \$3.50 \\ \$0.97 \\ + \$0.85 \\ \hline \end{array}$$

15. Carry on your fingers.
$$\begin{array}{r} 33 \\ \times 5 \\ \hline \end{array}$$

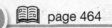

16. $4 \times 4 \times 4 =$
Carry on your fingers.

$$\begin{array}{r} 4 \\ \times\ 4 \\ \hline \end{array} \qquad \begin{array}{r} \\ \times\ 4 \\ \hline \end{array}$$

17. Do problem **17** on  page 464.

18. a. Draw a **square** with sides 6 cm long.

b. perimeter: _____

c. area: _____

Use work area.

19.

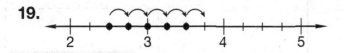

$2\frac{1}{2}, 2\frac{3}{4}, 3, 3\frac{1}{4}, 3\frac{1}{2},$ _____, _____, _____, _____, ...

Use work area.

20. Draw **two parallel line segments** that are **perpendicular** to these line segments.

Use work area.

Name _____

Teacher Notes:

• Review Hint #21 "Multiplication/ Division Fact Families" and Hint #27 "Ways to Show Division."

• Review "Missing Numbers" on page 7 and "Division" on page 8 in the *Student Reference Guide.*

• For additional practice, students may complete Targeted Practice 86.

• Division Facts
• Multiplication and Division Fact Families

New Concepts

• **Division Facts**

• In multiplication facts, the three numbers are called the **factors** and the **product.**

$$\text{factor} \times \text{factor} = \text{product}$$

• In division facts, the three numbers are called the **dividend,** the **divisor,** and the **quotient.**

• The **dividend** is the number *being divided.* The dividend is the largest number.

• The **divisor** is the number you are *dividing by.*

• The **quotient** is the *answer* in a division fact.

$$\text{dividend} \div \text{divisor} = \text{quotient}$$

$$\text{divisor} \overline{)\text{dividend}}^{\text{quotient}}$$

• **Multiplication and Division Fact Families**

• A **multiplication and division fact family** is a group of 3 numbers that make 2 multiplication facts and 2 division facts.

$4 \times 6 = 24$	$6 \times 4 = 24$
$24 \div 4 = 6$	$24 \div 6 = 4$

- The numbers at the bottom of the triangle *multiply* to the number at the top.

- When you learn **one** fact family, you know **four** facts.

Example

Write two multiplication facts and two division facts using the numbers 6, 7, and 42.

For the multiplication facts, the product has to be the biggest number. The other numbers can go in either order.

$$6 \times 7 = 42 \qquad 7 \times 6 = 42$$

For the division facts, the dividend has to be the biggest number. The other numbers can go in either order.

$$42 \div 6 = 7 \qquad 42 \div 7 = 6$$

- To find a *missing factor,* **divide.**

Example

Find the missing factor: $m \times 4 = 36$

Think of a multiplication problem with a missing factor as a division problem.

$$36 \div 4 = m$$

Because $36 \div 4 = 9$, we know that $9 \times 4 = 36$. The missing factor is **9.**

Lesson Practice

Find each quotient. Use a multiplication table for help.

a. $24 \div 3 =$ _____

b. $3\overline{)18}$

c. $18 \div 9 =$ _____

d. $2\overline{)8}$

e. $30 \div 5 =$ _____

f. $4\overline{)20}$

g. Write two multiplication facts and two division facts using the numbers **56, 7,** and **8.**

_____ × _____ = 56   _____ × _____ = 56

56 ÷ _____ = _____   56 ÷ _____ = _____

h. Write two multiplication facts and two division facts represented by the array below.

How many rows and columns?

☆ ☆ ☆ ☆ ☆ ☆ ☆
☆ ☆ ☆ ☆ ☆ ☆ ☆
☆ ☆ ☆ ☆ ☆ ☆ ☆

Find each missing factor.

i. $6 \times \square = 42$

Divide.

$\overline{)42}$

$\square =$ _____

j. $n \times 3 = 27$

Divide.

$\overline{)27}$

$n =$ _____

Written Practice page 468

1. $100
    $ 64

2. 10 cards for $0.35 each

$10 \times \$0.35 = \$$_____

© Saxon

3. See 📖 page 468.

a. digits: _____

b. words: _____

_____

‚‗‗‗‗‗‗‗‗‗‗‗‗‗‗‗‗‗‗‗‚
¦ Use work area. ¦
‚‗‗‗‗‗‗‗‗‗‗‗‗‗‗‗‗‗‗‗‚

---

4. a. Measure and label the sides of the triangle in **centimeters.**

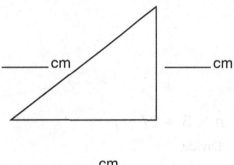

_____ cm

_____ cm

_____ cm

b. perimeter: _____

‚‗‗‗‗‗‗‗‗‗‗‗‗‗‗‗‗‗‗‗‚
¦ Use work area. ¦
‚‗‗‗‗‗‗‗‗‗‗‗‗‗‗‗‗‗‗‗‚

5. a. Complete this triangle **congruent** to the triangle in problem **4.**

Congruent means same size and shape.

3 cm

b. What kind of triangle is it?

_____

See the *Student Reference Guide.*

‚‗‗‗‗‗‗‗‗‗‗‗‗‗‗‗‗‗‗‗‚
¦ Use work area. ¦
‚‗‗‗‗‗‗‗‗‗‗‗‗‗‗‗‗‗‗‗‚

---

6. 10 quarters   ⟶

10 dimes   ⟶

10 nickels   ⟶

10 pennies   ⟶   +_____

© Saxon

7. half of a dozen

Use a multiplication table to divide.

_____

8. 1 ton = _____ lb

8 tons = _____ lb

See the *Student Reference Guide.*

9. fact family

Use work area.

10. What is the best measure of the mass of a raisin?

A 1 gram   **B** 1 kilogram

11. The picture shows the answer to which subtraction?

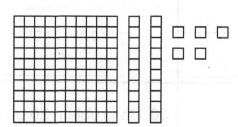

A 375	**B** 125	**C** 750
− 250	− 50	− 200

_____

12. Carry on your fingers.

a.   42
      × 8

b. Write your answer with a dollar sign and decimal point.

     34¢
   × 4

a. _____

b. _____

13.

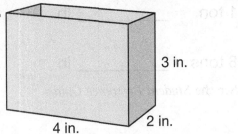

3 in.

4 in. 2 in.

a. cubes in bottom layer

b. number of layers

c. volume

Volume = length × width × height

a. _____

b. _____

c. _____

14. a.   90
         × 6

b.   80
       × 4

c.   60
       × 3

a. _____

b. _____

c. _____

15. $300
        − $166

16. $3.75
        + $2.87

17. 8 × 9 × 10 =

18. Divide.

       6
     × n   →   ⁾42
      42

n = _____

19. four and three fourths

_____

20. Do problem **20** on page 470.

_____

© Saxon

Name _____

Teacher Notes:

• Introduce Hint #29 "Measuring Liquids and Capacities of Containers."

• Refer students to "Liquids" on page 1 in the *Student Reference Guide.*

• Review "Equivalence Table for Units" on page 1 in the *Student Reference Guide.*

• Students will need a measuring cup, containers, and rice or other small objects to complete the activity.

• Capacity

New Concept

• **Capacity** is the amount of liquid a container can hold.

• In the United States, we measure capacity in units of **ounces** (oz), **cups** (c), **pints** (pt), **quarts** (qt), and **gallons** (gal).

• The chart below shows the relationships between cups, pints, quarts, and a gallon.

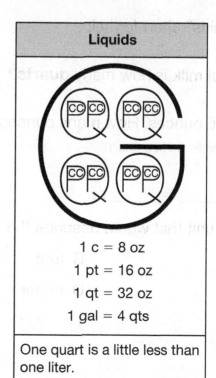

Liquids

1 c = 8 oz
1 pt = 16 oz
1 qt = 32 oz
1 gal = 4 qts

One quart is a little less than one liter.

 page 472

Measuring Capacity

Materials needed:

- measuring cup
- pint, quart, half gallon, and gallon containers
- rice, pinto beans, or other small objects
- funnel (optional)

Use your textbook to complete this activity.

- In the metric system, we measure capacity in units of **liters.**

- **One liter is a little more than a quart.**

  2 liters is a little more than a half gallon.

  4 liters is a little more than a gallon.

Lesson Practice

Use the "Liquids" chart for help.

a. A **gallon** of milk is how many **quarts?** _____ qt

b. A pint is 16 ounces. How many ounces is a quart? _____ oz

How many pints are in a quart?

16 oz × _____ = _____ oz

c. Circle the unit that would describe the amount of juice in a container.

A quart   **B** foot

C pound   **D** meter

d. Todd drank a glass of juice. Circle the measure below that best describes the amount of juice in a glass.

A 10 ounces

B 10 cups

C 10 pints

D 10 quarts

Written Practice page 474

1. 62

_____ freezing point of water in °F

2. half of 18

Use a multiplication table to divide.

3. sequence of doubles

Monday: 1 mi

Tuesday: 2 mi

Wednesday: 4 mi

Thursday: _____ mi

Friday: _____ mi

Saturday: _____ mi

4. half of the number of months in a year

5. What coins should he get back?

$2.00
− $1.39

_____ quarters, _____ dime, _____ penny

Use work area.

6. shortest to longest

meter   kilometer   centimeter

_____ , _____ , _____

shortest   longest

Use work area.

---

7. One quart is what **fraction** of a gallon?

How many quarts in a gallon?

---

8. The picture shows the answer to which multiplication?

A	21	**B**	31
	× 3		× 4

C	41	**D**	12
	× 3		× 3

---

9. Carry on your fingers.

a.   34
        × 6

b. Write your answer with a dollar sign and decimal point.

46¢
× 3

a. _____

b. _____

10. Do problem **10** on 📖 page 475.

© Saxon

11. A liter is closest in measure to a

　A pint.　　　**B** quart.

　C half-gallon.　**D** gallon.

_____

12. Divide.

$$\begin{array}{r} 7 \\ \times\ m \\ \hline 28 \end{array}$$ → $\overline{)28}$

$m =$ _____

13. sequence of doubles

1, 2, 4, 8, 16, _____, _____,

_____, ...

Use work area.

14.　$8.96
　　+ $4.78

15.　$11.00
　　− $ 5.75

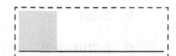

16. 5 × 5 × 5 =

Carry on your fingers.

$$\begin{array}{r} 5 \\ \times\ 5 \end{array}\qquad \begin{array}{r} \\ \times\ 5 \end{array}$$

_____

17. $6\overline{)42}$

Use a multiplication table to divide.

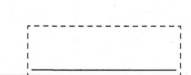

18. fact family

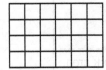

$\times$ _____ $\times$ _____ $\overline{)}$ $\overline{)}$

Use work area.

19. Each square is 1 square foot.

a. length

b. width

c. area

d. perimeter

a. _____

b. _____

c. _____

d. _____

20. Do problem **20** on page 475.

© Saxon

 page 476

Name _____

Teacher Notes:
- Refer students to "Even and Odd" on page 13 in the *Student Reference Guide.*
- Students will need counters to complete the activity.

• Even and Odd Numbers

New Concept

- **Even numbers** are the numbers we say when we count up from zero by 2.

  0, 2, 4, 6, 8, 10, 12, …

- **Odd numbers** are the numbers we say when we count up from one by 2.

  1, 3, 5, 7, 9, 11, 13, …

- If the **last digit** of a big number is *even,* then *the number is even.*

- If the **last digit** of a big number is *odd,* then *the number is odd.*

Example

There are 365 days in a common year. Is 365 even or odd?

The last digit of 365 is 5.

Five is an odd number, so 365 is **odd.**

- Even numbers can be divided into two equal groups.

- Odd numbers cannot be divided into two equal groups.

Activity  page 477

Even and Odd Numbers

Materials needed:
- counters

Use your textbook to complete this activity.

a. Circle the **even** number.

A 3   **B** 13

C 23   **D** 32

b. Can **28** students line up into two equal rows? Explain your answer.

Twenty-eight is an _____ number. All _____ numbers

can be divided into two equal groups, so 28 students _____ line

up in two equal rows.

c. Simon has $7. Nathan has $7. If they put their money together, will they

have an even number of dollars or an odd number of dollars? _____

$7 + $7 = $_____

d. Circle the name of the month that has an even number of days.

A July   **B** August

C September   **D** October

Written Practice   📖 page 479

1. $2.24
     $1.89
   + $1.18

2. Use your answer from problem **1.**

   $10.00

© Saxon

3. two hundred fifty thousand

4. half of a foot in inches

Use a multiplication table to divide.

5. Shade the circles to show $2\frac{1}{2}$.

 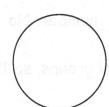 

Use work area.

6. Double each number.

a. $\begin{array}{r} 100 \\ \times\ \ 2 \\ \hline \end{array}$

b. $\begin{array}{r} 30 \\ \times\ \ 2 \\ \hline \end{array}$

a. _____

b. _____

7. Find **half** of each number.

Use a multiplication table to divide.

a. $2\overline{)10}$

b. $2\overline{)30}$

a. _____

b. _____

8. Which is an **even** number?

A 365 **B** 536

C 563 **D** 635

9. Can 15 counters be put into 2 equal groups?

Fifteen is an _____ number. No _____ number

can be divided into two equal groups, so 15 counters _____

be put into two equal groups.

Use work area.

10. a. $\begin{array}{r} 30 \\ \times\ \ 5 \\ \hline \end{array}$

b. Carry on your fingers.

$\begin{array}{r} \$24 \\ \times\ \ 4 \\ \hline \end{array}$

a. _____

b. _____

11. a. 1 quart = _____ pints

b. A pint is what **fraction** of a quart?

See the *Student Reference Guide.*

a. _____

b. _____

12. Use a multiplication table to divide.

    a. $8\overline{)48}$

    b. $36 \div 4 =$

a. _____

b. _____

13. expanded form

    521,769

    _____ + _____ + _____ + _____

    + _____ + _____

Use work area.

14. sequence of halves

    64, 32, 16, _____, _____, _____, ...

Use work area.

15. $496
   + $467

16. $10.00
   − $ 9.48

17. $4 \times 5 \times 6 =$

$$\begin{array}{r} 4 \\ \times\ 5 \\ \hline \end{array}$$

$$\times\ 6$$

18. Carry on your fingers.

$$\begin{array}{r} 36 \\ \times\ \ \ 3 \\ \hline \end{array}$$

19. Divide.

$$\begin{array}{r} 9 \\ \times\ n \\ \hline 72 \end{array} \longrightarrow \overline{}$$

$$n =$$

20. Measure the sides in centimeters and label the picture.

_____ cm

_____ cm

a. length

b. width

c. perimeter

Perimeter $\longrightarrow$ Add all sides.

d. area

Area = length $\times$ width

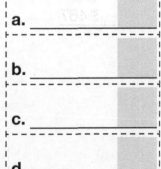

a. _____

b. _____

c. _____

d. _____

© Saxon

• Using a Multiplication Table to Divide by a One-Digit Number

New Concept

- To use a multiplication table to divide:

  1. Find the **row** that starts with the *smaller* number (the divisor).

  2. **Go to the right** until you find the *larger* number (the dividend).

  3. **Go up** to the top of the column. The number at the top is the quotient.

Example

For Game Day the teacher divided the 32 students into 4 equal teams. How many students were on each team?

The cue words *divided* and *each* help us see that this is a division problem.

The smaller number, 4, is the number we are dividing by. The larger number, 32, is the number we are dividing.

$$32 \div 4 =$$

1. Find the row that starts with 4.

2. Go to the right until we get to 32.

© Saxon

3. Go up to the top. The answer is 8.

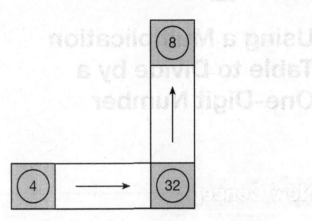

There were **8 students** on each team.

Lesson Practice

a. There are 12 inches in a foot. How many feet is 60 inches?

$12\overline{)60}$

b. Derek placed 32 books in 4 equal stacks. How many books were in each stack? _____

$32 \div 4 =$

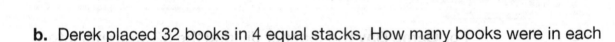

Use a multiplication table to find each quotient.

c. $56 \div 8 =$ _____   **d.** $84 \div 7 =$ _____

e. $9\overline{)72}$ **f.** $6\overline{)54}$

© Saxon

1. 5 erasers for 32¢ each

$$\begin{array}{r} 32¢ \\ \times 5 \\ \hline \end{array}$$

Write your answer with a dollar sign and decimal point.

2.

$$\begin{array}{r} 900 \\ \underline{625} \\ \end{array}$$

3. half of a dozen = _____

half of that number = _____

Use a multiplication table to divide.

4. 1 m   = _____ cm

$\frac{1}{2}$ meter = _____ cm

See the *Student Reference Guide*.

5. Instead of multiplying by 4, **double** twice.

a.   20
$\times 2$ $\times 2$

b.   21
$\times 2$ $\times 2$

a. _____

b. _____

© saxon

6. Carry on your fingers.

   a. $\begin{array}{r}\$14\\ \times\quad 6\\ \hline\end{array}$

   b. $\begin{array}{r}14¢\\ \times\quad 7\\ \hline\end{array}$

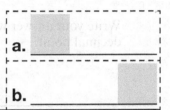

a. _____

b. _____

7. Which is an **even** number of cents?

A penny = _____¢

B nickel = _____¢

C dime   = _____¢

D quarter = _____¢

_____

8. How much is left in a gallon after one $\frac{1}{2}$ gallon and one quart are taken away?

See the *Student Reference Guide.*

1 gallon − $\frac{1}{2}$ gallon − 1 quart

1 gallon = _____ quarts

$\frac{1}{2}$ gallon = _____ quarts

© Saxon

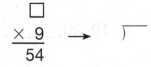

9. fact family

$\times$ ___ $\times$ ___) ‾‾) ‾‾

Use work area.

10. Divide.

$\square =$ ___

11. Do problem **11** on page 484.

12. The picture shows the answer to which multiplication?

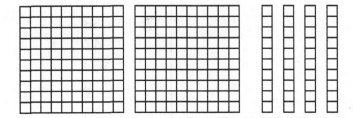

A 12
$\times$ 2

B 10 $\times$ 24 =

C 51
$\times$ 4

D 20
$\times$ 4

13. half of $24

Use a multiplication table to divide.

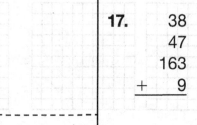

14. sequence of **doubles**

5, 10, 20, _____, _____, _____, ...

Use work area.

15. Use a multiplication table to divide.

    a. 24 ÷ 4 =

    b. 24 ÷ 6 =

    c. 24 ÷ 8 =

a. _____

b. _____

c. _____

16. $1.00
    − $0.42

17.   38
        47
     163
   +   9

18. $63
  + $45

19. $4 \times 3 \times 10 =$

20. Do problem **20** on page 485.

📖 page 486

• Equal Groups Problems, Part 2

Teacher Notes:
• Review Hint #28 "Word Problem Cues, Part 2."
• Review "Word Problem Keywords" on page 6 in the *Student Reference Guide*.

Name _____

New Concept

• Equal-groups stories have a multiplication pattern.

 Number of groups × Number in each group = Total

• The cue word for equal-groups stories is *each.*

• If the total is given, **divide** to find the answer.

Example

Twenty-eight children are going on a field trip. Seven cars are available to drive the children.

If the children are divided into equal groups, how many children will ride in each car?

The cue words *divided* and *each* tell us that this is an equal-groups story.

The total number of children is given: 28.

Only one of the factors, 7, is given. The other factor is missing.

$$7 \times ? = 28$$

To find a missing factor, we divide. We can find the answer on a multiplication table or by knowing the multiplication/division facts.

$$28 \div 7 = 4$$

Four children will ride in each car.

a. Sylvester has 40 pennies. He puts them in stacks with 5 pennies in **each** stack.

How many stacks does he make? _____

$40 \div 5 = ?$

b. There are 30 desks in the room. The teacher wants to arrange the desks

in 6 equal rows. How many desks will be in **each** row? _____

$6\overline{)30}$

Written Practice

📖 page 488

1. 1 BIG step   = 1 yard

1 BIG step   = _____ feet

12 BIG steps = _____ feet

2. $365
    $ 70
  _____

3. 16,000

_____

⌐ ⌐ ⌐ ⌐ ⌐ ⌐ ⌐
Use work area.
⌐ ⌐ ⌐ ⌐ ⌐ ⌐ ⌐

4. a. nearest hundred

$389 →

b. nearest hundred

$315 →

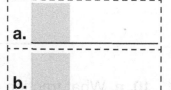

5. Estimate the total cost.

$389 →

$315 → + ___

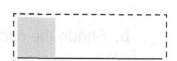

6. half of 80 seconds

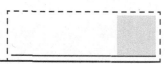

7. Instead of multiplying by 4, **double** twice.

a.
$$\begin{array}{r} 30 \\ \times\ 2 \end{array} \qquad \times\ 2$$

b. Carry on your fingers.

$$\begin{array}{r} 15 \\ \times\ 2 \end{array} \qquad \times\ 2$$

8. 30 desks with 5 desks in **each** row

Use a multiplication table to divide.

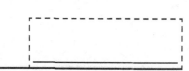

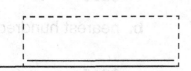

9. Do problem **9** on page 489.

_____

10. a. What fraction equal to $\frac{1}{2}$ does the shaded circle show? _____

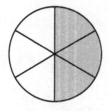

b. Shade the circle to show a fraction equal to $\frac{1}{2}$ with a **denominator** of 4.

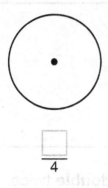

$\frac{\square}{4}$

Use work area.

11. Carry on your fingers.

a. $25
    × 6

b. Write your answer with a dollar sign and decimal point.

    15¢
    × 7

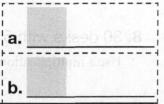

a.

b.

© Saxon

12.
```
    48
  –  w
  ───
    29
```

w = _____

Use work area.

13. sequence of **halves**

160, 80, 40, _____, _____, _____, ...

14. Use a multiplication table to divide.

a. 25 ÷ 5 =

a. _____

b. 21 ÷ 3 =

b. _____

c. 20 ÷ 4 =

c. _____

15. 5 × 6 × 7 =

```
    5
  × 6          × 7
```

_____

16.
```
   $5.00
 – $2.34
```

17. a.
```
    90
  ×  4
```

b.
```
    90
  ×  7
```

c.
```
    23
  × 10
```

a. _____

b. _____

c. _____

18. Which does **not** have an *obtuse angle*?

A 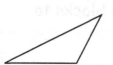 B   C   D

_____

© Saxon

19. Do problem **19** on 📖 page 490.

┌─────────────┐
│   │
│_____│
└─────────────┘

20. The map below shows Andy's home and Andy's school. Write directions **from Andy's home to school.**

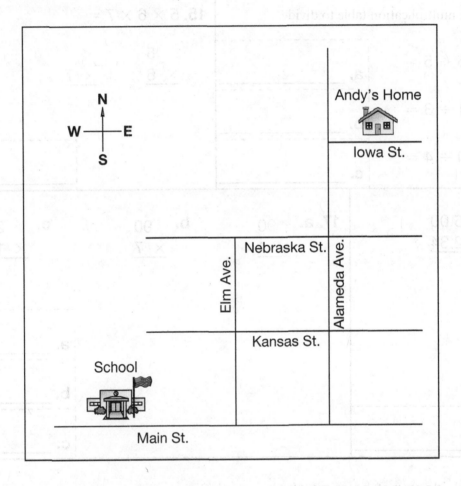

Start at Andy's home. Go west to _____ Avenue. Turn

_____ and go _____ 3 blocks to

_____ St. Turn right and go _____ 2 blocks

to school.

┌─────────────────┐
┆ Use work area. ┆
└─────────────────┘

Teacher Note:
• Students need scissors, a mirror, and a copy of **Lesson Activity 30** to complete this Investigation.

 page 491

Focus on
• Symmetry, Part 2

- A **line of symmetry** divides a figure into *mirror images.*

- Figures may have one line of symmetry, two lines of symmetry, or more.

- Some figures have no lines of symmetry.

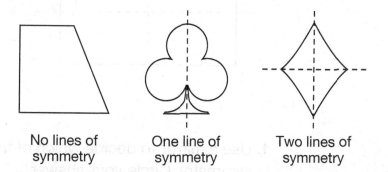

No lines of symmetry   One line of symmetry   Two lines of symmetry

- When a figure is folded across a line of symmetry, the two halves match exactly.

- Use this idea to create **symmetrical figures.**

 page 491

Creating Symmetrical Figures

Materials needed:

- 2 sheets of paper

- scissors

Use your textbook to complete this activity.

© Saxon

- We can use a mirror to find lines of symmetry in a figure.

- Place a mirror on the lines of symmetry in the figures below.

- When the mirror is placed correctly, you will see half of the original figure on your page and half of the figure "inside" the mirror.

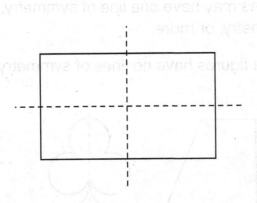

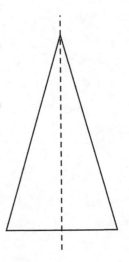

1. Use a mirror to decide which of these letters has a line of symmetry. Circle your answer.

A   **R**   B   **S**

C   **T**   D   **U**

2. Use a mirror to decide which of these quadrilaterals has a line of symmetry. Circle your answer.

A

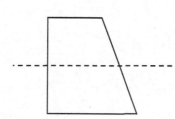

B

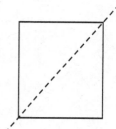

C

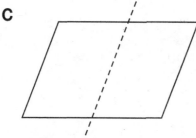

 **Activity 2** 📖 page 493

Lines of Symmetry

Materials needed:

- **Lesson Activity 30**

- ruler

- mirror

Get a copy of **Lesson Activity 30.** Use a mirror to look for lines of symmetry in the four shapes. When you find a line of symmetry, use a ruler to draw the line.

One shape on **Lesson Activity 30** has **one** line of symmetry.

One shape has **two** lines of symmetry.

One shape has **four** lines of symmetry.

One shape has **no** lines of symmetry. Circle that figure.

Try to find them all!

Name _____

Teacher Note:
• Review Hint #26 "Multiplication (Carrying on Fingers)."

• Multiplying Three-Digit Numbers, Part 1

New Concept

• To multiply a three-digit number:

   1. Multiply the ones.
   2. Multiply the tens.
   3. Multiply the hundreds.

• When a product is more than 10, write the ones and *carry on your fingers.* Add the carried number to the next product.

• Multiply every digit even if the digit is 0.

Example

Multiply: 7 × $250

1. Multiply the ones digit: 7 × 0 = 0.
Write 0 below the multiplication bar.

$$
\begin{array}{r}
\$2\,5\,0 \\
\times \quad\ 7 \\
\hline
0
\end{array}
$$

2. Multiply the tens digit: 7 × 5 = 35.
Write the 5 and carry the 3 on your fingers.

$$
\begin{array}{r}
\$2\,5\,0 \\
\times \quad\ 7 \\
\hline
5\ 0
\end{array}
$$

© Saxon

3. Multiply the hundreds digit: $7 \times 2 = 14$.
   Add 3 for the carried number: $14 + 3 = 17$.

$$\begin{array}{r} \$2\,5\,0 \\ \times\quad 7 \\ \hline \$1\,7\,5\,0 \end{array}$$

The product of 7 and $250 is **$1,750.**

Activity 📖 page 496

Estimation by Volume
This activity is optional.

Lesson Practice

Find each product. Carry on your fingers.

a. $\begin{array}{r} 400 \\ \times\quad 7 \\ \hline \end{array}$ **b.** $\begin{array}{r} \$300 \\ \times\quad 8 \\ \hline \end{array}$ **c.** $\begin{array}{r} 340 \\ \times\quad 6 \\ \hline \end{array}$ **d.** $\begin{array}{r} \$750 \\ \times\quad 4 \\ \hline \end{array}$

Written Practice 📖 page 497

1. each

Use a multiplication table to divide.

© Saxon

2. More likely, equally likely or less likely to draw a red marble?

Half of 18 marbles = _____ red

Half of 18 marbles = _____ blue

3. See the *Student Reference Guide* for help.

4. 18 grapes in 2 equal groups

Use a multiplication table to divide.

$$)\overline{}$$

5. sequence of **doubles**

$\frac{1}{2}$, 1, 2, _____ , _____ , _____ , ...

Use work area.

6.   76
      × 2

7. The picture shows the answer to which multiplication?

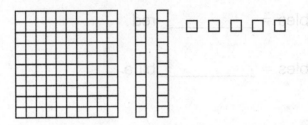

A $25 \times 10 =$

B $\begin{array}{r} 25 \\ \times\ \ 5 \\ \hline \end{array}$

C $\begin{array}{r} 21 \\ \times\ \ 5 \\ \hline \end{array}$

D $\begin{array}{r} 20 \\ \times\ \ 6 \\ \hline \end{array}$

8. 1 gal = _____ pt

9. The jar is $\frac{1}{2}$ full.

$200 \times 2 =$ _____ $\begin{array}{r} 200 \\ \times\ \ \ 2 \\ \hline \end{array}$

Use work area.

© Saxon

10.
$$\begin{array}{r} 20 \\ 30 \\ 40 \\ +\ m \\ \hline 100 \end{array}$$

$m = \underline{\hspace{3cm}}$

11. a.
$$\begin{array}{r} 60 \\ \times\ \ 3 \\ \hline \end{array}$$

b.
$$\begin{array}{r} 40 \\ \times\ \ 9 \\ \hline \end{array}$$

a. _____

b. _____

12. Complete this **rectangle** that is $1\frac{1}{4}$ inches long and $\frac{3}{4}$ inches wide. Then draw two lines of symmetry on the rectangle.

Use work area.

13. Use a multiplication table to divide.

a. $18 \div 3 =$

b. $18 \div 2 =$

c. $16 \div 8 =$

a. _____

b. _____

c. _____

14.
$$\begin{array}{r} \$6.75 \\ -\ \$5.68 \\ \hline \end{array}$$

15.
$$\begin{array}{r} \$1.00 \\ -\ \$0.47 \\ \hline \end{array}$$

16. 132
× 2

17. 100
× 6

18. 32
× 5

19. 600
× 5

20. a. Use a ruler to complete this rectangle that is 4 inches long and 3 inches wide.

4 in.

b. perimeter

b. _____

c. area

c. _____

Name _____

Teacher Note:
- For additional practice, students may complete Targeted Practice 92.

• Parentheses
• Using Compatible Numbers, Part 1

New Concept

- **Parentheses** tell us which part of a problem to do first.

• **Parentheses**
  - **Work inside the parentheses first.**

Example

Simplify: 12 − (6 − 2)

Do parentheses first: $6 - 2 = 4$.

Then we finish the problem.

$$12 - (6 - 2) =$$

$$\downarrow$$

$$12 - 4 = \mathbf{8}$$

Example

• **Using Compatible Numbers, Part 1**

- **Compatible numbers** are numbers that can be added or subtracted in your head.

- In an addition problem we can add the numbers in any order. Add the compatible numbers first.

- Look for numbers that add to 10 or 100.

$10 + 90 = 100$	$20 + 80 = 100$
$30 + 70 = 100$	$40 + 60 = 100$
$50 + 50 = 100$	$25 + 75 = 100$

© Saxon

Example

Add: 75 + 80 + 25

75 + 25 = 100. Add those numbers first in your head.

Add 100 + 80 to find the sum.

$$100 + 80 = \mathbf{180}$$

- We can use **compatible numbers** to estimate. Change the numbers in a problem to numbers that end in 25, 50, or 75.

Example

Jasmine had $8.79. She spent $4.24 at lunch. About how much money does Jasmine have left?

The word *about* tells us to estimate. We see that $8.79 is close to $8.75 and $4.24 is close to $4.25.

$$\begin{array}{r} \$8.75 \\ - \ \$4.25 \\ \hline \$4.50 \end{array}$$

Jasmine has about $4.50 left.

Lesson Practice

Work inside the parentheses first.

a. $12 - (6 \div 2)$

$\downarrow$

12 − _____ = _____

b. $(12 - 6) \div 2$

$\downarrow$

_____ ÷ 2 = _____

c. $12 \div (6 - 2)$

$\downarrow$

12 ÷ _____ = _____

d. $(12 \div 6) - 2$

$\downarrow$

_____ − 2 = _____

e. Compare: $(12 - 6) - 2$ $\qquad$ $12 - (6 - 2)$

$\downarrow$ $\qquad\qquad\qquad\qquad\qquad$ $\downarrow$

_____ $- 2 =$ $\qquad\qquad\qquad$ $12 -$ _____ $=$

For **f** and **g,** add compatible numbers first in your head. Then find the sum.

f. $30 + \overset{\bullet}{90} + \overset{\bullet}{110} =$ _____

g. $2 + \overset{\bullet}{7} + \overset{\bullet}{3} + \underset{\bullet}{9} + \underset{\bullet}{1} =$ _____

h. Paolo spilled the puzzle pieces on the playground. The puzzle had 800 pieces but Paolo could only find 627. **About** how many puzzle pieces were lost? Use compatible numbers to find your answer.

627 is close to 625.

$\qquad$ 800

$\qquad$ $-$ _____

(**Written Practice**) page 502

1. $ \$295.00$
$ \underline{\$\ \ 20.65}$

2. Use fraction manipulatives to compare.

$\dfrac{3}{4}$ $\bigcirc$ $\dfrac{1}{2}$

- - - - - - - - -
Use work area.
- - - - - - - - -

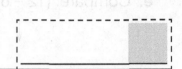

3. 24 pounds in 2 equal groups

4. Complete the **rectangular prism** below.

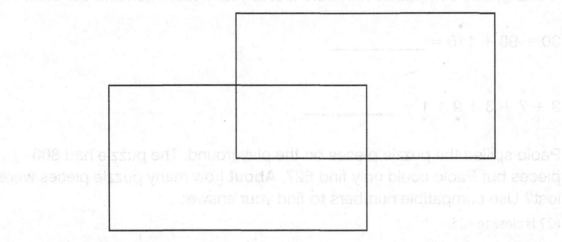

How many

a. faces?

b. edges?

c. vertices?

Use a manipulative for help.

a. _____

b. _____

c. _____

5. expanded form

895,283

_____ + _____ + _____ + ____ + ____ + ____

Use work area.

6. number of days in 1 year

× 2

© Saxon

7. Use compatible numbers to estimate.

$$824 \rightarrow 825$$
$$747 \rightarrow +\ 750$$

8. Each cube is 1 cubic inch.

    a. cubes in each layer   **b.** number of layers

    c. total number of cubes   **d.** volume

$$\text{Volume} = \text{length} \times \text{width} \times \text{height}$$

a. _____	b. _____
c. _____	d. _____

9. Estimate the sum.

$395 →

$598 → + _____

10.
$$\begin{array}{r} 60 \\ \times\ \ 4 \\ \hline \end{array}$$

11.
$$\begin{array}{r} 75 \\ \times\ \ 7 \\ \hline \end{array}$$

12. What **coins** should he get back?

$$\begin{array}{r} \$5.00 \\ -\ \$4.39 \\ \hline \end{array}$$

_____ quarters, _____ dime, _____ penny

      Use work area.

13. Write a multiplication fact for this rectangle.

_____ ✕ _____ = _____

14. 48, 24, 12, _____, _____, …

Use work area.

15. a. 30 ÷ 6 =

b. 35 ÷ 5 =

c. 32 ÷ 4 =

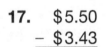

a. _____

b. _____

c. _____

16. $100 − ($62 + $9)

parentheses first

$62
+ $ 9

$100

−

17. $5.50
  − $3.43

18. (7 ✕ 80) + 40

parentheses first

80
✕ 7   +   40

19.   12
   ✕ 5

20. Do problem **20** on 📖 page 503.

© Saxon

Name _____

Teacher Note:
• Review Hint #11 "Estimating or Rounding."

• Estimating Products

New Concept

• To estimate a product:
  1. Round the larger factor.
  2. Multiply.

• Look for the cue word **about** to tell you to estimate.

Example

Tickets to the professional basketball game were $38 each. Mr. Jones wanted to buy 4 tickets. Estimate the total price of the 4 tickets.

1. Round the larger factor, $38.
   Because 8 is more than 5, round $38 up to $40.

2. Multiply to estimate the product.

$$\$38 \quad \longrightarrow \quad \begin{array}{r} \$40 \\ \times \quad 4 \\ \hline \$160 \end{array}$$

The total price of the tickets is **about $160.**

Lesson Practice

a. Estimate the total price of 4 water-park tickets at $19 each.

$$\$19 \quad \longrightarrow$$

$$\times \quad 4$$

b. If tickets to the football game are $32 each, about how much would

5 tickets cost? _____

$$\$32 \quad \rightarrow$$

$$\times \quad 5$$

c. Every day Alida walks around the track 4 times. She counted 489 steps for one lap. About how many steps does she take walking 4 laps?

_____

$$489 \quad \rightarrow$$

$$\times \quad 4$$

 Written Practice 📖 page 506

1. number of days in 1 week

$$\times \; 9$$

2. $1.12
$0.75

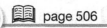
3. 2,200

_____

_____

¦ Use work area. ¦

4. Do problem **4** on 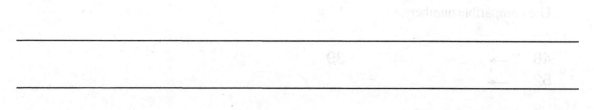 page 506.

5. standard form

3,000 + 700 + 40

¦ _____ ¦

¦ _____ ¦

6. Measure to the nearest quarter inch.

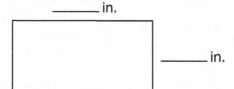

_____ in.

_____ in.

¦ Use work area. ¦

7.   quart   gallon   pint   cup

_____, _____, _____, _____

smallest   largest

¦ Use work area. ¦

8. 48 lb + 52 lb + 39 lb

Use compatible numbers.

48 →   39

52 →   + _____   + _____

---

9. parentheses first

(21 − 10) + 33

↓

_____ + 33 =

10. a.   16
        × 4

b.   24
       × 6

a. _____

b. _____

---

11. Estimate the product.

683 →

     × 4

---

12. 40 in 5 equal groups

_____⟌‾‾‾

13. Do problem **13** on page 507.

14. a. $40 \div 8 =$

b. $42 \div 7 =$

c. $45 \div 5 =$

a. _____

b. _____

c. _____

15.
$$\begin{array}{r} 412 \\ \times \quad 2 \\ \hline \end{array}$$

16.
$$\begin{array}{r} \$12.25 \\ - \ \$ \ 9.89 \\ \hline \end{array}$$

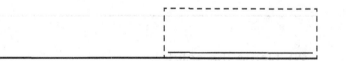

17. 80 + (70 × 6)

parentheses first

$$\begin{array}{r} 70 \\ \times\ \ 6 \end{array} \qquad + 80$$

18. parentheses first

(9 − 4) × 4

↓

_____ × 4 =

19. a. Which town is **east** of Redding?

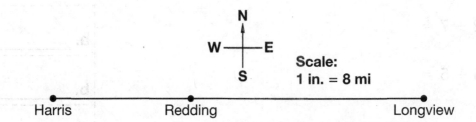

N

W ——|—— E

S

Scale:
1 in. = 8 mi

Harris   Redding   Longview

b. Measure the distance from Longview to Harris in inches. _____ in.

Every inch on the map is 8 miles.

Find the distance from Longview to Harris.

a. _____

b. _____

20. Name the solid: _____ _____

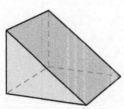

How many **faces?** _____

Use work area.

© Saxon

Name _____

• Using Compatible Numbers, Part 2

New Concept

- To estimate an answer, we often use round numbers.

- Other times we can use **compatible** numbers. Compatible numbers are easy to work with.

- These numbers are **multiples** of 100 or multiples of 25.

    Multiples of 100: 100, 200, 300, 400, 500, …

    Multiples of 25: 25, 50, 75, 100, 125, 150, …

Example

Use compatible numbers to estimate the cost of 4 board games at $24 each.

$25 is close to $24. Multiplying $25 by 4 is like counting quarters: 25, 50, 75, 100.

$$\$24 \longrightarrow \begin{array}{r} \$25 \\ \times \quad 4 \\ \hline \$100 \end{array}$$

The total price of the board games is **about $100.**

Lesson Practice

Use compatible numbers to estimate.

a. Estimate the **product** of 249 × 4.

$$249 \longrightarrow \begin{array}{r} 250 \\ \times \quad 4 \\ \hline \end{array}$$

b. When Alida walks her dog, she travels one mile in 24 minutes. About how

long would it take Alida to walk 2 miles? _____

$$24 \quad \rightarrow \quad \begin{array}{r} 25 \\ \times \quad 2 \\ \hline \end{array}$$

c. Estimate the **difference** of $678 and $354.

$$\begin{array}{r} \$678 \quad \rightarrow \quad \$675 \\ \$354 \quad \rightarrow \quad - \ \$350 \\ \hline \end{array}$$

Written Practice 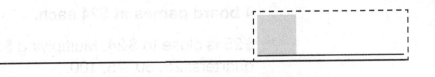 page 510

1. $\begin{array}{r} \$62.97 \\ \$ \ 4.41 \\ \hline \end{array}$

2. Find the number between 1 and 10 that has a product of 49 when multiplied by itself.

_____ × _____ = 49

3. Estimate the product.

$$82 \quad \rightarrow$$

$$\times \ 4$$

© Saxon

4. 1 mi = 5,280 ft

2 mi = _____ ft

$$\begin{array}{r} 5,280 \\ +\ 5,280 \\ \hline \end{array}$$

5. Fill in the blanks:

Four _____ equal a dollar, and four _____

equal a gallon.

Use work area.

6. 60 in 5 equal groups

$$\overline{)}$$

7. Does 254 round to 200 or 300?

254 →

8. Use compatible numbers to estimate.

23 →   _____ × 5 = $ _____

$$\begin{array}{r} \times\ \ \ 5 \\ \hline \end{array}$$

Use work area.

9. a. $\begin{array}{r} \$25 \\ \times\ \ 4 \\ \hline \end{array}$ **b.** $\begin{array}{r} 34 \\ \times\ \ 8 \\ \hline \end{array}$

a. _____

b. _____

10. A S_____ has _____ curved surface.

A C_____ has _____ curved surface and _____

flat surfaces.

Use work area.

11. place value of the 5

a. 4<u>5</u>,321

b. 23<u>5</u>

a. _____

b. _____

12. a. $\begin{array}{r} 30 \\ \times\ \ 4 \\ \hline \end{array}$ **b.** $\begin{array}{r} 90 \\ \times\ \ 6 \\ \hline \end{array}$

a. _____

b. _____

© Saxon

13. The picture shows the answer to which multiplication?

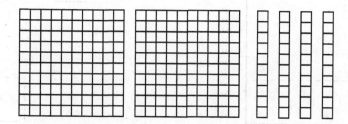

A	$\begin{array}{r} 40 \\ \times\ \ 6 \\ \hline \end{array}$	**B**	$\begin{array}{r} 20 \\ \times\ \ 7 \\ \hline \end{array}$
C	$\begin{array}{r} 12 \\ \times\ \ 2 \\ \hline \end{array}$	**D**	$\begin{array}{r} 40 \\ \times\ \ 2 \\ \hline \end{array}$

14. a. $48 \div 8 =$

b. $49 \div 7 =$

c. $42 \div 6 =$

a. _____

b. _____

c. _____

15. $7 \times 2 \times 5$ $\qquad$ $\begin{array}{r} 5 \\ \times\ \ 2 \\ \hline \end{array}$ $\qquad$ $\begin{array}{r} \ \ \ \\ \times\ \ 7 \\ \hline \end{array}$

16.   50
    $\times$ 9

17. $3 \times 7 \times 9$

            7
        $\times$ 3

            $\times$ 9

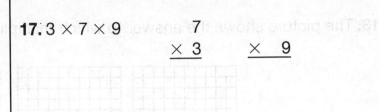

18. $100 - (3 \times 30)$

parentheses first

                    100

        30

    $\times$ 3 $-$ _____

19.   36
        a
        17
    $+$ 42
        99

20. Use a ruler to draw a **rectangle** that is 5 cm long and 4 cm wide.

Find the **area.**

$a =$ _____

Name _____

• Using Estimation to Verify Answers

New Concept

- When we use round numbers to find an answer, we get an **estimated answer.**

- The actual answer is called the **exact answer.**

- If the exact answer *is close* to the estimated answer, we say that the exact answer is **reasonable.**

- If the exact answer *is not close* to the estimated answer, we probably made a mistake and we should do the problem again.

Example

Francine bought a bat for $32, a mitt for $49, and a pair of batting gloves for $13. She calculated that she would need $94 for all three items. Is her total reasonable?

We round all three numbers and add to find an estimated total.

$$
\begin{array}{rcl}
\$32 & \rightarrow & \$30 \\
\$49 & \rightarrow & \$50 \\
\$13 & \rightarrow & +\ \$10 \\
\hline
& & \$90
\end{array}
$$

The estimated total ($90) is close to Francine's exact total ($94). So **Francine's total is reasonable.** She probably added correctly.

© Saxon

a. Roger bought a new bike seat for $31 and a helmet for $29. He calculated that he would need $90 to pay for both items. Is Roger's total reasonable?

$$\$31 \longrightarrow \underline{}$$

$$\$29 \longrightarrow \underline{} \; + \underline{}$$

The estimated total is $\underline{}$. Roger's exact total is

$\underline{}$. The estimated total is not close to the exact total,

so Roger's total $\underline{}$ reasonable.

b. Jackson estimates that 5 tickets to the football game will cost more than $300. If tickets are $32 each, is Jackson's estimate reasonable? If not, about how much would 5 tickets cost?

$$\$32 \longrightarrow \underline{}$$

$$\underline{} \times \; \underline{} 5$$

My estimate is $\underline{}$. Jackson's estimate is $\underline{}$.

The estimates $\underline{}$ close, so Jackson's estimate

$\underline{}$ reasonable. Five tickets would cost

about $\underline{}$.

© Saxon

c. Every day Alida walks around the track 5 times. She counted 489 steps for one lap. She estimates that she will walk 2,500 steps in 5 laps. Is her estimate reasonable?

$$489 \longrightarrow \underline{\qquad}$$

$$\underline{\times \quad 5}$$

My estimate is _____ steps. Alida's estimate is _____

steps. The estimates _____ close, so her answer

_____ reasonable.

Written Practice   📖 page 514

1. Estimate the product.

$$\$62 \longrightarrow \underline{\qquad}$$

$$\underline{\times \quad 7}$$

2.   100
       $\underline{36}$

3. Is Rachael's estimate reasonable?

$$193 \longrightarrow \underline{\qquad}$$

$$\underline{\times \quad 6}$$

My estimate is _____. Rachael's estimate is _____. The

estimates _____ close, so her answer _____ reasonable.

Use work area.

4. a.
$$\begin{array}{r} 400 \\ \times\ \ \ 3 \\ \hline \end{array}$$

b.
$$\begin{array}{r} \$500 \\ \times\ \ \ \ 6 \\ \hline \end{array}$$

c.
$$\begin{array}{r} 430 \\ \times\ \ \ 7 \\ \hline \end{array}$$

d.
$$\begin{array}{r} \$320 \\ \times\ \ \ \ 5 \\ \hline \end{array}$$

a. _____   b. _____   c. _____   d. _____

5. halfway between 1 and 2

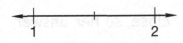

6. 1 yd = 36 in.

2 yd = _____ in.

$$\begin{array}{r} 36 \\ \times\ \ \ 2 \\ \hline \end{array}$$

7. Estimate the product.

38 $\longrightarrow$

$$\begin{array}{r} \times\ \ \ 5 \\ \hline \end{array}$$

8. 1 quart = _____ cups

9. Shade one fourth of the circle.

10. Estimate the difference.

$602 $\longrightarrow$

$298 $\longrightarrow$ $-\underline{}$

Use work area.

© Saxon

11. a. $\begin{array}{r} \$35 \\ \times\ \ 4 \\ \hline \end{array}$ **b.** $\begin{array}{r} 21 \\ \times\ \ 3 \\ \hline \end{array}$ **c.** $\begin{array}{r} 43 \\ \times\ \ 2 \\ \hline \end{array}$

a. _____ b. _____ c. _____

12. $\begin{array}{r} 700 \\ \times\ \ \ 5 \\ \hline \end{array}$

_____

13. $\begin{array}{r} 460 \\ \times\ \ \ 3 \\ \hline \end{array}$

_____

14. $\begin{array}{r} 375 \\ 658 \\ +\ \ 74 \\ \hline \end{array}$

_____

15. $370 - (9 \times 40)$

parentheses first

$\begin{array}{r} 40 \\ \times\ \ 9 \\ \hline \end{array}$

$\begin{array}{r} 370 \\ -\quad\ \ \\ \hline \end{array}$

_____

16. Is Lori's estimate reasonable?

$\begin{array}{r} 31 \ \longrightarrow \\ \times\ 6 \\ \hline \end{array}$

My estimate is _____. Lori's estimate is _____.

The estimates _____ close, so her answer

_____ reasonable.

Use work area.

17. a. $28 \div 4 =$

b. $36 \div 6 =$

c. $48 \div 6 =$

a. _____

b. _____

c. _____

18. Do problem **18** on 📖 page 515.

_____

19. Count up by $\frac{1}{4}$.

$\frac{1}{4}, \frac{1}{2}, \frac{3}{4}, 1, 1\frac{1}{4}, 1\frac{1}{2},$ _____, _____, _____, _____, ...

Use work area.

20. The box is filled with 1-cm cubes.

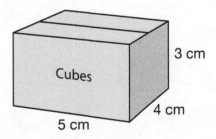

Cubes

3 cm
4 cm
5 cm

a. cubes in bottom layer

b. number of layers

c. total number of cubes

d. volume

a. _____ b. _____

c. _____ d. _____

© Saxon

📖 page 516

• Rounding to the Nearest Dollar

New Concept

• To round dollars and cents, read the number of cents.

   If there are *50¢ or more,* **round up** to the next dollar.

   If there are *less than 50¢,* **round down.**

Example

The price of a box of crayons is $3.15 and a set of colored markers is $1.89. Estimate the total price of the two items.

Round each price to the nearest dollar and then add.

Read the number of cents in $3.15.
There are less than 50¢. Round down to $3.

Read the number of cents in $1.89.
There are more than 50¢. Round up to $2.

$$\begin{array}{rcr}
\$3.15 & \rightarrow & \$3 \\
\$1.89 & \rightarrow & +\ \$2 \\
\hline
& & \$5
\end{array}$$

The total price for the crayons and markers is **about $5.**

Lesson Practice

For problems **a–d,** round each dollar and cent amount to the nearest dollar.

a. $4.90 → _____

b. $6.25 → _____

© Saxon

c. $8.19 →  _____

d. $6.79 → _____

e. Estimate the total price of a rubber ball that costs $2.95 and a plastic bat

that costs $5.82. _____

$2.95 → _____

$5.82 → ___+___

f. Estimate the total price of a bottle of milk at $1.89, a box of cereal at $3.92,

and a bag of fruit at $4.17. _____

$1.89 → _____

$3.92 → _____

$4.17 → ___+___

Written Practice 📖 page 518

1. 150
  118
  _____

2. 1 dozen = 12 eggs

  10 dozen = _____ eggs

3. $4.50 is between what two dollar amounts? $_____ and $_____

Round $4.50 to the nearest dollar.

$4.50 → $_____

⌐ Use work area. ¬

4. Find sets of 10.

5 + 1 + 2 + 5 + 8 + 7 =

5. odd numbers between 10 and 20

_____, _____, _____, _____, _____

⌐ Use work area. ¬

6. a.   500
        ×   4

b. $800
        ×   3

Carry on your fingers.

c.   720
        ×   5

d. $370
        ×   2

⌐ a. _____
  b. _____
  c. _____
  d. _____ ¬

© Saxon

7. $(50 + 21) + 17$

parentheses first

$$\begin{array}{r} 50 \\ + \ 21 \\ \hline \end{array} \qquad \begin{array}{r} \\ + \ 17 \\ \hline \end{array}$$

8. $\begin{array}{r} 300 \\ \times \quad 3 \\ \hline \end{array}$

9. Complete this drawing of a triangular prism.

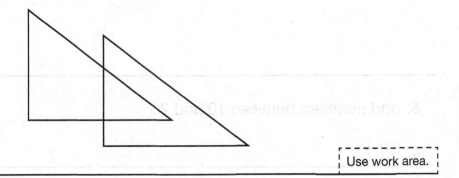

Use work area.

10. 1 gal = 4 qt

$\frac{1}{2}$ gal = _____ qt

11. halfway between 3,000 and 4,000

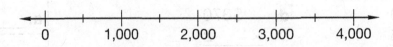

12. Count up by $\frac{1}{4}$.

2, $2\frac{1}{4}$, $2\frac{1}{2}$, _____, _____, _____, _____, ...

Use work area.

13. Carry on your fingers.

a.	15	**b.**	21	**c.**	45
	$\times\ \ 4$		$\times\ \ 9$		$\times\ \ 8$

a. _____ **b.** _____ **c.** _____

14. Estimate the product.

$12 $\longrightarrow$

$\times\ 9$

15. $20.00
     $-$ $ 1.99

16. $(63 + 37) \times 2$

parentheses first

63
$+ 37$

$\times\ \ 2$

17. Is Jonathan's estimate reasonable?

11 →

$$\times\ \ 6$$

My estimate is _____ minutes. Jonathan's estimate

is _____ minutes. The estimates _____ close, so

his answer _____ reasonable.

┌─────────────────┐
┆ Use work area. ┆
└─────────────────┘

18. Use compatible numbers to estimate.

a. 248 → 250
$$\times\ \ \ 4$$

b. 19 → 20
$$\times\ \ 5$$

┌─────────────────┐
┆ **a.** _____ ┆
├─────────────────┤
┆ **b.** _____ ┆
└─────────────────┘

19. a. 27 ÷ 3 =

b. 56 ÷ 7 =

c. 63 ÷ 9 =

┌─────────────────┐
┆ **a.** _____ ┆
├─────────────────┤
┆ **b.** _____ ┆
├─────────────────┤
┆ **c.** _____ ┆
└─────────────────┘

20. Circle every even number.

152   365   438

┌─────────────────┐
┆ Use work area. ┆
└─────────────────┘

Name _____

Teacher Notes:
- Review Hint #26 "Multiplication (Carrying on Fingers)."
- For additional practice, students may complete Targeted Practice 97.

• Multiplying Three-Digit Numbers, Part 2

New Concept

- To multiply a three-digit number:

   1. Multiply the ones.
   2. Multiply the tens.
   3. Multiply the hundreds.

- When a product is more than 10, write the ones and *carry on your fingers.* Add the carried number to the next product.

- Multiply every digit even if the digit is 0.

Example

Multiply: 7 × 308

1. Multiply the ones digit: $7 \times 8 = 56$.
Write the 6 and *carry the 5* on your fingers.

$$
\begin{array}{r}
30\boxed{8} \\
\times \quad \boxed{7} \\
\hline
6
\end{array}
$$

2. Multiply the tens digit: $7 \times 0 = 0$.
Add 5 for the carried number: $0 + 5 = 5$.

$$
\begin{array}{r}
3\,\textcircled{0}\,8 \\
\times \quad 7 \\
\hline
5 \quad 6
\end{array}
$$

3. Multiply the hundreds digit: $7 \times 3 = 21$. We write 21.

$$
\begin{array}{r}
3\,0\,8 \\
\times \quad\quad 7 \\
\hline
2\,1\,5\,6
\end{array}
$$

The product of 7 and 308 is **2,156.**

Lesson Practice

Find each product. Carry on your fingers.

a.
$$
\begin{array}{r}
135 \\
\times \quad 6 \\
\hline
\end{array}
$$

b.
$$
\begin{array}{r}
213 \\
\times \quad 7 \\
\hline
\end{array}
$$

c.
$$
\begin{array}{r}
\$275 \\
\times \quad 4 \\
\hline
\end{array}
$$

d.
$$
\begin{array}{r}
\$232 \\
\times \quad 3 \\
\hline
\end{array}
$$

e.
$$
\begin{array}{r}
706 \\
\times \quad 8 \\
\hline
\end{array}
$$

f.
$$
\begin{array}{r}
\$204 \\
\times \quad 9 \\
\hline
\end{array}
$$

Written Practice

page 522

1. The uppercase letter below is the ninth letter of the alphabet. Draw **two lines of symmetry** on the letter.

Use work area.

2. $39.95
      $ 2.60

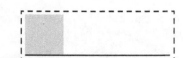

3. Estimate the sum.

   $4.67   ⟶

   $7.23   ⟶   + _____

4. length of a pencil

   A   15 cm

   B   15 m

   C   15 km

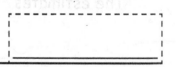

5. Divide 17 into 2 almost equal groups.

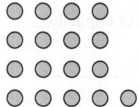

How many are in each group? _____ and _____

Use work area.

6. A window is **twice** as wide as it is high.

35 in.

How wide is the window?

_____

7. Is Susan's estimate reasonable?

$22   →

            ×   3

My estimate is $_____.   Susan's estimate is $_____.

The estimates   _____   close, so her answer

_____ reasonable.

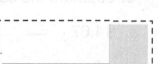

| Use work area. |

_____

8. Fill in the blanks with units of capacity.

Doubling a cup makes a   _____.

Doubling that makes a   _____.

Doubling that makes a   _____.

Doubling that makes a gallon.

| Use work area. |

9. Estimate the product. Write a number sentence.

_____ mi × 5 = _____ mi

18 →

$$\begin{array}{r} \times\ 5 \\ \hline \end{array}$$

Use work area.

10. How many cubes are there in all?

volume

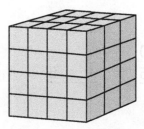

_____

11. a.   210
$$\begin{array}{r} \times\quad 4 \\ \hline \end{array}$$

b.   34
$$\begin{array}{r} \times\quad 7 \\ \hline \end{array}$$

a. _____

b. _____

12. Use a multiplication table to divide.

a. $2\overline{)12}$

b. $3\overline{)12}$

a. _____

b. _____

13. Round to the nearest dollar.

$5.38 →

 _____

14.   190
$$\begin{array}{r} \times\quad 4 \\ \hline \end{array}$$

_____

15.   230
$$\begin{array}{r} \times\quad 5 \\ \hline \end{array}$$

_____

16. $ 65
   $350
$$\begin{array}{r} +\ \$\quad 9 \\ \hline \end{array}$$

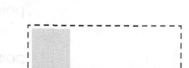 _____

17. $6 + (5 \times 80)$

parentheses first

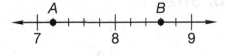

$$\begin{array}{r} 80 \\ \times\ \ 5 \end{array} \qquad \begin{array}{r} \\ +\ \ \ 6 \end{array}$$

_____

18. Use a multiplication table to divide.

a. $42 \div 7 =$

b. $36 \div 4 =$

c. $64 \div 8 =$

a. _____

b. _____

c. _____

19. Name the **mixed numbers** on the number line.

```
      A           B
  ├───●─┼─┼─┼─●─┼─→
  7         8         9
```

point A: _____

point B: _____

20. Use a ruler to draw a **rectangle** that is 5 cm long and 3 cm wide.

a. Find the **perimeter.**

b. Find the **area.**

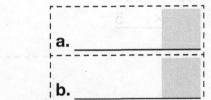

a. _____

b. _____

Name _____

📖 page 525

Teacher Note:
• Review Hint #26 "Multiplication (Carrying on Fingers)."

• Estimating by Weight or Mass

New Concept

Example

About 400 pennies have a mass of 1 kilogram. Create a table to estimate the number of pennies in 5 kilograms.

About 400 pennies have a mass of 1 kilogram.

Either multiply **or** count up by 400 to find the number of pennies in more than 1 kilogram.

Number of Pennies	400	800	1,200	1,600	2,000
Mass of Pennies	1 kg	2 kg	3 kg	4 kg	5 kg

About **2,000 pennies** have a mass of 5 kilograms.

Example

Alison knows that a pint of water weighs about a pound. She weighs a pitcher of water and finds that it weighs 7 pounds. The empty pitcher weighs 3 pounds. How many pints of water are in the pitcher?

The weight of the pitcher full of water is 7 pounds.
The pitcher without any water weighs 3 pounds.

Subtract to find the weight of the water in the full pitcher.

$$\begin{array}{ll} 7 \text{ pounds} & \text{full pitcher} \\ -\ 3 \text{ pounds} & \text{empty pitcher} \\ \hline 4 \text{ pounds} & \text{water} \end{array}$$

The water in the pitcher weighs 4 pounds.

Every pound is about 1 pint of water, so 4 pounds of water is about **4 pints.**

© Saxon

Activity 📖 page 527

Estimating by Mass
This activity is optional.

Lesson Practice

a. An empty bucket weighs 1 pound. When filled with water, the bucket weighs 9 pounds. A pint of water weighs about 1 pound. About how many

pints of water were in the bucket? _____

First, find the weight of the water.

full bucket

−____ empty bucket

____ water

b. If 1 kilogram of pennies is about 400 pennies, then 6 kilograms of pennies is about how many pennies? Complete the chart to find the answer.

Number of Pennies	400					
Mass of Pennies	1 kg	2 kg	3 kg	4 kg	5 kg	6 kg

Written Practice page 527

1. $31.76
   $23.50

© Saxon

2. 1 gal = _____ qt

  5 gal = _____ qt

3. a. 136
    × 8

b. $151
    × 9

  a. _____

  b. _____

4. 20
  − n
  ‾8‾

  n = _____

5. Estimate the sum.

  $5.49 →

  $3.29 → + ___

6. 5
  × M →
  ‾40‾

  m = _____

7. 1 gallon = _____ cups

  1 half gallon = _____ cups

8. halfway between 2,000 and 3,000

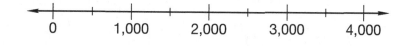

9. Estimate the product.

$7.75   →

$$\times \; 6$$

10. About 4 small apples are in 1 pound. Complete the table to estimate the number of small apples in 6 pounds.

Number of Apples	4					
Weight of Apples	1 lb	2 lb	3 lb	4 lb	5 lb	6 lb

Use work area.

11. a.   150
$$\times \quad 4$$

b.   630
$$\times \quad 3$$

c.   35
$$\times \quad 7$$

a. _____

b. _____

c. _____

12. a. $4\overline{)12}$

b. $6\overline{)12}$

a. _____

b. _____

© Saxon

13. The picture shows the answer to which multiplication?

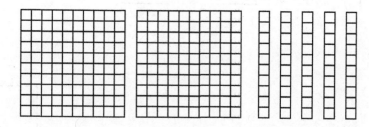

A	25	**B**	50	**C**	20	**D**	100
	$\times\ \underline{\ \ 5}$		$\times\ \underline{\ \ 5}$		$\times\ \underline{\ \ 5}$		$\times\ \underline{\ \ 3}$

14. a. $28 \div 4 =$

b. $42 \div 6 =$

c. $54 \div 9 =$

a. _____

b. _____

c. _____

15. $\begin{array}{r} \$12.45 \\ -\ \$\ 5.75 \\ \hline \end{array}$

16. $\begin{array}{r} 215 \\ \times\ \ \ 3 \\ \hline \end{array}$

17. (70 × 5) – 50

parentheses first

$$\begin{array}{r} 70 \\ \times\ 5 \end{array} \qquad \begin{array}{r} - \quad 50 \end{array}$$

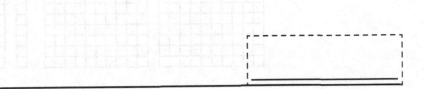

18.
$$\begin{array}{r} 470 \\ 63 \\ 7 \\ +\ \ 86 \\ \hline \end{array}$$

---

19. Use a centimeter ruler to measure.

   a. length   **b.** width

   c. area   **d.** perimeter

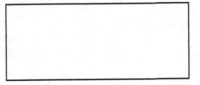

a. _____

b. _____

c. _____

d. _____

---

20. _____ min ÷ _____ = _____

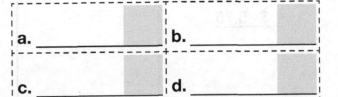

• Effects of Estimation

New Concept

- To estimate an answer, we round the numbers.

- If we *round up,* the estimated answer will be **a little more** or greater than, the exact answer.

- If we *round down,* the estimated answer will be **a little less** or less than, the exact answer.

Example

Deb bought 4 gallons of milk for $2.89 per gallon. To estimate the total cost, Deb multiplied 4 × $3. Will Deb's estimate be greater than or less than the exact cost?

Deb rounded the price of the milk from $2.89 to $3.00

$$\$2.89 \quad \longrightarrow \quad \$3.00$$

Deb *rounded up.*

Her estimated price will be **greater than** the exact price.

Lesson Practice

a. Sal bought a gallon of milk for $2.89 and a box of cereal for $3.95. He added $3 and $4 to estimate the total price. Is Sal's estimate greater

than or less than the exact price? _____ than

© Saxon

b. Thom is paid $9.15 per hour. Estimate how much Thom is paid for working

8 hours. _____

$9.15 →

  × 8

Is your estimate greater than or less than Thom's exact pay?

_____ than

Written Practice

📖 page 532

1. 1 yd = _____ ft

  100 yd = _____ ft

2. Write a multiplication fact for this rectangle.

_____ × _____ = _____

3. Is the estimate greater than or less than the exact price?

$7.99 → $8

$8.90 → $9

_____ than

© Saxon

4. 1 lb = 2 sweatshirts

10 lb = _____ sweatshirts

5. a. 227
× 2

b. $260
× 3

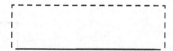

a. _____

b. _____

6. $8.95
$2.89
+ $0.43

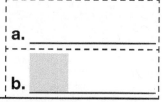

7. Which pair of fractions is not equivalent?

Use fraction pieces for help.

A $\frac{1}{2}$ and $\frac{2}{4}$ **B** $\frac{2}{3}$ and $\frac{3}{4}$

C $\frac{2}{6}$ and $\frac{1}{3}$ **D** $\frac{3}{6}$ and $\frac{1}{2}$

8. 1 gallon = _____ cups

9. Estimate the difference.

$12.05 ⟶ _____

$ 2.95 ⟶ − _____

10. How many cubes are there in all?

11. Use compatible numbers to estimate.

a. 252 ⟶ 250
× 2

b. 23 ⟶ 25
× 3

a. _____

b. _____

12. a. 40
× 4

b. 62
× 6

a. _____

b. _____

13. Draw **two lines of symmetry** on the figure.

Use work area.

14. $(25 + 75) \times 4$
     parentheses first

$$\begin{array}{r} 25 \\ + \ 75 \\ \hline \end{array} \qquad \begin{array}{r} \times \quad 4 \\ \hline \end{array}$$

15. $\begin{array}{r} 75 \\ \times \ 3 \\ \hline \end{array}$

16. $\begin{array}{r} 1{,}306 \\ - \ 567 \\ \hline \end{array}$

17. 708
    $\times$ 6

18. a. $56 \div 8 =$

b. $45 \div 9 =$

c. $63 \div 7 =$

a. _____

b. _____

c. _____

19. Measure each segment to the nearest **centimeter.**

a. _____

b. _____

a. _____

b. _____

20. Write a fraction with a **numerator of 2** and a **denominator of 5.**

Use words to name the fraction:

_____

Use work area.

© Saxon

Name _____

• Multiplying Dollars and Cents

New Concept

- Multiplying dollars and cents is the same as multiplying a three-digit number.

- To multiply dollars and cents:

    1. Multiply pennies.
    2. Multiply dimes.
    3. Multiply dollars.
    4. Write the dollar sign and the decimal point.

    The decimal point always goes two digits from the right.

- When a product is more than 10, write the ones and *carry on your fingers.* Add the carried number to the next product.

- Multiply every digit even if the digit is 0.

Math Language

A **decimal point** separates dollars from cents in money amounts.

$12.34

↑

decimal point

Example

Multiply: 3 × $7.75

1. Multiply pennies: 3 × 5 = 15. Write the 5 and carry 1.

$$\begin{array}{r} \$7.7\boxed{5} \\ \times\ \ \ \boxed{3} \\ \hline 5 \end{array}$$

2. Multiply dimes: $3 \times 7 = 21$. Add 1 for the carried number: $21 + 1 = 22$. Write the 2 and carry 2.

$$\begin{array}{r} \$7.7\,5 \\ \times \quad 3 \\ \hline 2\,5 \end{array}$$

3. Multiply dollars: $3 \times 7 = 21$. Add 2 for the carried number: $21 + 2 = 23$. Write 23.

$$\begin{array}{r} \$7\,7\,5 \\ \times \quad 3 \\ \hline 2\,3\,2\,5 \end{array}$$

Because this is dollars and cents, write a dollar sign at the front of the number. Write the decimal point two digits from the right.

$$\begin{array}{r} \$7.75 \\ \times \quad 3 \\ \hline \$23.25 \end{array}$$

The total is **$23.25**.

Lesson Practice

Find each product. Remember to write the dollar sign and decimal point. The decimal point goes two digits from the right.

a.
$$\begin{array}{r} \$4.00 \\ \times \quad 6 \\ \hline \end{array}$$

b.
$$\begin{array}{r} \$3.05 \\ \times \quad 7 \\ \hline \end{array}$$

c.
$$\begin{array}{r} \$3.40 \\ \times \quad 5 \\ \hline \end{array}$$

d.
$$\begin{array}{r} \$2.35 \\ \times \quad 4 \\ \hline \end{array}$$

© Saxon

1. 32 books in 4 equal stacks

_____

2. Is the estimate greater than or less than the exact price?

$2.29 → $2

_____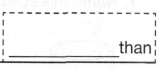
_____than

3. Write as a multiplication.

4 qt + 4 qt + 4 qt + 4 qt + 4 qt

_____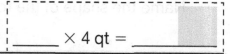
_____ × 4 qt = _____

4. Draw **one line of symmetry** on the letter.

B

_____   Use work area.

5. Estimate the difference.

$14.92 →

$ 7.21 →   − _____

_____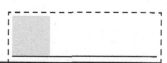

© Saxon

6. Use a centimeter ruler to draw a segment **5 centimeters long.**

Measure the segment to the **nearest inch.**

7. Name this solid. _____

Name the shape of the top and bottom faces. _____

¦ Use work area. ¦

8. $1.51
   ×   4

9. Write the mixed number two and two thirds.

10. 5 × 12 = 60

    12 × 5 = ?

© Saxon

11. 1 in. = 5 mi

4 in. = _____ mi

12. halfway between 1 inch and $1\frac{1}{2}$ inch
Use an inch ruler for help.

13. Estimate the product.

$415 $\longrightarrow$

$$\times \quad 2$$

14. a. 40   **b.**   260   **c.** $1.25
$$\times \ 5 \qquad \times \ 3 \qquad \times \ 4$$

a. _____

b. _____

c. _____

15. Add compatible numbers first.

$$50 + \overset{\bullet}{90} + \overset{\bullet}{110} =$$

16. a. $32 \div 4 =$

b. $48 \div 6 =$

c. $63 \div 9 =$

a. _____

b. _____

c. _____

17. $\begin{array}{r} 60 \\ \times\ \ 4 \\ \hline \end{array}$

_____

18. $\begin{array}{r} 376 \\ 28 \\ 205 \\ +\ \ \ 9 \\ \hline \end{array}$

_____

19. $\begin{array}{r} n \\ -\ \ 3 \\ \hline 15 \end{array}$

$n =$ _____

20. One box of pens has a mass of about 100 grams. Complete the table to estimate the mass of 6 boxes of pens.

Boxes of Pens	1	2	3	4	5	6
Mass of Pens	100 g					

Use work area.

© Saxon

📖 page 538

Focus on
• Evaluating Estimates

Teacher Notes:

• Students need a half-dozen egg carton (or a dozen egg carton cut in half) and enough marbles to fill the 6 egg cups to complete this activity.

• If students have completed the optional activities in Lesson 91 and Lesson 98 using Lesson Activity 31, use the textbook to complete this investigation.

• Ian wants to estimate the number of words in a 6-page long science lesson.

• Ian counted 198 words on one page of the science lesson.

1. How could Ian **estimate** the number of words in the whole 6-page lesson?

To _e_____, Ian could round the number

of words on one page and then multiply by _____.

• Jerry, Talia, and Ian each estimated the number of words in the entire lesson.

• Each student counted the number of words on a different page, rounded that number, and multiplied by 6.

• The three estimates are shown in the table below.

Student	Estimate
Ian	1,200
Jerry	1,300
Talia	1,000

- After making their estimates, the students counted all the words on all 6 pages of the lesson. **The lesson had 1,245 words.**

2. How can the students find who made the closest estimate?

Jerry's estimate is more than the exact number.

He can subtract the _____ number from

his estimate. Ian and Talia's _____ are

less than the exact number. They can **S**_____

their estimates from the exact number.

3. Whose estimate was closest? _____

Ian	Jerry	Talia
1,245	1,300	1,245
− 1,200	− 1,245	− 1,000

 page 538

Evaluating Estimates

Materials needed:

- half-dozen egg carton

- marbles or counters

The half-dozen egg carton has 6 small cups. Number the cups from 1 to 6. Then fill all the cups with marbles. Put any extra marbles away.

To estimate the total number of marbles, we will count the marbles in each cup and multiply by 6.

© Saxon

Cup 1

Count the number of marbles in Cup 1 and write the number.

Count for Cup 1: _____

Multiply that number by 6 to make an estimate:

$$\times\ 6$$

Estimate for cup 1: _____

Cup 2

Count the number of marbles in Cup 2 and write the number.

Count for Cup 2: _____

Multiply that number by 6:

$$\times\ 6$$

Estimate for cup 2: _____

Cup 3

Count the number of marbles in Cup 3 and write the number.

Count for Cup 3: _____

Multiply that number by 6:

$$\times\ 6$$

Estimate for cup 3: _____

Cup 4

Count the number of marbles in Cup 4 and write the number.

Count for Cup 4: _____

Multiply that number by 6:

$$\underline{\times\ 6}$$

Estimate for cup 4: _____

Cup 5

Count the number of marbles in Cup 5 and write the number.

Count for Cup 5: _____

Multiply that number by 6:

$$\underline{\times\ 6}$$

Estimate for cup 5: _____

Cup 6

Count the number of marbles in Cup 6 and write the number.

Count for Cup 6: _____

Multiply that number by 6:

$$\underline{\times\ 6}$$

Estimate for cup 6: _____

Exact Total

Add the **counts** for each cup to find the exact number of marbles in all the cups.

Cup 1 _____

Cup 2 _____

Cup 3 _____

Cup 4 _____

Cup 5 _____

+ _____ Cup 6

_____ exact total

Compare Estimates

Complete the table below with the **estimate** from each cup.

Estimates

Cup	1	2	3	4	5	6
Number of Marbles						

1. What is the greatest estimate? _____

2. What is the lowest estimate? _____

Evaluate Estimates

Subtract to find which estimate is closest to the exact total.

- If the estimate is *less than* the exact total, **subtract the estimate.**

- If the estimate is *more than* the exact total, **subtract the exact total.**

Cup 1   **Cup 2**   **Cup 3**

___ ___   ___ ___   ___ ___

Cup 4   **Cup 5**   **Cup 6**

___ ___   ___ ___   ___ ___

3. Which cup made the estimate **closest** to the exact

total? cup _____

4. Which cup made the estimate **furthest** from the exact

total? cup _____

Name _____

• Dividing Two-Digit Numbers

Teacher Notes:

• Introduce Hint #30 "Short Division."

• For additional practice, students may complete Targeted Practice 101.

New Concept

Math Language

The **dividend** is the number you are dividing.

The **divisor** is the number you are dividing by.

The **quotient** is the answer in a division problem.

• Some divisions have a two-digit dividend and a *two-digit quotient:*

$$90 \div 6 = 15$$

• To solve problems with two-digit quotients, we will use a division box and divide one digit at a time.

• Your textbook uses long division.

• We will use **short division.** Long division is not allowed.

1. Divide the first digit.
Think: "How many times will the divisor go into the first digit **without going over?**"

How many times will 6 go into 9 without going over 9?

$$6 \times 1 = 6 \qquad 6 \times 2 = 12$$

So 6 goes into 9 **one time** without going over.

2. Write the digit above the first digit in the division box.

$$\begin{array}{r} 1 \\ 6{\overline{)9\;0}} \end{array}$$

3. Multiply in your head the digit and the divisor.

$$6 \times 1 = \mathbf{6}$$

4. Subtract that number from the first digit in the division box. This is the "left over" number.

$$9 - 6 = \mathbf{3}$$

© Saxon

5. Write the "left over" number next to the second digit in the division box. This creates a new number.

$$\frac{1}{6)9\ ^30}$$

6. Divide the new number by the divisor. You can use a multiplication table for help.

$$30 \div 6 = \mathbf{5}$$

7. Write that answer above the second digit in the division box.

$$\frac{1\ \ 5}{6)9\ ^30}$$

- Rules for short division:

    Any number "left over" goes in front of the next digit.

    Write a digit above every digit in the division box.

Example

Maria is putting a collection of 48 postcards into a photo album. Each page can hold 3 postcards. How many pages can she fill?

Write the division in a division box and use short division.

1. Think: How many times will 3 go into 4 without going over?

$$3 \times 1 = 3 \qquad\qquad 3 \times 2 = 6$$

Three goes into 4 one time.

2. Write "1" above the 4.

$$\frac{1}{3)4\ \ 8}$$

3. Multiply: $3 \times 1 = 3$.

© Saxon

4. Subtract: $4 - 3 = 1$.

5. Write "1" next to the 8 to create a new number.

$$3\overline{)4\ ^18}$$ with 1 above

6. Divide: $18 \div 3 = 6$.

7. Write "6" above the 8.

$$\begin{array}{r} 1\ 6 \\ 3\overline{)4\ ^18} \end{array}$$

The quotient is 16. Maria can fill **16 pages.**

Lesson Practice

Follow the instructions to answer problem **a.**

a. To display his rock collection, Juan glues 5 rocks on each card. How many cards does he need for 75 rocks?

$$5\overline{)7\ 5}$$

1. How many times will 5 go into 7 without going over? _____

2. Write that number above the 7.

3. Multiply that number and the divisor: $5 \times$ _____ = _____

4. Subtract the product: $7 -$ _____ = _____

5. Write the "left over" number in front of the 5 in the division box to create a new number.

6. Divide the new number by the divisor: _____ $\div 5 =$ _____

7. Write that number above the 5 in the division box.

What is the quotient? _____

Use short division to answer problems **b** and **c**.

b. Shelly collected 54 shells that she will store in plastic bags. If she puts

3 shells in each bag, how many bags of shells will she have? _____

$$3\overline{)5\ 4}$$

c. If 76 horn players line up in 4 rows, how many players will be in each row?

_____

$$4\overline{)7\ 6}$$

Written Practice 📖 page 543

---

1. 36 books in 9 equal stacks

2. Lora has $8. Does she have enough money?

$$\begin{array}{r} \$2.39 \quad \rightarrow \quad \$2.50 \\ \times \qquad 3 \\ \hline \end{array}$$

_____

---

3. short division

$$6\overline{)7\ 8}$$

_____

4. $3\overline{)5\ 4}$

_____

5. $$\begin{array}{r} 24 \\ -\ w \\ \hline 3 \end{array}$$

$w =$ _____

© Saxon

6. Use an inch ruler to draw a segment **4 inches long.**

Measure the segment to the **nearest centimeter.**

7. What is the 15th number in this sequence?

Saying the numbers out loud will help.

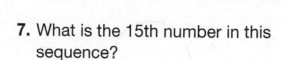

100, 200, 300, 400, 500, ...

8. fact family

$\times$ ___ $\times$ ___   ⌐___   ⌐___

Use work area.

9. halfway between $1\frac{1}{4}$ inches and $1\frac{3}{4}$ inches

Use an inch ruler for help.

10. $248
   $\times$ 4

11. Use a ruler to draw a **square** with sides $\frac{1}{2}$ inch long.

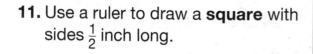

Find the **perimeter.**

12. 36 photos on 6 equal pages

© Saxon

13. Do problem **13** on 📖 page 544.

14. 1992
    1492

15. a. 24
    × 6

b. $2.30
    × 5

a. _____

b. _____

16. Draw one line of symmetry on this semicircle.

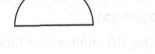

Use work area.

17. a. 28 ÷ 7 =

b. 56 ÷ 8 =

c. 36 ÷ 9 =

Use work area.

18. Estimate the sum.

$5.17 ⟶

$6.98 ⟶

$8.89 ⟶ + _____

Use work area.

19. least to greatest

Use fraction pieces for help.

$\frac{3}{4}$ $\frac{1}{2}$ $\frac{2}{3}$

_____, _____, _____
least   greatest

Use work area.

20. Which symbol makes the problem work?

24 □ 2 = 12

A +

B −

C ×

D ÷

© Saxon

• Sorting

New Concept

- **Sorting** means to put objects or numbers into groups based on how they are the same and how they are different.

- Objects can be sorted based on color, size, shape, or other reasons.

- Numbers can be sorted by even and odd, number of digits, type of digits, or other reasons.

- The reason for sorting is called the **sorting rule.**

Example

Sort the following numbers into two groups: even numbers and odd numbers.

26, 73, 54, 49, 31, 80

Even numbers end with even digits (0, 2, 4, 6, 8). All the other numbers are odd.

We look at each number and make two lists:

Even numbers: 26, 54, 80

Odd numbers: 73, 49, 31

© Saxon

a. Describe the sorting rule for the numbers in these two groups:

Group A: 10, 60, 40, 20, 70

Group B: 12, 23, 74, 31, 58

All the numbers in Group A end with _____.   All the numbers

in Group B do not end with _____.

b. Jill has a collection of action figures. Describe some ways she could sort the figures.

Jill could sort the action figures by _____

_____

_____ .

Written Practice   page 547

1. 24 children in 3 equal teams

┌ ─ ─ ─ ─ ─ ─ ─ ┐
└ ─ ─ ─ ─ ─ ─ ─ ┘

2. 75, 23, 98, 43, 82, 11, 90, 86

Even numbers: _____, _____, _____, _____

Odd numbers: _____, _____, _____, _____

┌ ─ ─ ─ ─ ─ ─ ─ ┐
¦ Use work area. ¦
└ ─ ─ ─ ─ ─ ─ ─ ┘

3. (275 + 375) − 200

parentheses first

4. 1 cup **doubled** is how many cups?

How many **pints** is that many cups?

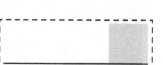

5. Use an inch ruler to draw a segment $\frac{2}{4}$ inch long.

What fraction is equivalent to $\frac{2}{4}$ inch?

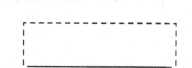

6. Draw rows of 3 Xs until there are 27 Xs in all.

X   X   X

How many rows are there in all?

7. If 3 × (4 × 5) = 60, then what is (3 × 4) × 5?

parentheses first

8. expanded form

875,632

_____ + _____ + _____ + _____

+ _____ + _____

> Use work area.

9. halfway between 300 and 600

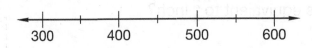

10. $\frac{1}{4}$ jar = 300 pennies

1 jar = _____ pennies

Because the jar is about _____ full with 300 pennies,

I can m_____ 300 by 4 to estimate the full jar.

> Use work area.

11. 108
     × 3

12. 3 × 5 × 8

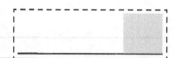

13. Describe the sorting rule.

Group A: 0, 1, 4, 5, 8

Group B: 10, 32, 35, 57, 79

All the numbers in Group A have _____ digit. All the

numbers in Group B have _____ digits.

_____ ⌐ Use work area. ⌐

14.   1826
        _1776_

15. a.   14   **b.** $2.50
        × _7_   × __3_

a. _____

b. _____

16. Estimate the product.

$78   →

        × _7_

17. a. $30 \div 6 =$

b. $40 \div 5 =$

c. $64 \div 8 =$

a. _____

b. _____

c. _____

18. short division

$2\overline{)7\ \ 6}$

19. $3\overline{)8\ \ 1}$

20. Estimate the sum.

$3.19 \ \longrightarrow$

$4.89 \ \longrightarrow$

$4.89 \ \longrightarrow \quad + \ \_\_\_\_\_$

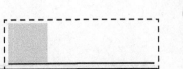

Name _____

 page 549

Teacher Notes:
• Review Hint #15 "Place Value Through Thousands."
• Review "Place Value" on page 13 in the *Student Reference Guide*.

• Ordering Numbers Through 9,999

New Concept

• **Ordering** numbers means writing them from *least to greatest* or *greatest to least*.

• We **compare** all the numbers.

• To compare numbers through 9,999:

  1. Compare thousands.

  2. If two or more numbers have the same thousands, compare hundreds.

  3. If two or more numbers have the same hundreds, compare tens.

  4. If two of more numbers have the same tens, compare ones.

• Writing the numbers in a column can help us compare.

Example

Write these numbers in order from least to greatest.

3,672	3,712	372

Write the numbers in a column to compare.

Line up the ones digits so that the same place values are aligned.

3,672

3,712

372

© Saxon

1. Compare thousands.

The top two numbers have 3 thousands, but 372 has no thousands. The least number is 372.

2. Compare hundreds in 3,672 and 3,712.

We see that 3,672 has 6 hundreds and 3,712 has 7 hundreds. The greatest number is 3,712.

Write the numbers from least to greatest.

372   3,672   3,712
least   greatest

Lesson Practice

a. The birth years in Roger's family are as follows:

1998   2002   1976   1974

Arrange these years from **earliest to latest.**

_____, _____, _____, _____
earliest   latest

b. In 2000, the population of Blanco County was 8,418. The population of Castro County was 8,285. The population of Archer County was 8,854. List the **names** of the 3 counties in order from **least population to greatest.**

_____, _____, _____
least   greatest

Blanco   8,418

Castro   8,285

Archer   8,854

c. Robinson compared the price of a game at three different stores. Here are the prices:

$18.85 $19.25 $17.98

Arrange the prices in order from **least to greatest.**

$_____ , $_____ , $_____

    least   greatest

Written Practice   page 551

1. 24 quarters in stacks of 4

2. Name this **six-sided** figure.

3. short division

$$5\overline{)7\ 5}$$

4. $4\overline{)8\ 8}$

5. Draw one line of symmetry on this D.

D

Use work area.

6. Get a 1 foot ruler with inches and centimeters.

How long is the ruler to the **nearest centimeter?**

7. Can 25 books be separated into two equal stacks?

© Saxon

8. short division

$7\overline{)8\ 4}$

9. $8\overline{)5\ 6}$

10. least to greatest

2,654   2,913   2,987   2,398

_____, _____, _____, _____
    least   greatest

Use work area.

11. Write the sum in words.

$\begin{array}{r} \$750 \\ + \ \$840 \\ \hline \end{array}$

words: _____

_____ dollars

Use work area.

12. Estimate the product.

294   →

$\begin{array}{r} \times\ \ \ 3 \\ \hline \end{array}$

13. Use a ruler to draw a rectangle that is one inch long and $\frac{1}{2}$ inch wide. Find the **perimeter.**

© Saxon

14. a.   6   **b.**   6
    + _a_   × _c_
    24   24

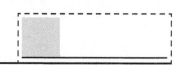

a. _a_ = _____

b. _c_ = _____

15. $4.20
   ×   6

16. The figure on the left is a **cube**. The figure on the right is a **rectangular prism.**

 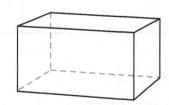

How are the figures alike and different?

Use manipulatives for help.

Both figures have _____ faces, _____ edges, and _____

vertices. The cube has faces that are all the _____ size.

Use work area.

© Saxon

17. a. $27 \div 3 =$

b. $45¢ \div 5 =$

c. $\$36 \div 6 =$

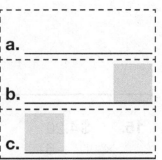

a. _____

b. _____

c. _____

---

18. $\$10.00 - (\$5.85 + 89¢)$

parentheses first

19. 1 km = _____ m

3 km = _____ m

---

20. Describe the sorting rule.

Group A: 11, 25, 36, 48, 59

Group B: 125, 238, 374, 431, 578

All the numbers in Group A have _____ digits. All the

numbers in Group B have _____ digits.

© Saxon

Teacher Note:
• Review the **Geometry** section of the *Student Reference Guide.*

• Sorting Geometric Shapes

New Concept

• We can **sort** or **classify** shapes by how they are alike or different.

Math Language

A **polygon** is a flat, closed shape with only straight sides.

• Some examples of sorting rules for shapes:

> polygons or not polygons
>
> number of sides
>
> types of triangles
>
> polygons or solids
>
> number of faces, edges, or vertices
>
> flat or curved surfaces

• Use pattern blocks or solids manipulatives for help.

Example

Sort these figures into polygons and figures that are not polygons. Then describe the sorting rule.

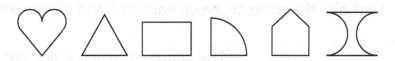

Polygons are flat, closed shapes with only straight sides. Sort the figures.

Polygons   Not Polygons

The sorting rule is **shapes with curved sides are not polygons.**

© Saxon

a. Sort these polygons into two groups: triangles and quadrilaterals. Circle the triangles.

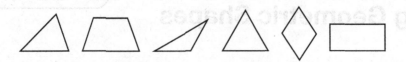

b. Describe how the solids in Group 1 are alike. Describe how the solids in Group 1 are different from the solids in Group 2.

Group 1	Group 2

The solids in Group 1 are prisms because they have   f_____

that are the same shape on each end and all the other faces are

r_____.   The solids in Group 2 are not   p_____.

Written Practice   page 556

1. 48 in 6 equal rows

2. 121 cm

    114 cm

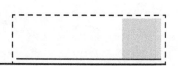

3. Draw columns of 4 dots until there are 20 dots in all.

How many columns are there?

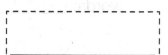

4. Estimate each answer.

    a. $396 →

        $419 → + _____

    b. $587 →

        $259 → − _____

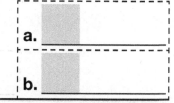

5.   18
     − _m_
     ———
      3

_m =_ _____

6. 1 kg = _____ g

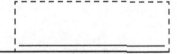

7. Use words to write the 15th number in this sequence.

Saying the numbers out loud will help.

1,000, 2,000, 3,000, 4,000, ...

words: _____ thousand

Use work area.

8. Which of the following equals one quart?

A 3 cups   **B** 4 pints

C 2 pints   **D** 2 cups

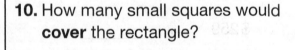

9. If 56 ÷ 7 = 8, then what does 56 ÷ 8 equal?

fact family

10. How many small squares would **cover** the rectangle?

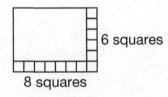

6 squares

8 squares

11. Is drawing red less likely, equally likely, or more likely than drawing blue?

$$\begin{array}{r} 5 \text{ blue marbles} \\ + \underline{} \text{ red marbles} \\ \hline 10 \text{ total marbles} \end{array}$$

There are _____ blue marbles and _____ red marbles.

Drawing red is _____ likely as drawing blue.

Use work area.

12.

$$\begin{array}{r} 365 \\ \times 4 \end{array} \qquad + 1$$

13. $(24 + 80) - 44$

parentheses first

14. Draw a picture of 24 flowers in 4 equal rows.

How many flowers are in each row?

15. a. $0.24
          $\times \qquad 5$

b. $0.24
          $\times \qquad 4$

a. _____

b. _____

16. 1 package = 70 crackers

4 packages = _____ crackers

_____

17. a. 36¢ ÷ 4 =

b. 36 ÷ 6 =

c. 35 ÷ 7 =

a. _____

b. _____

c. _____

18. expanded form

6,877

_____ + _____ +

_____ + _____

Use work area.

19. Use compatible numbers to estimate.

$2.56 →

$\times \qquad 8$

20.   721
        $\times \qquad 2$

_____

© Saxon

Teacher Notes:
• Review the **Geometry** section of the *Student Reference Guide*.
• For additional practice, students may complete Targeted Practice 105.

• Diagrams for Sorting

New Concept

• We can **sort** or **classify** numbers and shapes into lists based on a counting rule.

• Instead of sorting into lists, we can also sort into circles.

Example

The circles below are labeled "Even numbers" and "Odd numbers." Write these numbers in the correct circles.

15, 26, 7, 14, 30, 21

Even numbers end in an even digit: 0, 2, 4, 6, or 8. The other numbers are odd.

Write the even numbers in the "Even numbers" circle. Write odd numbers in the "Odd numbers" circle.

Even numbers   Odd numbers

26   14   15
                        7
    30
                      21

• In a **Venn diagram,** two sorting circles overlap.

Venn diagram

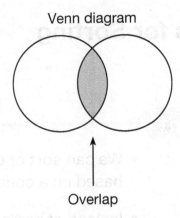

Overlap

• If a number or shape could go in **both circles,** write it in the overlap part.

Example

In the Venn diagram below, the circles are labeled "P" for parallel sides and "R" for right angle. Draw the polygons in the correct parts of the Venn diagram.

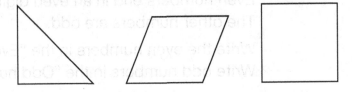

The triangle has a right angle but no parallel sides.
Draw it in the "R" circle.

The parallelogram has parallel sides but no right angles.
Draw it in the "P" circle.

The square has parallel sides **and** right angles.
Draw it in the overlap part.

P   R

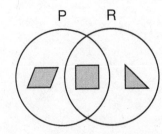

a. The circles below are labeled "Quadrilaterals" and "Triangles." Draw the shapes in the correct circles.

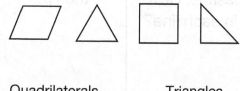

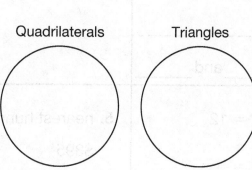

b. In the Venn diagram below, the circles below are labeled "Q" for **quadrilaterals** and "R" for **right angle.** Draw the shapes in the correct parts of the diagram.

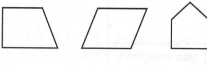

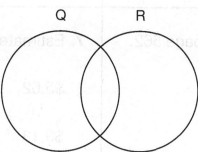

Written Practice 📖 page 561

1. 1 yd = _____ ft

$0.75

© Saxon

2. Forty-one students stood in two lines as equally as possible. How many students were in each line?

Draw a picture for help.

┌─────────────────────┐
│   │
│ _____ and _____ │
└─────────────────────┘

3. Draw **two lines of symmetry** on the H.

H

┌─────────────────┐
│ Use work area. │
└─────────────────┘

4. 1 dozen   = 12

    2 dozen   = _____

    1 paper clip   = _____ g

    2 dozen paper clips = _____ g

┌─────────────────┐
│ Use work area. │
└─────────────────┘

5. nearest hundred dollars

   $395

6. Do problem **6** on 📖 page 562.

7. Estimate the total price.

   $5.62 ⟶

   $3.18 ⟶

   $1.20 ⟶ + _____

8. In what **place** is the 7?

   a. 3,6<u>7</u>4

   b. 36<u>7</u>

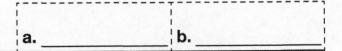

a. _____   b. _____

© Saxon

9. halfway between 500 and 1000

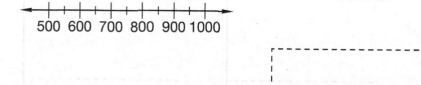

500 600 700 800 900 1000

```
10. $3.23   →

          ×
        _____
        $12.00
```

Patrick rounded $3.23 down to $_____.   So the actual price

will be _____ than his estimated price.

┌─────────────────┐
┆ Use work area. ┆
└─────────────────┘

11. Use a ruler to draw a **square** with sides 2 cm long.

Find the **perimeter.**

12. Write as a multiplication and find the total.

60 sec + 60 sec + 60 sec +
60 sec + 60 sec

_____ × 60 sec = _____ sec

┌──────────────┐
┆ Use work area. ┆
└──────────────┘

13. Divide.

```
       6
    ×  n    →    )‾‾‾
    ─────
      48
```

┌────────────────┐
┆ n = ┆
└────────────────┘

14.   365
     $\times$ 3

15.   400
     $\times$ 8

16. $81 \div 9 =$

17. short division

$2\overline{)9\ 2}$

18. a. $81 \div 9 =$

b. $32 \div 4 =$

c. $42 \div 7 =$

a. _____

b. _____

c. _____

19. sequence of **doubles**

5, 10, 20, 40, _____, _____, _____

Use work area.

20. How many 1-foot square tiles will **cover** the floor?

10 ft

8 ft

Name _____

• Estimating Area, Part 1

New Concept

• Multiply length and width to find the area of a rectangle.

Area = length × width

• Not all figures are rectangles.

• To estimate area, we use a **grid** of squares.

1. Put a dot in every full square.

2. Put an X in every square that is about half-full.

3. Count up the area. Every dot is 1 square unit and every X is $\frac{1}{2}$ square unit.

Example

Every square in the grid is one square meter. What is the area of the pond?

Look at the figure and draw:

　　a dot in every full square.

　　an X in every half-full square.

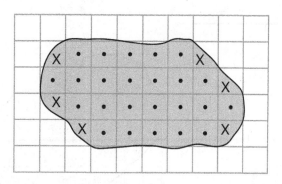

Every dot is 1 square meter. Count 24 dots for 24 square meters.

Every X is $\frac{1}{2}$ square meter. Count 6 Xs for 3 square meters.
The total area of the pond is **27 square meters.**

Lesson Practice

a. Find the area of this figure. Every square is 1 square inch.

Put a dot in every full square.
Put an X in every half-full square.
Count the dots as 1 and the Xs as $\frac{1}{2}$ square inch.

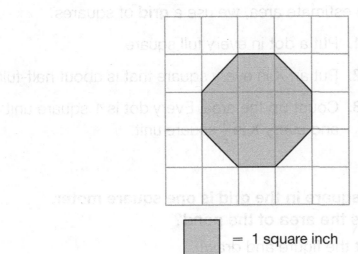

☐ = 1 square inch

b. Estimate the area of this figure. Every square is 1 square yard.

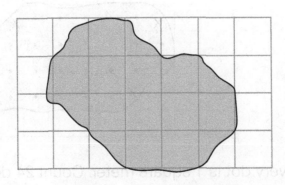

☐ = 1 square yard

© Saxon

1. 1 yd = _____ ft

11 yd = _____ ft

_____

2. short division

$3\overline{)7\ \ 2}$

_____

3.   575
      $\times$ 3

_____

4. ..., 600, 700, 800, _____, _____, _____, ...

‖ Use work area. ‖

5.   1 ft = 12 in.

8 × _____ in. = _____ in.

‖ Use work area. ‖

6. halfway between $1\frac{1}{2}$ inches and 2 inches

Look at a ruler for help.

7. Estimate the product.

$$487 \quad \longrightarrow$$

$$\underline{\times \quad 3}$$

8. a. Estimate the sum. **b.** Calculate the sum.

$$\$608 \quad \longrightarrow$$

$$\$487 \quad \longrightarrow \quad \underline{+}$$

$$\begin{array}{r} \$608 \\ + \ \$487 \\ \hline \end{array}$$

a.

b.

9. If $11 \times 12 = 132$, then what does 12×11 equal?

fact family

10. thousands place

a. 23,478

b. 375,129

a.

b.

© Saxon

11. Complete this drawing of a **cube.**

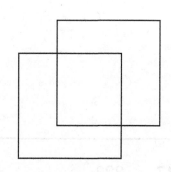

How many **vertices**?

12. expanded form

365

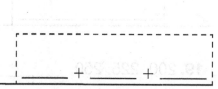

_____ + _____ + _____

13. Use a ruler to draw a rectangle that is 2 cm long and 1 cm wide.

a. perimeter

b. area

a. _____

b. _____

14. a. $\begin{array}{r} \$1.45 \\ \times \quad 7 \\ \hline \end{array}$ **b.** $\begin{array}{r} \$0.45 \\ \times \quad 4 \\ \hline \end{array}$

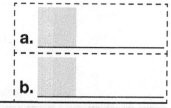

a. _____

b. _____

15. a. $16 \div 2 =$

b. $36 \div 6 =$

c. $24 \div 3 =$

a. _____

b. _____

c. _____

---

16. $\begin{array}{r} 173 \\ \times \quad 7 \\ \hline \end{array}$

17. $\begin{array}{r} 322 \\ \times \quad 8 \\ \hline \end{array}$

18. $\begin{array}{r} 500 \\ \times \quad 7 \\ \hline \end{array}$

---

19. 200, 225, 250, _____, _____, _____, ...

Use work area.

---

20. Every square is 1 square inch. Find the area.

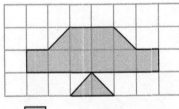

▨ = 1 square inch

Name _____

📖 page 569

Teacher Note:

• Students will need a copy of **Lesson Activity 23**; a small-grid transparency; and a small, simple black-and-white picture to complete the activity.

• Drawing Enlargements

New Concept

• An **enlargement** is a drawing that is the same as a small drawing, only bigger.

 Activity 📖 page 570

Drawing Enlargements

Materials needed:

• **Lesson Activity 23**

• small-grid transparency

• a small, simple picture to copy

Find a picture that you would like to enlarge. The picture should be small, about the size of a cartoon.

Put the picture on your desk.

Then put the small-grid transparency on top of your picture. The transparency should completely cover your picture.

Tape the transparency to your desk so that it will not move.

The grid transparency divides your picture into small squares.

Get a copy of **Lesson Activity 23**. The squares on **Lesson Activity 23** are larger than the squares on the grid transparency.

Find the top and left small square that covers a part of your picture. Copy that part of the picture into a larger square on the top and left of **Lesson Activity 23**. You have *enlarged* that part of the picture.

Copy the rest of your picture one square at a time until you have enlarged the whole picture.

1. Is Bea **more likely** to draw a striped marble or a black marble?

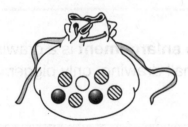

2. Write the names in order from **oldest to youngest.**

Name	Birth Year
Jessica	1993
Matt	1980
Samantha	2000
Paul	1997

oldest _____

_____

youngest _____

Use work area.

© Saxon

3. Use a ruler to draw a **square** with sides $1\frac{1}{2}$ inches long.

Find the **perimeter.**

4. Which does **not** equal 15?

A $15 + 0 =$ _____

B $15 - 0 =$ _____

C $15 \times 0 =$ _____

D $15 \times 1 =$ _____

5. short division $5\overline{)9\ 0}$

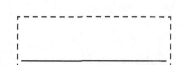

6. $\begin{array}{r} 111 \\ \times\ \ \ 3 \\ \hline \end{array}$

7. short division   3)3 9

8. 100 pennies in 10 equal piles

9. In what **place** is the 5?

  a. 5̲24

  b. 36,45̲2

  a. _____

  b. _____

10. Draw a **rectangle** 3 cm long and 2 cm wide.

  Find the **area.**

© Saxon

11. Sort the shapes.

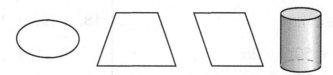

Polygons Not polygons

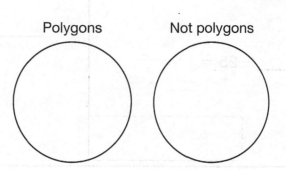

Use work area.

---

12. nearest dollar

$5.58 →

---

13. Carry on your fingers.

$$\begin{array}{r} \$7.50 \\ \times 5 \end{array}$$

---

14. $$\begin{array}{r} \$1.20 \\ \times 3 \end{array}$$

---

15. a. 56 ÷ 7 =

b. 63 ÷ 7 =

c. 24 ÷ 4 =

a. _____

b. _____

c. _____

---

16. Sort the numbers.

34 88 17 61 81 22 98 23

Even numbers Odd numbers

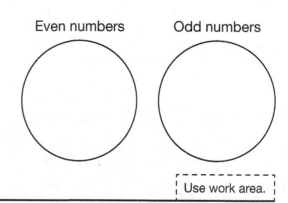

Use work area.

© Saxon

17. parentheses first

$$(50 + 50) \;\; - 25$$

↓

_____ − 25 =

18. (99 + 1) × 4

↓

_____ × 4 =

19. The triangle below is **obtuse.**

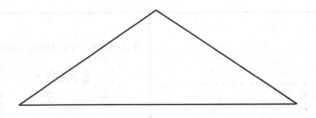

How many angles are **obtuse?** _____ angles

How many angles are **acute?** _____ angles

Use work area.

20. 3 mi = 21 min

1 mi = _____ min

© Saxon

Name _____

📖 page 573

Teacher Note:
• Students will need a copy of **Lesson Activity 33**; an inch-grid transparency, a centimeter-grid transparency, and an erasable marker or crayon to complete the activity.

• Estimating Area, Part 2

New Concept

- To estimate area, we use a grid of squares.

  1. Put a dot in every full square.

  2. Put an X in every square that is about half-full.

  3. Count up the area. Every dot is 1 square unit and every X is $\frac{1}{2}$ square unit.

Activity 📖 page 574

Estimating Area with a Grid

Materials needed:

- **Lesson Activity 33**
- inch-grid transparency
- centimeter-grid transparency
- erasable marker or crayon

In this activity we will estimate the area of the shapes on **Lesson Activity 33.**

Every square on the inch-grid transparency is *1 square inch.*

Every square on the centimeter-grid transparency is *1 square centimeter.*

For each shape, place the inch or centimeter grid over the shape. Line up a side or corner of the shape with a side or corner of the grid.

Do not move the grid once you have started counting the area.

- Place the **centimeter** grid on top of shape **1**. Slide or turn the grid so that a straight line in the grid is on top of a straight line in the shape.

- Use your marker or crayon to draw a dot in any square that is completely inside the shape.

- Draw an X in any square that is half inside the shape.

- Count up the area. Every dot is 1 square centimeter and every X is $\frac{1}{2}$ square centimeter.

1. The estimated area of shape **1** is _____ square centimeters.

Use the same steps to estimate the areas of shapes **2–6**. Use the centimeter-grid (smaller squares) to estimate in square cm and the inch-grid (larger squares) to estimate in square inches.

2. _____

3. _____

4. _____

5. _____

6. _____

© Saxon

1. least likely number

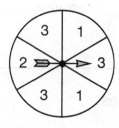

2. Estimate the total.

312 →

624 →

511 → + _____

3. Is your estimated answer in problem **2** greater than or less than the exact answer?

_____ than

4. Use a ruler to draw a rectangle that is $1\frac{1}{2}$ inches long and $1\frac{1}{4}$ inches wide.

Draw **two lines of symmetry** on the rectangle.

Use work area.

© Saxon

5. $18.95 $12.95 $17.95

$ _____ , $ _____ , $ _____
    least   greatest

---

6. 1 roll of pennies = 50 pennies

1 roll of pennies = _____ dimes

_____ rolls of pennies = 50 dimes

---

7. 16 oz = 1 pt

1 qt = _____ pt

1 qt = _____ oz

---

8. Describe the sorting rule.

Group A: $\frac{2}{2}, \frac{3}{3}, \frac{4}{4}, \frac{5}{5}, \frac{6}{6}$

Group B: $\frac{1}{2}, \frac{1}{3}, \frac{1}{4}, \frac{1}{5}, \frac{1}{6}$

All the fractions in Group A have the _____ number in the

numerator and the denominator. All the fractions in Group B have a

n_____ of 1.

© Saxon

9. $(10 + 15) \div 5 =$

```
┌─────────────┐
│             │
│ _____ │
└─────────────┘
```

10. short division $2\overline{)6\ \ 8}$

```
┌─────────────┐
│             │
│ _____ │
└─────────────┘
```

11.   1,376   2,147   1,859

_____, _____, _____
     least   greatest

```
┌──────────────────┐
│ Use work area.   │
└──────────────────┘
```

12. How many small cubes in the prism?

Volume = length $\times$ width $\times$ height

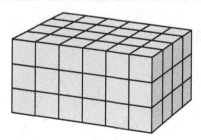

```
┌─────────────┐
│             │
│ _____ │
└─────────────┘
```

13.   700
       $\times$ 3

```
┌─────────────┐
│             │
│ _____ │
└─────────────┘
```

14.   36
     $\times$ 4

15. $0.75
     $\times$ 6

16. Estimate the total.

    153   $\longrightarrow$

              +   5

17. $4.50
     $\times$ 3

18.   451
     $\times$ 2

19.   61
     $-$ m
     24

   m =

20. Complete the triangular prism.

   How many **vertices**?

© Saxon

Name _____

• Points on a Grid

New Concept

• A **point on a grid** is the place where two lines intersect.

• If we number the lines on a grid, we can name the points using a pair of numbers in parentheses called **coordinates.**

The *first number* tells how many lines to move **right.**

The *second number* tells how many lines to move **up.**

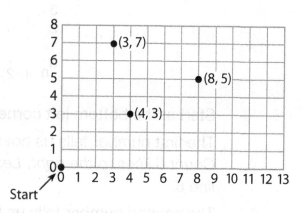

• **Always start at (0, 0) in the bottom left corner.**

Example

Write the coordinates of point *A* on the grid.

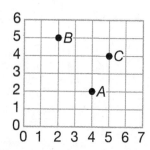

Find point *A* on the grid.

Start at the bottom left corner (0, 0).

Count to the right until you get to the line with point *A*.
Point *A* is right 4 lines.

Count up from line 4 until you get to point *A*.
Point *A* is up 2 lines.

The coordinates for point *A* are 4 to the right and 2 up **(4, 2).**

Example

Name the letter of the point that has the coordinates (6, 3).

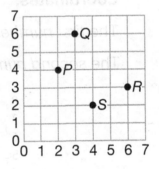

Start at the bottom left corner (0, 0).

The first number tells us how many lines to go to the right.
Count 6 lines to the right. Leave your finger or pencil tip on line 6.

The second number tells us how many lines to go up.
Count 3 lines up.

We are at point *R*. **Point *R*** has the coordinates (6, 3).

Write the coordinates for each point.

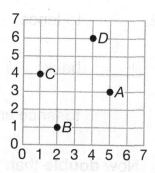

a. Point A (_____, _____)

b. Point B (_____, _____)

c. Point C (_____, _____)

d. Point D (_____, _____)

Name the letter of the point that has these coordinates.

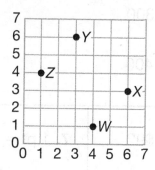

e. (6, 3) Point _____

f. (1, 4) Point _____

1.   286
        72

2.   to fence

    +____   back

        to fence and back

        Now **double** that.

3. 1 in. = 4 mi

    2 in. = _____ mi

4. 8 × 5 × 7

        8
    × 5   × 7

5. Which of the following is the best choice to estimate 579−329?

    A 600 − 300   **B** 500 − 300

    C 600 − 400   **D** 500 − 400

6. Does $8.65 round to $8 or $9?

7. 1 pt = 1 lb

    a. 1 gal = _____ pt

        1 gal = _____ lb

    b. 5 gal = _____ lb

Use work area.

© Saxon

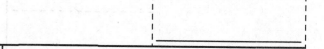

8. Add mentally.

$$50 + 90 + 150 + 20 + 10 =$$

---

9. a. 123 ◯ 132

10. 1 m = _____ cm

b. 5 + 7   7 + 5

↓   ↓

____ ◯ ____

Use work area.

---

11. How many small cubes in the prism?

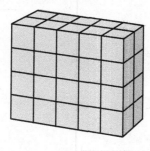

---

12. Write as a multiplication problem and find the total.

12 in. + 12 in. + 12 in. + 12 in. + 12 in. + 12 in.

_____ × _____ = _____

Use work area.

13.   1,152   1,215   1,125

_____ , _____ , _____
   least   greatest

Use work area.

© Saxon

14. short division

$$3\overline{)7\ 8}$$

15.
$$
\begin{array}{r}
420 \\
\times\ \ \ 4 \\
\hline
\end{array}
$$

16. Use a multiplication table to divide.

a. $27 \div 3 =$

b. $28 \div 7 =$

c. $42 \div 6 =$

a. _____

b. _____

c. _____

17.
$$
\begin{array}{r}
94 \\
\times\ \ 2 \\
\hline
\end{array}
$$

18. short division

$$4\overline{)5\ 2}$$

19. a.
$$
\begin{array}{r}
\$2.50 \\
\times\ \ \ \ 4 \\
\hline
\end{array}
$$

b.
$$
\begin{array}{r}
\$2.50 \\
\times\ \ \ \ 8 \\
\hline
\end{array}
$$

a. _____

b. _____

20. Describe the sorting rule.

Group A: 0, 2, 4, 6, 8

Group B: 1, 3, 5, 7, 9

All the numbers in Group A are _____. All the numbers in

Group B are _____.

Use work area.

© Saxon

Name _____

Teacher Notes:

- Review Hint #31 "Graphing Coordinates."
- Students will need a copy of **Lesson Activity 34** to complete the activity.

• Dot-to-Dot Design

New Concept

- To find a point on a grid, use the coordinates.

  The *first number* tells how many lines to move **right**.

  The *second number* tells how many lines to move **up**.

- Always start at (0, 0) in the bottom left corner.

 📖 page 583

Dot-to-Dot Design

Materials needed:
- **Lesson Activity 34**
- ruler

Get a copy of **Lesson Activity 34.**

Draw a dot for every set of coordinates on **Lesson Activity 34.** Write the number of each dot on the grid.

When you have finished drawing dots, use a ruler to draw straight lines between the dots to make a drawing. Start at dot 1 and draw a line to dot 2. Then draw from dot 2 to dot 3, and so on.

1. $7.50
      × 3

Use work area.

2.   7,862   5,798   9,365

_____ , _____ , _____
  least   greatest

Use work area.

3. Name this shape: _____

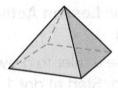

How many **edges**? _____

How many **vertices**? _____

Use work area.

4. Do problem **4** on  page 584.

Group _____

© Saxon

5. nearest dollar

$7.75 →

6. Estimate the difference.

395 →

504 → – _____

7. Draw a line of symmetry on the shape.

Use work area.

8. Draw a square with sides 2 inches long.

Find the **perimeter.**

© Saxon

9. Write each comparison in words.

   a. 2×3 3×2

          $\downarrow$ $\downarrow$

       ____ ◯ ____

    Two times three is _____ three times two.

   b. $0.05 ◯ 50¢

    _____ cents is _____ fifty cents.

> Use work area.

10. If $60 \div 5 = 12$, then what does $60 \div 12$ equal?

11. expanded form

    366

    _____ + _____ + _____

12. Estimate the product.

   92 →

      $\times\ \ 9$

13. Which symbol works in both problems?

$1 \square 1 = 1$ $2 \square 2 = 1$

A +   **B** −

C ×   **D** ÷

14. short division

$2\overline{)3\ 8}$

15.   51
      $\times\ \ \ 3$

16. $1.25
      $\times\ \ \ \ 4$

17. a. $64 \div 8 =$

b. $63 \div 9 =$

c. $60 \div 10 =$

a. _____

b. _____

c. _____

---

18. $5 \times 9 \times 2$

$$\begin{array}{r} 9 \\ \times\ 5 \end{array} \qquad \begin{array}{r} \\ \times\ 2 \end{array}$$

_____

---

19. Use a ruler to find the next three numbers.

$2, 2\frac{1}{4}, 2\frac{1}{2},$ _____, _____, _____, ...

Use work area.

---

20. Write a multiplication fact for the array.

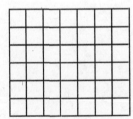

_____ $\times$ _____ $=$ _____

© Saxon

📖 page 586

Focus on
• Planning a Design

Teacher Notes:
• Review Hint #31 "Graphing Coordinates."
• Students will need a copy of **Lesson Activities 35** and **36** to complete this investigation.

1. Look at the design below.

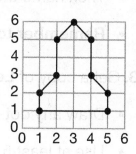

- To write directions for the design, we can start at any dot. We start at (1, 1).

- Now we want to trace around the design and name every dot we come to.

- From (1, 1), we go to (5, 1). Then to (5, 2).

- Finish the directions for drawing this design. The last point is the same as the first.

1. (1, 1)   **6.**

2. (5, 1)   **7.**

3. (5, 2)   **8.**

4.   **9.**

5.   **10.** (1, 1)

© Saxon

2. Get a copy of **Lesson Activity 35.**

- Draw a triangle on the grid. Choose any three points that are not all in a straight line.

- Write directions for drawing your triangle on **Lesson Activity 35.**

- Start at any point in your triangle. Name its coordinates.

- Then name the coordinates for the other points in order.

- **Remember to end at the same point you began.**

3. Get a copy of **Lesson Activity 36.**

- Draw any dot-to-dot design you want on the grid.

- Use at least 5 dots in your design.

- Use only straight lines—no curves.

- When you are finished with your design, write directions for drawing your design on **Lesson Activity 36.**

- Make sure to write the coordinates of the points in order and begin and end at the same point.

© Saxon